Professional Wrestling and the Commercial Stage

Professional Wrestling and the Commercial Stage examines professional wrestling as a century-old, theatrical form that spans from its local places of performance to circulate as a popular, global product.

Professional wrestling has all the trappings of sport, but is, at its core, a theatrical event. This book acknowledges that professional wrestling shares many theatrical elements such as plot, character, scenic design, props, and spectacle. By assessing professional wrestling as a neglected but prototypical case study in the global business of theatre, Laine argues that it is an exemplary form of globalizing, commercial theatre. He asks what theatre scholars might learn from pro wrestling, and how pro wrestling might contribute to conversations beyond the ring, by considering the laboring bodies of the wrestlers, and analyzing wrestling's form and content.

Of interest to scholars and students of theatre and performance, cultural studies, and sports studies, *Professional Wrestling and the Commercial Stage* delimits the edges of wrestling's theatrical frame, critiques established understandings of corporate theatre, and offers key wrestling concepts as models for future study in other fields.

Eero Laine is Assistant Professor of Theatre at the University at Buffalo, State University of New York. He is the co-editor of *Performance and Professional Wrestling* (2017).

Routledge Advances in Theatre and Performance Studies

Women's Playwriting and the Women's Movement, 1890–1918
Anna Farkas

Theatrical Performance and the Forensic Turn
James Frieze

Mummers' Plays Revisited
Peter Harrop

Hypertheatre
Contemporary Radical Adaptation of Greek Tragedy
Olga Kekis

After the Long Silence
The Theatre of Brazil's Post-Dictatorship Generation
Cláudia Tatinge Nascimento

The Bible and Modern British Drama
From 1930 to the Present-Day
Mary F. Brewer

Moving Relation
Touch in Contemporary Dance
Gerko Egert

The Dramaturgy of the Door
Stuart Andrews and Matthew Wagner

Professional Wrestling and the Commercial Stage
Eero Laine

For more information about this series, please visit: www.routledge.com/Routledge-Advances-in-Theatre–Performance-Studies/book-series/RATPS

Professional Wrestling and the Commercial Stage

Eero Laine

LONDON AND NEW YORK

First published 2020
by Routledge
2 Park Square, Milton Park, Abingdon, Oxon OX14 4RN

and by Routledge
52 Vanderbilt Avenue, New York, NY 10017

Routledge is an imprint of the Taylor & Francis Group, an informa business

© 2020 Eero Laine

The right of Eero Laine to be identified as author of this work has been asserted by him in accordance with sections 77 and 78 of the Copyright, Designs and Patents Act 1988.

All rights reserved. No part of this book may be reprinted or reproduced or utilized in any form or by any electronic, mechanical, or other means, now known or hereafter invented, including photocopying and recording, or in any information storage or retrieval system, without permission in writing from the publishers.

Trademark notice: Product or corporate names may be trademarks or registered trademarks, and are used only for identification and explanation without intent to infringe.

British Library Cataloguing-in-Publication Data
A catalogue record for this book is available from the British Library

Library of Congress Cataloging-in-Publication Data
A catalog record has been requested for this book

ISBN: 978-0-8153-5399-7 (hbk)
ISBN: 978-1-351-13439-2 (ebk)

Typeset in Bembo
by Wearset Ltd, Boldon, Tyne and Wear

Contents

Acknowledgments vi

Introduction: Professional wrestling and the commercial stage 1

1 Productive theatre and professional wrestling: The business of kayfabe 18

2 Form and content: Professional wrestling's troubling theatrics 39

3 Hardcore wrestling: Deregulation and theatrical danger 59

4 Trading likenesses: Wrestling labor and the branded body 80

5 A stock theatre company: WWE and theatrical value 103

Conclusion 121

Bibliography 130
Index 145

Acknowledgments

This book has benefitted from innumerable conversations, exchanges, and arguments both formal and spontaneous. The work here is the culmination of many years of writing and thinking about this topic, and I am especially indebted to those who have worked with me and on the subject matter. I am especially thankful for those kind and critical readers whose comments and feedback have advanced and improved this project.

My thinking around professional wrestling emerged from my doctoral studies at the Graduate Center of the City University of New York, where David Savran's guidance, advocacy, and mentorship (along with some well-placed preliminary skepticism) pushed the work beyond its initial limits and boundaries. His comments and questions reshaped and directed the project in ways that have become central to my thinking about theatre and performance more broadly. Also at the Graduate Center, Edward Miller's candidness and probing inquiries into this work greatly benefitted the project. His advising and caring engagement were incredibly important as I developed this work. This book would not exist had it not been for a rousing and rather loud discussion of artistic and theatrical merits of professional wrestling in a seminar many years ago. Maurya Wickstrom led that seminar discussion and has since offered substantial and thoughtful critical responses to various aspects of this work in writing and at conferences. Maurya was also fundamental to this work by insisting that I attend a performance related to labor and wrestling co-created and performed by Broderick Chow at the Performance Studies international conference in Leeds. I have since had the pleasure of working with Broderick on a good number of projects. His camaraderie and insight have made him a dear friend whose scholarship and ideas have clearly and substantially advanced my own.

Many thanks to Ben Piggott, Lucia Accorsi, Laura Soppelsa, and the rest of the team at Routledge. Ben encouraged the idea of an edited volume on wrestling and performance when Claire Warden, Broderick Chow, and I pitched it to him at the International Federation for Theatre Research conference in Warwick and has been a thoughtful and determined presence in this work ever since. Text from the chapter I published in that volume (Eero

Laine. "Stadium Sized Theatre: WWE and The World of Professional Wrestling" in *Performance and Professional Wrestling*, edited by Broderick Chow, Eero Laine, and Claire Warden, 39–47. London and New York: Routledge, 2017. ©Eero Laine) appears throughout this book and most substantially in the Introduction, Chapter 1, and Chapter 5. The work is reproduced with permission of The Licensor through PLSclear. Claire Warden was kind enough to initially reach out to invite me as a co-editor of that project that would become *Performance and Professional Wrestling*. She has impressively led the field of professional wrestling studies through her scholarship as well as through her work as a wrestling promoter and remains a champion of the continually emerging field of professional wrestling.

The volume with Claire and Broderick took shape as a number of other publications were developing on professional wrestling, and I have been lucky to work alongside many of those moving the conversation forward across disciplines. I am honored to be part of these developments with Sam Ford, Nell Haynes, Dru Jeffries, Andrew Kannegeiser, CarrieLynn Reinhardt, Andrew Zolides, and many, many others. A special note of thanks must be extended to those whose work laid the foundations for the field into which this book emerges: Sharon Mazer, Heather Levi, Nicholas Sammond, and R. Tyson Smith. Of this group, Sharon Mazer stands out as both groundbreaking in her book-length study of professional wrestling and many other contributions to the field and as a fierce interlocutor and collaborator.

The work has been funded by a number of sources and in a variety of ways from conference grants to research funds. The funding facilitated many conference presentations and interactions with colleagues at the American Society for Theatre Research, American Theatre in Higher Education, International Federation for Theatre Research, Performance Studies international, and many other symposia and academic gatherings. Significantly, the Martin A. Tackle American Theatre Research Award funded visits to The National Wrestling Hall of Fame in Stillwater, Oklahoma, The National Wrestling Hall of Fame Dan Gable Museum in Waterloo, Iowa, as well as the Professional Wrestling Hall of Fame and Museum, which I visited when it was located in Amsterdam, New York (it is currently located in Wichita Falls, Texas).

My deep appreciation to the many friends and colleagues who have worked alongside me and whose presence and engagement have been essential to my labor and thinking: Anick Boyd, Kevin Byrne, Michelle Liu Carriger, Anne Donlon, Rayya El Zein, Drew Friedman, Jacob Gallagher-Ross, Donatella Galella, Nell Haynes, Stefanie A. Jones, Ana Martinez, Patrick McKelvey, Shawn Rice, Carly Smith, Jared Simard, Chris Alen Sula, Aaron Thomas, Janet Werther, Catherine Young, and Peter Zazzali. Through Performance Studies international and its Future Advisory Board, I have gained immensely from the friendship and collegiality of Felipe Cervera, Shawn Chua, Panayiotoa Demetriou, Joãoa Florêncio, Areum Jeong, Azedeh

Sharifi, Evelyn Wan, and Asher Warren. Maaike Bleeker and then Sean Metzger have impressively led that organization during my time working with it and have both done so much to open opportunities for scholars at all levels of their careers.

At the University at Buffalo a junior faculty leave afforded the time to finish this book. I also thank the students in my first year seminar, Performance and Pro-Wrestling, who engaged the subject with both seriousness and a sense of novelty that moved our discussions into a variety of performance forms and social issues. Thank you also to my UB colleagues who have made space for this work and who have offered their encouragement and support: Barbara Bono, Anne Burnidge, Meredith Conti, Christian Flaugh, Lindsay Brandon Hunter, Lynne Koscielniak, Carla Mazzio, Ariel Nereson, Cathy Norgren, and Elizabeth Otto.

Finally and essentially, my immense gratitude to Christine Marks, whose intellect and humor have fostered my own and whose thoughtfulness has shaped me deeply in my work and thinking for more than a decade. Her generosity and kindness are matched only by her intelligence, and it is impossible to imagine this project without her critically engaged feedback, relentless support, and loving partnership.

Introduction
Professional wrestling and the commercial stage

Professional wrestling is theatre. Even as it is mediated, broadcast, and reproduced and resold, the live event sits at the core of professional wrestling. The wrestlers, costumed in bedazzled briefs, glossy sports bras, singlets, capes, masks, gowns, tuxedos, and street clothes speak in booming tones over PA systems and weave wordless stories out of shared repertoires of physicality. Their bodies speak through sweaty impacts and bloodied brows—agony and triumph, arrogance and humility, desire and disgust. It's overwhelming. It's amazing. It's hard to watch. The ring, the epicenter of the professional wrestling world, is surrounded by audience members: dozens, hundreds, thousands, one hundred thousand people chanting in unison. Each syllable of the wrestlers' names and slogans echoes off the hard concrete of the stadium, hands and feet beating out rhythms, crude musical scores of adoration and derision: thunderous boos, sustained standing ovations, intervals of boredom, pops of excitement, hilarity, absurdity, and disbelief. From ringside to the cheap seats and broadcast, simulcast, streaming into living rooms and onto phone screens around the world, pro wrestling rumbles outward, always circling back to bodies on the mat—the pre-show, the mid-card, the main event. The next match is scheduled for one fall! You can't deny professional wrestling its theatricality.

Recognizable across continents and languages from *lucha libre* in Mexico to *puroresu* in Japan to established customs and family lineages and legacies around the world, professional wrestling is a tradition, an institution, a ritual even while it is a fleeting entertainment, a carnival trick, and a flippant waste of time. It is both widespread and overlooked, closely examined but empty of meaning. Styles change and storylines shift, characters are taken up as icons spanning generations or disappear after a single performance. In formal terms: across traditions and histories professional wrestling is scripted or predetermined, live entertainment performed in front of an audience by actors portraying characters. And it is spectacular.

Roland Barthes saw as much in even the "most squalid Parisian halls" of the 1950s.[1] For Barthes, the wrestling event, the bodies in apparent conflict and framed by the ring, is to be considered alongside the other "great solar

2 Pro wrestling and the commercial stage

spectacles, Greek drama and bullfights," because in them "a light without shadow generates an emotion without reserve."[2] Professional wrestling, as I understand it, following Barthes, "sits between the two forms; the emotion, the blood and sweat, and the spectacle are set centre stage and enacted by clearly labouring bodies."[3] In pro wrestling, we witness the physicality and bloody pain of the bullfight intertwining the pathos of Aeschylus, Sophocles, Euripides. Barthes is emphatic:

> There are people who think that wrestling is an ignoble sport. Wrestling is not a sport, it is a spectacle, and it is no more ignoble to attend a wrestled performance of suffering than a performance of the sorrows of Arnolphe or Andromaque.[4]

As Aristotle reminds us, even if it is "the least artistic" of the six elements of tragedy, "spectacle has, indeed, an emotional attraction of its own."[5]

Which is not to say that professional wrestling is somehow short of plot. Rather, professional wrestling plots, referred to by fans and those in the business as "angles" and "feuds," are what drive the action, what motivates the characters played by the wrestlers to return to the ring to finally settle the score, defend their honor, get revenge, prove themselves as the best. "As one match ends," Sharon Mazer reminds us, "the stage is invariably set for a return encounter."[6] An angle can last for a single show or it might span weeks, years, decades even. And maybe it is in this stretching of time, in knowing that the often flimsy resolution offered tonight will only hold until the next event, that any catharsis is fleeting, that the deus ex machina is actually exposition—maybe this is what makes pro wrestling, for many, not quite theatre or at least not legitimately so. That is, professional wrestling may be theatre, yet something about it doesn't feel like theatre. Something about it seems other than theatre, maybe even excessive to theatre. Plots and characters spilling outward and beyond the narratives contained in a single play, from night to night, city to city, ring to ring. You can't sit in the library and read a professional wrestling script.

I am quite interested in this idea that professional wrestling is not somehow like the other things we study as theatre scholars (even as the economic underpinnings are quite nearly the same).[7] I suspect the feeling has something to do with class formations and taste within the field of theatre studies, while at the same time it is linked to the practical impulses of undergraduate and graduate training—no one that I know of is advocating for pro wrestling modules to be added to the BA and BFA curriculum, you can't get an MFA in pro wrestling. (But now that I write that, I hope I am proven wrong.) Nevertheless, this book takes it for granted that professional wrestling is theatre.

It should be stated outright and will be made clear, I hope, that the project does not uncritically celebrate or otherwise argue for a canonical pedestal on which to place professional wrestling. Rather the project seeks out those aspects of professional wrestling that, through its perceived similarities and differences with theatre proper, might actually reveal how theatre circulates and otherwise functions as a live, globalizing product. And while its popularity is certainly one reason to investigate professional wrestling, I am happy to suggest that millions of viewers can, in fact, be wrong.[8] To put it another way, while such popularity, I think, demands academic attention, there is no value—theoretically, aesthetically, or politically—in *celebrating* a performance form simply because it is immensely popular.

People often ask me if I like professional wrestling or if I am a fan. The short answer is yes. The long answer is that I am deeply skeptical of the form or rather much of the content that seems to fit so neatly within the form, but I have come to really appreciate and stand in awe of the work, the physical labor, and the heart that such labor takes. Like Sharon Mazer noted when confronted with the same questions now over twenty years ago, it's hard not to be drawn in by it all. It is hard to not be a fan.[9] Perhaps like the "hard-core fans" Mazer describes herself in relation to, I've teared up while watching wrestling, cheered and laughed wildly, and found myself exhausted afterwards. But I have also read my phone waiting for a match to end and skipped major events only to check the reviews the next day.[10] Yet, it takes an amazing bravery to appear semi-clothed in front of thousands of incredibly critical and often antagonistic viewers. And it is that sort of absurd bravery that brings me back and seems to even welcome my skepticism. It is what makes me a fan but makes me also deny it a little bit. Like Mazer, I am drawn to the ability to chant "boooring" during a match when highly paid "superstars" are just phoning it in.[11] I appreciate the ability and even encouragement to shout down a racist character's rant or boo at sexist plots and find myself wishing I could do such things in the theatre. Those expressions are encouraged at pro wrestling matches and one will even find others to do them with as we witness today, as Mazer did, "breathtaking flight, incidents of fierce fighting, genuine intimacy, and a sense of community."[12] That is, for some theatre and performance scholars, like Mazer, like myself, the promised community of theatre might actually be found ringside (or even in the ring).

And yet, I am wary of the trap of popular culture, where scholars search for and find immense truths about human nature and being and becoming in the heart of popular or disposable forms of art. In part because I do not think that a lot of contemporary theatre, with its suburban sets and psychological hang-ups, somehow holds any more depth of meaning than professional wrestling. I don't expect everyone to agree with me of course, but once one starts to directly compare the forms, it's hard not to see the similarities. Another project might build on Gerald Craven and Richard Moseley's 1972 study "Actors on the Canvas Stage: The Dramatic Conventions of Professional Wrestling," and sort through the various theatrical elements of pro wrestling from the costuming to the lighting to performer training to close readings of plots and storylines.[13] This is important work and I hope others will continue and deepen this line of inquiry.[14] Somewhat differently from those studies, this book is significantly less concerned with the ritual or carnivalesque aspects of professional wrestling and while I do spend some time on aesthetics and match logics or dramaturgical structure, I am far more interested in what professional wrestling might actually have tell us about commercial theatre and performance. That is, strong comparisons between wrestling and theatre have been made in the academy for some time: Mark Elliot Workman's ethnographic work on fans and others in the wrestling industry in the late 1970s finds many teetering on a designation between theatre and sport while others, like his interviewee "Nate," begin with the "basic premise that professional wrestling is a form of theater, not a form of sport."[15] It is clear that professional wrestling is theatre to those who watch it and to many in the business, and also to many others outside of theatre studies (Workman, for instance, earned his PhD in Folklore and Folklife). Yet, in theatre studies, wrestling remains a theatrical outlier. Rather than trying to bring wrestling towards the center of the discipline, however, I think we might approach it as outsider example that is actually essential to theatre, the omission that reinforces the form.

That is to say, the exclusion of pro wrestling from theatre studies is just as, if not more, important than what it might mean to somehow make it canonical. This book, then, intervenes in theatre studies to examine a century-old, embodied, narrative form that extends from its local places of performance through globally mediated live events. Considering its international popularity and connections to financial markets, professional wrestling provides a testing ground for many theoretical concepts and ideas—from the ontological nature of theatre to the connection between performer and character to the possibilities of theatrical circulation in a global economy. Indeed, I propose that the wrestling promotion WWE (World Wrestling Entertainment, Inc., formerly World Wrestling Federation) is a model, yet surprisingly underexamined, example of a publicly traded, transnational theatre company.[16]

At a national conference, I was once asked if we really needed to go so far out of our way to discuss these issues. The question might have been something like: "In order to properly examine commercial or for-profit theatre, do we really need to take this detour through professional wrestling?" Well, yes, but I do not think we are going out of our way. Wrestling is not a detour; rather, I think that if we want to study commercial theatre we must go *through* professional wrestling. Theatre isn't getting less commercial, and the actors, designers, and technicians studying theatre in most universities and theatre schools enter a world that is much more like the theatrical economy of professional wrestling than, say, that of state-sponsored repertory theatres.[17] That is, we must confront the growing, conspicuous (and perhaps perturbing) similarities between the industries of theatre and professional wrestling in order to understand what we are studying as theatre scholars and how we define our field.

You can probably blame musical theatre for this book on professional wrestling. The forms share some structural similarities, of course—flashy costumes, touring productions, recognizable tropes, devoted fanbases, sometimes stilted dialogue that is amplified by microphones and leads into spectacular sequences not bound by the genre of theatrical realism (in pro wrestling characters break into fights not songs, but this is a quibble). Perhaps not incidentally, there has been a serious and dedicated study of musical theatre over the past two decades that has, in many ways, coincided with the increased attention given to other less literary forms of live entertainment. Not that the study of pro wrestling and musical theatre have run directly parallel, but the formal study of musical theatre has marked a number of openings in the fields of theatre and performance studies. Stacy Wolf in 2016 noted that:

> Musical Theatre Studies, whose presence as a viable academic field is not much more than a decade old, is spreading out in all directions of chronology, geography, approach, and methods. Scholars trained in theatre studies, dance studies, and musicology and ethnomusicology are becoming more comfortable with each other's intellectual tendencies and conventions, sharing our analytical languages and epistemological assumptions.[18]

This move towards shared academic conventions was also innovative for undergraduate curricula, which

> for generations consisted of knowledgeable professors—typically longtime fans of musicals and collectors of trivia who listed facts and dates and told stories (many of them fascinating and crucial to understanding how musicals are made but with no critical framework).[19]

In other words, it is not that that musical theatre went somehow unstudied or untaught, but it was not formalized as a field. In some ways, then, professional wrestling studies is just a decade or so behind musical theatre studies. The wave of theses and dissertations beginning in the early 2000s and the recent formation of the Professional Wrestling Studies Association begin to point towards a field that is congealing across disciplines with a not insignificant amount of research emerging from the fields of theatre and performance studies.[20]

David Savran's 2004 *Theatre Survey* article "Towards a Historiography of the Popular" traces historical shifts that led to the study of musical theatre and makes a case for its continued study: "As the so-called legitimate theatre became increasingly and irreversibly literary, high modernist, and haut bourgeois to distinguish itself from motion pictures, the theatrical forms categorized as popular have declined or expired—with the important exception of the Broadway musical."[21] Professional wrestling may not have expired as other popular forms might have, but as a genre of live entertainment worthy of study and legitimation, it was eclipsed by the theatrical stage itself. More importantly, professional wrestling is quite similar to musical theatre because, as Savran prompts us, musical theatre "is able to provide a virtual laboratory in which to study the circulation of the artwork-as-commodity."[22] Indeed, both professional wrestling and musical theatre are often unabashedly commercial, for-profit, and developed, designed, and circulated with money at the forefront of many creative decisions and actions. What is also noteworthy here, in many ways, is the fact that, while Savran notes the immense popularity of the Broadway musical and his surprise at how underrepresented it is in theatre textbooks and scholarship, it is useful and important for theatre scholars well beyond its popularity.

Indeed, what interests me in professional wrestling is less its popularity or even the possibility of instrumentalizing it to further legitimize popular forms ("Look! Another form that resembles canonical theatre!"). As David Saltz explains in 2008, citing work on popular culture and theatre going back to the 1970s, including Savran's "Toward a Historiography of the Popular," among others: Within the field of theatre studies,

> we have reached the point where the very act of demarcating popular entertainment as a discrete topic … runs the risk of reinforcing a deeply problematic dichotomy between populist and elitist art that a virulently anti-intellectual strand of the political Right has co-opted to discredit progressive and transgressive artists and thinkers.[23]

The question of popular forms or entertainment in some sort of contradistinction from exclusive forms or proper art is a moot point and even a politically regressive one.[24] Professional wrestling may not fit neatly in some narratives of the stage, but as a theatrical form with decidedly working class roots, to exclude it from considerations of theatre may draw one's progressive claims into question. As I have argued in the past: if you want to see how live performance circulates under capitalism, if you want to see how a publicly traded theatre company functions, if you have interest in the larger structures of the performing arts, you should really pay attention to professional wrestling.[25]

If I might go even one step further, I would invite the many musical theatre scholars who are swayed by Savran's appeal to study musical theatre as an industry and through its methods of circulation (and production and consumption) to also consider professional wrestling, among other commercial forms. And if one is interested in popular forms, pro wrestling likely has more to offer than those forms of theatre that are more closely tied to the upper parts of the middle classes. Rather than focusing on the genre of theatre that is broadly construed as musical theatre, or even the Broadway musical, theatre scholars might cluster according to the broader category of commercial theatre or theatre driven by a profit motive—productive theatre as I refer to it in this book. Such an encompassing category would, of course, include musical theatre, but would also take in the many other for-profit forms and productions from Marvel Live to the Harlem Globetrotters to the Blue Man Group to Disney on Ice to Cirque du Soleil.[26] We might also then examine the production companies that produce such work. For instance, rather than close readings and analyses of the productions themselves, we might have a look behind the curtain to consider the massive supply chains and institutions necessary in order to stage a live piece of theatre that travels and circulates. Professional wrestling offers such an example and, I hope, this book begins to explicate some of the possibilities for such studies in theatre and performance studies. What follows is a brief review of other studies meant to situate this book within what is a rapidly accelerating interdisciplinary field of professional wrestling studies, followed by an overview of the chapters of the book.

Wrestling scholarship

The growing interdisciplinary field has seen a wide range of articles and at least two book-length studies every year since 2016 and, from what I can tell, the field is on track to continue such a trend.[27] That year marked the initial release of *Performance and Professional Wrestling*, edited by Broderick Chow, Claire Warden, and myself.[28] Certainly more significantly, professional wrestling has received increased attention due to political events in 2016, notably the campaign and election of Donald Trump to the office of US president. The connections between wrestling and politics were noted widely, with the *New York Times* asking "Is Everything Wrestling Now?"[29] Recall also that CNN got dragged into a virtual Twitter war (largely fought by proxies on both sides) when Trump "sent out a tweet containing video in which he pummels a person with a CNN logo as its head."[30] The idea that politics was like professional wrestling was no longer just something wrestling fans pointed out.

There has been no shortage of articles on the topic in the popular press and a number of scholars have weighed in as well. Sharon Mazer's *TDR* article "Donald Trump Shoots the Match" quite effectively explained the many historical connections between Donald Trump and professional wrestling, even if Claire Warden, Broderick Chow, and myself felt that it threw the professional wrestling baby out with the presidential bathwater, as it were.[31] Echoing WWE's rebranding of professional wrestling as "sports entertainment," Kira Hall, Donna M. Goldstein, and Matthew Bruce Ingram call Trump's spectacular performance "political entertainment."[32] And in the forthcoming volume *Professional Wrestling: Politics and Populism*, Mazer takes up the matter again in "A Mega Power Implodes: Donald Trump, Presidential Performativity, and Professional Wrestling," while in the same volume

Heather Levi explains "Why It Mattered: Wrestling Dramaturgy in the 2016 Presidential Election," providing a reading of the 2016 election in wrestling terms that should prove fundamental for future examinations of presidential politics and wrestling.[33]

The turn to professional wrestling in light of a Trump presidency is interesting, but perhaps not unexpected. Trump is famously indebted to the genre of reality television and, indeed, professional wrestling itself. And while it is good to see professional wrestling studies flourishing, what is ultimately disconcerting in this flurry of work, and I have stated this before, is not the realization that the presidency is now like professional wrestling, but that it takes someone like Trump for many to realize it. Of course politics is like professional wrestling, which is in some ways to say that of course politics is theatrical. Professional wrestling provides a neat low-brow comparison that apparently sullies Trump's reputation even as theatre is rarely far from the discussion.

Probably the first major academic book on professional wrestling, Gerald W. Morton and George M. O'Brien's *Wrestling to Rasslin': Ancient Sport to American Spectacle* was published in 1985 as WWE was ascending towards national and international notoriety.[34] The book includes an entire chapter on "Professional Wrestling's Roots in Theatrical Traditions," which goes to lengths to explain how "professional wrestling has elements of the morality play, allegory, the Noh Drama, and classical theatre."[35] Even if in the end, however, Morton and O'Brien decide that professional wrestling is more an American ritual than theatre, the formal comparisons between professional wrestling and various forms of theatre are hard to ignore. The concluding chapter of the book opens with a Bible passage describing Jacob wrestling with a man all night long and concludes that wrestling is ritual and "it is a ritual particularly American because is dramatizes characters and conflicts that are especially significant to contemporary American culture."[36] Morton and O'Brien's analysis of pro wrestling as theatre and as ritual has endured in many ways and would become the premise of many studies that followed. For instance, five years later (1990), Michael R. Ball's *Professional Wrestling as Ritual Drama in American Popular Culture* analyzed a number of regional and national professional wrestling promotions to make the case for wrestling as a social and cultural ritual.[37]

While Morton and O'Brien and Ball certainly set the stage for professional wrestling studies (along with a number of theses and dissertations dating back to the 1970s), I do not think one can overstate the lasting impact of Sharon Mazer's 1998 *Professional Wrestling: Sport and Spectacle*. Blending ethnographic field work with performance and literary theory, Mazer opened the field for further serious inquiry. The book has become so essential to the ways that we think of and understand professional wrestling that many of Mazer's insights might now be considered common knowledge for wrestling fans and scholars. Even if, I think, general sentiment has tipped over to thinking of wrestling as theatre (or at least in a broader sense, theatrical performance), it was Mazer who put forward the notion of wrestling as simultaneously engaging sport and theatre, even as wrestling could never fully be either.[38] A lot has changed in professional wrestling since Mazer first wrote about it, but a lot has stayed the same and academic interest has greatly increased.

The 2000s saw many additional studies, including Patrice Oppliger's 2004 *Wrestling and Hyper-Masculinity*, which presents a media critique of the form through theories of masculine performance and gendered behavior.[39] In the book, she sets out to create a link between viewing professional wrestling and masculinist behavior such as verbal and physical aggression and violence. Perhaps most interestingly here, Oppliger includes "The Appeal of Theatrics" as a section of a chapter entitled "The Appeal of Professional Wrestling," citing also the "Appeal of Violence," the "Appeal of the Gross Out," the "Appeal of Exploiting Class," and the "Appeal of Exploiting Women" as reasons that fans tune in.[40] In considering the attraction of the theatrical in wrestling, Oppliger notes that "Wrestling's audiences have more influence over the programming than almost any other form of entertainment."[41] It is in fact this feature that makes the form so flexible and adaptable and is also largely why many of the other "appeals" listed by Oppliger might not apply in the same way they maybe once did as audiences and social awareness change.

The 2005 volume *Steel Chair to the Head*, edited by Nicholas Sammond, featured chapters on lucha libre,[42] Latino wrestlers,[43] female fandom,[44] S/M narratives,[45] wrestling logic and structure,[46] economics,[47] and wrestling as a potentially "progressive, transgressive, or regressive (or all of these at different moments)" representation of traditional notions of family and social bonds.[48] In the volume, Roland Barthes' essential article "The World of Wrestling" is followed by Henry Jenkins's "'Never Trust a Snake': WWF Wrestling as Masculine Melodrama" and Sharon Mazer's "'Real Wrestling'/'Real' Life."[49] In a particularly brilliant piece of editing, Sammond reprinted what has become a sort of triptych of articles on the ways we might understand professional wrestling—from semiotics to a gendered genre to "a totalizing worldview."[50] Finally, Sammond's introduction, which is subtitled "A Brief and Unnecessary Defense of Professional Wrestling," takes up professional wrestling as a popular art form and still stands today as an indispensable explication of what professional wrestling affords academic examination.

Following *Steel Chair to the Head* were two historical studies published in 2006 and two ethnographic studies, one in 2008 and another in 2014. Of the historical studies, one was quite focused (Chad Dell's *Revenge of Hatpin Mary: Women, Professional Wrestling, and Fan Culture in the 1950s*) and one was sprawling, covering over 100 years of wrestling history (Scott M. Beekman's *Ringside: A History of Professional Wrestling*).[51] Dell's study provides a close look at the gendered performance of professional wrestling and its fandom in the 1950s, considering the often masculinist spaces of wrestling halls and the ways that "in the case of wrestling, television sanitized the performance by resituating it within the home" and offered an intimate perspective on the action, a close-up previously reserved for those privileged fans who could afford ringside seats."[52] Beekman's *Ringside*, in contrast, offers a broad survey of professional wrestling as an athletic performance form in the United States.[53]

Heather Levi's 2008 *The World of Lucha Libre: Secrets, Revelations, and Mexican National Identity* examines lucha libre (translated literally as "free fight" or "free wrestling"), the professional wrestling form developed and most prominently practiced in Mexico.[54] The book provides an historical and cultural analysis of lucha libre through the discursive lenses of gender, cultural identity, and nationalism. Levi focuses on Mexican lucha libre and draws connections to North American trade, electoral politics, problems of authenticity, and the media. Sociologist R. Tyson Smith's 2014 book *Fighting for Recognition: Identity and the Performance of Violence in Professional Wrestling* examines pro wrestling as "physical theatre where spectators pay to be entertained by performers acting out a fight."[55] Smith's and Levi's books are notable for their in-depth ethnographies, with Smith spending years with a wrestling promotion and Levi standing out as one of the only wrestling researchers at the time to actually get in the ring and train with wrestlers.

As noted, wrestling scholarship has recently seen a rather impressive increase in work. Benjamin Litherland's 2018 *Wrestling in Britain: Sporting Entertainments, Celebrity and Audiences* is the sole authored manuscript on wrestling in Britain. Citing *Steel Chair to the Head* and *Performance and Professional Wrestling*, Litherland acknowledges that the field has largely been shaped by theatre and media studies: "Influenced by Barthes, and often taking a semiotic approach, at their core, most of these studies are attracted to professional wrestling's 'fakery,' its illusions, spectacle and dramatic tendencies and the meanings, representations and ideologies therein."[56] Litherland's study stands out for taking up sports directly and considering wrestling's history in Britain through a sports sociology lens. Finally, there are four edited volumes that have been or will be published between 2018 and the end of 2020: Aaron D. Horton's *Identity in Professional Wrestling: Essays on Nationality, Race and Gender*, CarrieLynn D. Reinhard and Christopher J. Olson's *Convergent Wrestling: Participatory Culture, Transmedia Storytelling, and Intertextuality in the Squared Circle*; Dru Jeffries' *#WWE: Professional Wrestling in the Digital Age*, and Nell Haynes, Eero Laine, Heather Levi, and Sharon Mazer's *Professional Wrestling: Politics and Populism*.[57] These volumes, in many ways, do continue the scholarly threads outlined by Litherland. And in many ways this book does as well. Litherland warns us that to consider pro wrestling as some sort of easy sport/theatre hybrid "risks taking sport, and for that matter theatre, to be an unchanging, natural phenomenon."[58] Indeed. But where Litherland's approach is to suspend assumptions about what sport is or what sport does in order to study professional wrestling through the broad view of cultural studies, I am situating professional wrestling squarely as theatre. It is an inverted rhetorical move in that I am doubling down on the assumption of professional wrestling as theatre, taking decades of scholarship on pro wrestling's theatricality and claiming the form as theatre. So, the semiotics and playful encounters in and out of the ring are quite interesting to me, but even more so are the mechanisms that make pro wrestling necessarily studied as a theatrical form.

Chapters

The book proceeds from the general to the specific, beginning with a broad overview of professional wrestling and its connections to the commercial stage through to a closer examination of WWE, the largest and currently most profitable professional wrestling company. The first chapter of this book functions as a broader theoretical introduction by examining the business of professional wrestling as it comes to bear on the economics of theatre and other live performance. The chapter considers the fact that performance offers a difficult issue for global capitalism: how to circulate and sell something like a theatrical performance that is otherwise generally considered ephemeral and not replicable? To begin to answer such a question, the chapter rehearses the economic arguments of Adam Smith and Karl Marx on the idea of productive labor. Whereas Smith considered labor to be productive only if it created something tangible, Marx defined labor from the perspective of the capitalist, wherein any labor that produces a profit is considered productive. This distinction is useful in understanding live performance today as a way of reading expanding theatrical industries as productive, even if nothing material is produced. This discussion is related to recent trends in both theatre studies and business marketing that emphasize experiences over raw goods and the ways that theatre and performance function within contemporary economies. The chapter attempts to connect such matters in relation to the wrestling concept of *kayfabe*, which is roughly the presentation of pro wrestling as a legitimate competition and also implies a wider-reaching theatricality.

The second chapter picks up with an examination of the professional wrestling form held in opposition to its content. This chapter thus pulls apart the notions of form and content and takes up Kristoffer Diaz's 2014 Pulitzer Prize-nominated play, *The Elaborate Entrance of Chad Deity*, and Claire Luckham's play from the late 1970s and early 1980s, *Trafford Tanzi*, in order to examine and critique professional wrestling's long history of racist, misogynistic, and otherwise troubling representations and stereotypes. Here, I consider the more disconcerting aspects of professional wrestling as primarily theatrical problems. In doing so, I am particularly interested in the ways that we might separate the content of pro wrestling (the often politically regressive characters and plots) from the theatrical wrestling form (the faux competition and even the ring itself) and what such a distinction might do in terms of how we assess and study such performances broadly. This chapter thus encourages a broader reading of popular theatre and its circulation, and does so through theatrical representations of the performance form.

This leads in to the third chapter, which examines hardcore-style wrestling as a form that troubles even the seemingly neat considerations of form and content. Indeed, hardcore-style professional wrestling is taken up as perhaps the ideal site in which to examine the conceit that professional wrestling is "predetermined, not fake." Hardcore wrestling style exemplifies an aesthetic of what I term "extreme authenticity," which stages a form of violence that echoes and reverberates with both reality television and some forms of performance art. The bloody and overtly painful acts of hardcore wrestling stage the real potential of the performers' wage labor as they struggle and bleed in a predetermined, theatrical competition. The chapter thus investigates the differences between theatrical and performed violence and the possible political implications of performing such bloody spectacles as those found in hardcore wrestling.

Such discussions give way to the fourth chapter, which addresses the physical work of wrestlers and figures wrestlers as performers who labor both in the ring and in every other area of their lives as they maintain their physiques through training regimens and special diets. The chapter continues with a close consideration of wrestlers as workers, whose images, names, and gestures are often trademarked property of the wrestling promotions for which they work. The chapter introduces the legal concept of likeness as a potentially useful analytic for considering a wide range of performance and theatre. Likeness and its legal protections allow celebrities to protect their visage, name, and identity, and are particularly important in making the images of wrestlers saleable and tradeable through current trademark law. The model of branding that divorces the brand from material goods, using goods simply as a means to deliver a brand, is given new consideration when the disposable brand delivery tools are actors performing outsized identities in often dangerous wrestling maneuvers. The discussion attempts to make legible the various ways that theatrical performance can be made replicable and saleable in a global economy. In addition to professional wrestling, this chapter draws on a number of examples from US case law, which offer further illustrations of how live entertainment circulates globally today.

The fifth chapter focuses explicitly on WWE as a publicly traded, commercial theatre company with a global reach. Unlike other forms of performance and theatre, commercial theatre not only performs for audiences in the theatre, but for shareholders, economists, and business analysts. The staged production is at once a product of the market and an extension of the corporation while, at the same time, the performance influences share price and consumer perception of the company itself. This is true, I argue, whether the people onstage are wrestling or performing in *Lion King* or any other live entertainment owned by a for-profit corporation, particularly those that issue public stock. The chapter is principally interested in the ways that WWE stages its theatrical entertainments and corporate identity, performing for a variety of spectators around the world, including a multinational fan base, shareholders, and various corporate partners. This chapter's methodology scrutinizes global corporate finance as storylines affect stock prices and financial concerns come to acutely affect characters and performers. Working through the character of Mr. McMahon and a plot that spanned the ring, stadium, and stock market, the chapter examines the ambiguities that emerge between corporation and theatrical fictions. The conclusion points to the possibilities for future study of professional wrestling and considers the importance and troubles of working through academic disciplines to study an interdisciplinary form. The conclusion also notes the many recent developments in professional wrestling studies and offers some suggestions for how else theatre studies might engage with professional wrestling and similar entertainments

Finally, a note on images, or the lack thereof. As I believe should be clear after reading the chapter on likeness, professional wrestling promoters are often remiss to offer what they consider their intellectual property to anyone for any reason, even under what should be considered fair use. For instance, after months of emailing with the publisher, I was not able to procure the image rights to the back of Mick Foley's book *Have a Nice Day: A Tale of Blood and Sweatsocks* for any price. The images in Foley's book are all reprinted with permission of WWE and other promotions and are listed in a section on image permissions. Even though the back cover was not listed in that section and a particular copyright owner was not named (which seemed to imply the image was created by and for the publisher), I was encouraged to contact WWE. Many emails to WWE without response for another project have made clear to me that I will likely never get approval for a wrestling image from WWE. Others seem to have better luck. This is perhaps something we should be familiar with in the field of theatre and performance studies, where production photos are not always available. Like the theatre it is, in many ways, professional wrestling has to be seen to be understood. Promoters understand this and leverage the visual in order to make money. Maybe someone will procure all the many rights for images and produce a beautiful coffee-table-ready academic book on professional wrestling. Until then, professional wrestling images circulate widely on the internet. I can only recommend that you do an image search for the back cover of Mick Foley's book and for the images of wrestlers and wrestling moves and other visual material as they are mentioned in the book. In the end, there is very little that might be seen in a picture from a pro wrestling event that you cannot infer from the writing if you have seen even a few minutes of professional wrestling. It is a live, narrative form and we should probably start considering it in relation to the many other live, narrative forms that we already easily consider theatre.

Notes

1 Roland Barthes, *Mythologies*, trans. Annette Lavers (New York: Hill and Wang, 1972), 13.
2 Barthes, *Mythologies*, 13.
3 Eero Laine, "Kayfabe: Optimism, Cynicism, and Critique," *Professional Wrestling: Politics and Populism*, eds. Nell Haynes, Eero Laine, Heather Levi, Sharon Mazer, Enactments, Richard Schechner, series editor (Calcutta: Seagull Books/University of Chicago Press, forthcoming).
4 Barthes, *Mythologies*, 13.
5 Aristotle, *Poetics*, trans. S.H. Butcher, part 6, http://classics.mit.edu/Aristotle/poetics.1.1.html. For an extended comparison of professional wrestling and Aristotle's elements of tragedy, see Gerald W. Morton and George M. O'Brien, *Wrestling to Rasslin: Ancient Sport to American Spectacle* (Bowling Green, OH: Bowling Green State University Popular Press, 1985), 118–124.
6 Sharon Mazer, *Professional Wrestling: Sport and Spectacle* (Jackson, MS: University of Mississippi Press, 1998), 19.
7 See Eero Laine, "Stadium Sized Theatre: WWE and The World of Professional Wrestling," in *Performance and Professional Wrestling*, eds. Broderick Chow, Eero Laine, and Claire Warden (London: Routledge, 2017), 39–47; and Chapter 1 in this book.
8 It is a common refrain among many fan-scholars and historians of popular culture that something might be made respectable because it is widely consumed and may have elements that resemble more distinguished cultural form. Especially considering the overt misogyny and racism present in 1990s and early-2000s wrestling, the sentiment that "Fifty Million Viewers Can't Be Wrong" is troublingly stated even as the question of why so many people engage with professional wrestling is a useful inquiry (Michael Atkinson, "Fifty Million Viewers Can't Be Wrong: Professional Wrestling, Sports Entertainment, and Mimesis," *Sociology of Sport Journal* 19 (2002): 47–66).
9 Mazer, *Professional Wrestling*, 172.
10 Mazer, *Professional Wrestling*, 172–173.
11 Mazer, *Professional Wrestling*, 173.
12 Mazer, *Professional Wrestling*, 173.
13 Gerald Craven and Richard Moseley, "Actors on the Canvas Stage: The Dramatic Conventions of Professional Wrestling," *Journal of Popular Culture* 6, no. 2 (Fall 1972): 326–336.
14 See for instance: Stephen Di Benedetto, "Playful Engagements: Wrestling with the Attendant Masses," in *Performance and Professional Wrestling*, eds. Broderick Chow, Eero Laine, and Claire Warden (London: Routledge, 2017), 26–36; Michael Ball, *Professional Wrestling As Ritual Drama in American Popular Culture* (Lewiston, NY: Edwin Mellen Press, 1990). See also a number of theses and dissertations: Allen Turowetz, "An Ethnography of Professional Wrestling: Elements of a Staged Contest" (MA Thesis, McGill University, 1974); Mark Elliot Workman, "The Differential Perception of a Dramatic Event: Interpretations of the Meaning of Professional Wrestling Matches (PhD Diss., University of Pennsylvania, 1977); Terry McNeil Saunders, "Play, Performance and Professional Wrestling: An Examination of a Modern Day Spectacle Of Absurdity" (PhD Diss., University of California, Los Angeles, 1998); Dalbir Singh Sehmby, "Professional Wrestling, Whooo!: A Cultural Con, an Athletic Dramatic Narrative, and a Haven for Rebel Heroes" (MA Thesis, University of Alberta, 2000); David Eugene Everard, "Wrestling Dell'arte: Professional Wrestling as Theatre" (MA Thesis, University of Victoria, 2002).

15 Workman, "Perception of a Dramatic Event," 226.
16 For the sake of simplicity and in keeping with the practice of World Wrestling Entertainment, Inc., WWE is not referred to by its former names or acronyms.
17 See Peter Zazzali, *Acting in the Academy: The History of Professional Actor Training in US Higher Education* (New York: Routledge, 2016).
18 Stacy Wolf, "Musical Theatre Studies," *Journal of American Drama and Theatre* 28, no. 1 (Winter 2016), https://jadtjournal.org/2016/03/23/musical-theatre-studies/.
19 Wolf, "Musical Theatre Studies."
20 Eero Laine, Professional Wrestling Scholarship: Legitimacy and Kayfabe," *The Popular Culture Studies Journal* 6, no. 1 (2018): 97–99; Professional Wrestling Studies Association, https://prowrestlingstudies.org/.
21 Savran, "Toward a Historiography of the Popular" *Theatre Survey* 45, no. 2 (November 2004): 212.
22 Savran, "Toward a Historiography," 213.
23 David Saltz, "Editorial Comment: Popular Culture and Theatre History," *Theatre Journal* 60, no. 4 (December 2008): front matter.
24 Also see Rodman, Gil. "Notes on Reconstructing the 'Popular,'" *Critical Studies in Media Communication* 33, no. 5 (2016): 388–398; and, Stuart Hall, "Notes on Deconstructing the Popular," in *People's History and Socialist Theory*, ed. Raphael Samuel (London: Routledge, 1981), 227–240; both are discussed in relation to professional wrestling in Laine, "Kayfabe: Optimism, Cynicism, and Critique."
25 Laine, "Stadium Sized Theatre."
26 In 2005, Susan Bennett reminded the field of its neglect of commercial theatre: "Though its audiences have been large and enthusiastic, critical practice has, apparently, found it of little or no interest to our sophisticated and theoretically informed theatre historiography and dramatic criticism." Susan Bennett, "Theatre/Tourism," *Theatre Journal* 57, no. 3 (October 2005): 407.
27 The *Professional Wrestling Studies Journal* has recently emerged under the auspices of the Professional Wrestling Studies Association.
28 Broderick Chow, Eero Laine, and Claire Warden, eds., *Performance and Professional Wrestling* (London: Routledge, 2017).
29 Jeremy Gordon, "Is Everything Wrestling?" *New York Times*, May 27, 2016, www.nytimes.com/2016/05/27/magazine/is-everything-wrestling.html.
30 Chris Cillizza, "Why Pro Wrestling is the Perfect Metaphor for Donald Trump's Presidency," The Point with Chris Cillizza, CNN, July 2, 2017, www.cnn.com/2017/07/02/politics/trump-wrestling-tweet/index.html.
31 Sharon Mazer. "Donald Trump Shoots the Match," *TDR: The Drama Review* 62, no. 2 (Summer 2018):175–200; Claire Warden, Broderick Chow, and Eero Laine, "Working Loose: A Response to 'Donald Trump Shoots the Match' by Sharon Mazer," *TDR: The Drama Review* 62, no. 2, T238 (Summer 2018): 201–215; Sharon Mazer, "Sharon Mazer Responds to Warden, Chow, and Laine," *TDR: The Drama Review* 62, no. 2 (Summer 2018): 216–219.
32 Kira Hall, Donna M. Goldstein, and Matthew Bruce Ingram, "The Hands of Donald Trump: Entertainment, Gesture, Spectacle," *HAU: Journal of Ethnographic Theory* 6, no. 2 (Autumn 2016): 93.
33 Sharon Mazer, "A Mega Power Implodes: Donald Trump, Presidential Performativity, and Professional Wrestling," in *Professional Wrestling: Politics and Populism*, eds. Nell Haynes, Eero Laine, Heather Levi, Sharon Mazer, Enactments, Richard Schechner, series editor (Calcutta: Seagull Books/University of Chicago Press, forthcoming); Heather Levi, "Why It Mattered: Wrestling Dramaturgy in the 2016 Presidential Election," in *Professional Wrestling: Politics and Populism*, eds. Nell Haynes, Eero Laine, Heather Levi, Sharon Mazer, Enactments, Richard

Schechner, series editor (Calcutta: Seagull Books/University of Chicago Press, forthcoming).
34 Morton and O'Brien, *Wrestling to Rasslin*.
35 Morton and O'Brien, *Wrestling to Rasslin*, 104.
36 Morton and O'Brien, *Wrestling to Rasslin*, 156.
37 Ball, *Professional Wrestling as Ritual Drama*.
38 Mazer, *Professional Wrestling*, 21.
39 Patrice A. Oppliger, *Wrestling and Hypermasculinity* (Jefferson, NC: McFarland and Company, 2004).
40 Oppliger, *Wrestling and Hypermasculinity*, 139–160.
41 Oppliger, *Wrestling and Hypermasculinity*, 145.
42 Heather Levi, "The Mask of the Luchador: Wrestling, Politics, and Identity," in *Steel Chair to the Head: The Pleasure and Pain of Professional Wrestling*, ed. Nicholas Sammond (Durham, NC: Duke University Press, 2005), 96–131; Carlos Monsiváis, "The Hour of the Mask as Protagonist: El Santo versus the Skeptics on the Subject of Myth," in *Steel Chair to the Head: The Pleasure and Pain of Professional Wrestling*, ed. Nicholas Sammond (Durham, NC: Duke University Press, 2005), 88–95.
43 Phillip Serrato, "Not Quite Heroes: Race, Masculinity, and Latino Professional Wrestlers," in *Steel Chair to the Head: The Pleasure and Pain of Professional Wrestling*, ed. Nicholas Sammond (Durham, NC: Duke University Press, 2005), 232–259.
44 Catherine Salmon and Susan Clerc, "'Ladies Love Wrestling, Too': Female Wrestling Fans Online," in *Steel Chair to the Head: The Pleasure and Pain of Professional Wrestling*, ed. Nicholas Sammond (Durham, NC: Duke University Press, 2005), 167–191.
45 Lucia Rahilly, "Is *RAW* War? Professional Wrestling as Popular S/M Narrative," in *Steel Chair to the Head: The Pleasure and Pain of Professional Wrestling*, ed. Nicholas Sammond (Durham, NC: Duke University Press, 2005), 213–231.
46 Laurence DeGaris, "The 'Logic' of Professional Wrestling," in *Steel Chair to the Head: The Pleasure and Pain of Professional Wrestling*, ed. Nicholas Sammond (Durham, NC: Duke University Press, 2005), 192–212.
47 Douglas Battema and Philip Sewell, "Trading in Masculinity: Muscles, Money, and Market Discourse in WWF," in *Steel Chair to the Head: The Pleasure and Pain of Professional Wrestling*, ed. Nicholas Sammond (Durham, NC: Duke University Press, 2005), 260–294.
48 Nicholas Sammond, "Squaring the Family Circle: WWF Smackdown Assaults the Social Body," in *Steel Chair to the Head: The Pleasure and Pain of Professional Wrestling*, ed. Nicholas Sammond (Durham, NC: Duke University Press, 2005), 133.
49 Roland Barthes, "The World of Wrestling," in *Steel Chair to the Head: The Pleasure and Pain of Professional Wrestling*, ed. Nicholas Sammond (Durham: Duke University Press, 2005), 23–31; Henry Jenkins III, "'Never Trust a Snake': WWF Wrestling as Masculine Melodrama," in *Steel Chair to the Head: The Pleasure and Pain of Professional Wrestling*, ed. Nicholas Sammond (Durham, NC: Duke University Press, 2005), 33–66; Sharon Mazer, "'Real Wrestling'/'Real' Life," in *Steel Chair to the Head: The Pleasure and Pain of Professional Wrestling*, ed. Nicholas Sammond (Durham, NC: Duke University Press, 2005), 67–87.
50 Mazer, "'Real Wrestling' /'Real' Life," 68.
51 Chad Dell, *The Revenge of Hatpin Mary: Women, Professional Wrestling, and Fan Culture in the 1950s* (New York: Peter Lang Publishing, 2006); Scott M. Beekman, *Ringside: A History of Professional Wrestling in America* (Westport, CT: Praeger, 2006).
52 Dell, *Revenge of Hat Pin Mary*, 18.
53 Beekman, *Ringside*.

54 Heather Levi, *The World of Lucha Libre: Secrets, Revelations, and Mexican National Identity* (Durham: Duke University Press, 2008). Levi's book is the primary study of lucha libre in Mexico published in English. Nell Haynes has examined lucha in the context of Bolivia in a series of articles that are essential reading for considering lucha and professional wrestling in a global context: Nell Haynes, "Global Cholas: Reworking Tradition and Modernity in Bolivian Lucha Libre," *The Journal of Latin American and Caribbean Anthropology* 18, no. 3 (2013): 432–446; Nell Haynes, "UnBoliviable Bouts: Gender and Essentialisation of Bolivia's Cholitas Luchadoras," in *Global Perspectives on Women in Combat Sports: Women Warriors around the World*, ed. Alex Channon and Christopher R. Matthews (London: Palgrave Macmillan, 2015), 267–283; Nell Haynes, "Kiss with a Fist," *Journal of Language and Sexuality* 5, no. 2 (2016): 250–275.
55 R. Tyson Smith, *Fighting for Recognition: Identity and the Performance of Violence in Professional Wrestling* (Durham, NC: Duke University Press, 2014), 1.
56 Benjamin Litherland, *Wrestling in Britain: Sporting Entertainments, Celebrity and Audiences* (London: Routledge, 2018), 2.
57 Aaron D. Horton, ed., *Identity in Professional Wrestling: Essays on Nationality, Race and Gender* (Jefferson, NC: McFarland, 2018); CarrieLynn D. Reinhard and Christopher J. Olson, eds., *Convergent Wrestling: Participatory Culture, Transmedia Storytelling, and Intertextuality in the Squared Circle* (London: Routledge, 2019); Dru Jeffries, ed., *#WWE: Professional Wrestling in the Digital Age* (Indiana University Press, forthcoming); Nell Haynes, Eero Laine, Heather Levi, and Sharon Mazer, eds., *Professional Wrestling: Politics and Populism*, Enactments, Richard Schechner, Series Editor (Calcutta: Seagull Books, forthcoming).
58 Litherland, *Wrestling in Britain*, 3.

Chapter 1

Productive theatre and professional wrestling
The business of kayfabe

Professional wrestling has always functioned with a theatrical business model, wherein live events drive ticket sales and profits. More directly: "the business of professional wrestling is the business of theatre" and vice versa.[1] While pro wrestling emerged from carnivals and athletic troupes of the late 1800s, it became more theatrical (including performances on literal stages) as theatre in Europe and especially the US was becoming more "artistic," less popular, and ostensibly moving away from commercial interests.[2] Journalist Marcus Griffin describes professional wrestling in his 1937 book *Fall Guys: The Barnums of Bounce* as "probably the greatest entertainment spectacle today, containing acrobatics, comedy, buffoonery, pantomime, tragedy, interlude, curtain, and afterpiece."[3] Griffin's is the earliest book-length study of the theatricality of professional wrestling and it directly links theatre and pro wrestling through overlapping aspects of production and the work of the performers:

> There are all the elements of theatre including the producer, publicity man, advance agent, stage manager, and prompter. Like Shakespeare's famed line, wrestlers "suit the action to the word and the word to the action," and thus create in their bouts what is known as heat, or as Pope expressed it, "they awaken the soul by tender strokes of art."[4]

While Griffin perhaps stretches some of his more literary connections too far, his book otherwise includes dramaturgical-like analyses of the various ways matches begin, proceed, and finish; information regarding how wrestling promoters and wrestlers tour and stage their shows; journalistic accounts of individuals working behind the scenes; and other presumed (theatrical) secrets of the trade.

Wrestling as secret theatre (or not-so-secret theatre, as the case may be) is built into its very performance and, indeed, is integral to the pro wrestling business model. In a way, the performance of pro wrestling inverts the idea of theatre where cast and crew acknowledge the fictions of the show and the audience willfully suspends disbelief during the performance. In professional wrestling, wrestlers and promoters have insisted on the idea that what they do is not theatrical and the audience plays along both during the performance and the rest of the time as well. This has taken different turns throughout the history of professional wrestling and today there is an acknowledgment that wrestling is certainly theatrical, but it is also "not fake." Even those fans who have historically challenged the claims to sport are already playing the wrestling game. If the promoter and the wrestlers present a product that is highly theatrical and claim it is not and someone decides to start an argument about it, they have already succumbed to the broader spectacle of the pro wrestling game.

This shared theatricality is often referred to as *kayfabe*. Kayfabe is a central idea for professional wrestling and has had different notions over time, but, in short, it is the presentation of professional wrestling as sport that is not pre-determined. Kayfabe is central to professional wrestling's theatrical and financial interests and also describes a wide range of social practices. It is often construed as simple deception or even lying, and some of the etymological evidence presented in this chapter supports such a reading. Kayfabe need not be forceful deception; rather, today, kayfabe is most frequently that which is the easiest to believe.

Wrestlers have historically gone to significant lengths and expended impressive amounts of labor to protect kayfabe; for those watching wrestling it is fairly easy to just accept it or not think too deeply about it. David Shoemaker cites a wrestling fan from 1931:

> As far as I know the shows are honest. But even if they're not I get a big kick out of them, for they are full of action and all the outward signs of hostile competition. It is either honest competition or fine acting and in either case I get a real show.[5]

Shoemaker suggests that fans have been in on kayfabe for the better part of the past century, which is to say there wasn't nearly as much concern about the truth or theatricality of pro wrestling from fans as there might have been from pro wrestling's critics. A reprinted article in an issue of the *Literary Digest* from 1932 supports such a reading, offering the notion that "maybe the chief reason wrestling is popular is that it is not wrestling."[6]

Indeed, as early as 1930, the *New York Times* reported that pro wrestling had "passed into the status of theatrical classification."[7] The headline read: "Wrestling Placed Under New Status: Commission Rules Clubs Must List Matches as Shows or Exhibitions."[8] It would not be the last time the wrestling industry was "exposed" for its overt theatricality and it certainly did not greatly alter the way the events were promoted. Just one year after the reclassification, the same athletic commission official (former wrestler William Muldoon) who changed the status of professional wrestling issued his objections to a proposed wrestling event that was to be held in a less than sportive location. His statement for the *New York Times*:

It would be just as ridiculous for New Yorkers to stage a wrestling match at the Metropolitan Opera or to present an opera in Madison Square Garden as for the Westchester County Centre to be desecrated by a bout of professional wrestling.[9]

It seems, however, that the lack of clarity from organizing bodies on the topic of wrestling's nature as sport or theatre did not hurt professional wrestling as a source of entertainment. By the middle of the twentieth century, professional wrestling had spread to many countries throughout Europe and would also gain especially strong followings in Japan and Mexico. Today, the business connections between theatre and wrestling described by Griffin in the 1930s—the producers, publicity people, and advance agents—are wrapped up in a finely polished, corporate package by WWE, which is based in the United States but frequently holds events throughout the world.

Throughout their varied histories, theatre and professional wrestling have shared a business model that is based in a live event that resists replication and requires workers to labor in front of and for customers. While the aesthetics of the forms and even labor pools at times appear distinct, the labor that generates profit for the promoter functions in the same way. In thinking about professional wrestling and/as theatre, I begin by asking, "What does live entertainment produce?" What is the theatrical product? This is, I think, a central question for theatre and one that has seemingly obvious and counterintuitive answers. I am interested in the ways that theatre and performance (and thus professional wrestling) make money without producing tangible goods. This is perhaps as obvious as professional wrestling itself, but frequently the very obviousness of labor in the theatre obscures such labor. Theatre produces an event, an experience, a moment in time that is purchased for the price of admission. In that same consideration, once the show is over, all that is left is the detritus of the event. Some of these materials might turn out to be collectors' items or souvenirs or reused for future productions and a good amount is even thrown away. So, other than the labor that is expended before and during the act of theatre, the theatrical goods that remain sit perhaps awkwardly between souvenirs and garbage.

Those are broad categories, of course, and Christopher B. Balme suggests we might define theatrical goods as almost anything "that might enter economic circulation: texts, production concepts, songs, dance routines, costumes, and of course, the performers themselves."[10] And while he acknowledges the performances of a play as "invariably the beginning of the commodification process," he notes the ways that theatrical productions circulate past the performances themselves, sometimes through media.[11] In theatre and professional wrestling, the live performance forms the nucleus of the form itself and the act of profit making.

Despite the common sentiment that the theatre is no place to make a living, the performing arts are quite profitable, just not necessarily for the laborers or the artists themselves. According to some measures, in 2016 the performing arts contributed 4.3 percent to the US GDP or about 800 billion dollars.[12] For comparison, in the 2015–16 season, Broadway grossed 1.373 billion dollars, and in the 2016–17 season, 1.449 billion dollars.[13] WWE grossed about half of that: 729 million dollars in 2016 and a little over 800 million dollars in 2017.[14] Both Broadway and WWE represent just a fraction of the money in the performing arts, but they are useful examples, if for no other reason than their financial transparency. Indeed, professional wrestling is, along with Broadway, exemplary of how theatre and other narrative-driven, live events make money despite the many apparent limitations that present themselves. And while the commercial stage that pro wrestling occupies is more often than not a stadium rather than a historic touring theatre or new arts complex, the logic of professional wrestling at the business level is not unlike any other commercial theatre.

This chapter considers the ways in which the theatricality of professional wrestling has made it more productive. The theatricalization of the performance form over the course of the twentieth century allowed producers and promoters to capitalize on the possibility of having narrative command over sport or otherwise unpredictable events. The chapter begins with an overview of what I call productive theatre, what is often referred to as commercial or for-profit theatre. The idea of productive theatre stems from a reading of Marx and his conception of productive labor that is in contradistinction to Adam Smith's goods-based notion of the term. The connections between commercial theatre and professional wrestling, taking both as forms of productive theatre, follows and leads into a consideration of the theatrical logic of professional wrestling and the further explication of the term kayfabe. Kayfabe is the theatrical overlay to professional wrestling that for parts of pro wrestling history presented the fake sport as real, unfixed, and unscripted. In this chapter, I consider the etymology of the term as it stretches back to a secret carnival dialect in order to explore the ways that professional wrestling operates today. In particular, I am interested in how professional wrestling models production for other performance forms.

Productive theatre

Professional wrestling performs labor, but nothing tangible is produced. However, rather than trying to find a continuum or a precise moment of commodification, we might look to the labor of the performers. Michael Shane Boyle's *Theatre Survey* article, "Performance and Value: The Work of Theatre in Karl Marx's Critique of Political Economy," discusses the central economic arguments regarding theatre and production between Adam Smith and Karl Marx.[15] Boyle reminds us that Adam Smith places performers and musicians among many other "unproductive" professions whose "services generally perish in the very instant of their performance."[16] Indeed, for Smith,

The labour of some of the most respectable orders in the society is, like that of menial servants, unproductive of any value, and does not fix or realize itself in any permanent subject, or vendible commodity, which endures after that labour is past, and for which an equal quantity of labour could afterwards be procured.[17]

Because nothing tangible remains after laboring, because no raw materials are transformed, Smith considered a wide swath of labor (from royalty to lawyers to singers) to be unproductive because "Like the declamation of the actor, the harangue of the orator, or the tune of the musician, the work of all of them perishes in the very instant of its production."[18] The labor may vanish; however, Boyle reminds us that it does not vanish "before it has transformed socially into the form of a capitalist commodity. Marx moves the actor's performance that Smith describes as unproductive into a new set of social relations through which the very same labor yields surplus value."[19] That is, Smith only considered labor to be productive if it produced tangible goods; however, for Marx, when these so-called "unproductive" laborers are employed by another person, something *is* produced: surplus value for the capitalist.

As if to highlight his distinction from Smith, Marx uses the labor of the actor as an extreme example of one who labors but creates no tangible good. For Marx, "Actors are productive workers, not in so far as they produce a play, but in so far as they increase their employer's wealth."[20] In his *Theories of Surplus Value*, Marx is entirely clear that from the standpoint of the capitalist, it does not matter if laborers produce widgets or arias: "Productive and unproductive labour is here throughout conceived from *the standpoint of the possessor of money, from the standpoint of the capitalist.*"[21] Capital is produced and thus the labor is productive—the widget or the aria are both equalized under the regime of wage labor.

Any laborer, whether an actor or "even a clown, according to this definition, is a productive labourer if he works in the service of a capitalist (an entrepreneur) to whom he returns more labour than he receives from him in the form of wages"[22] Thus, productive labor is labor that benefits the capitalist (or capital), that provides surplus value (as opposed to revenue or another use-value). Professional wrestlers, like other performers, need not produce any material goods in order to be productive for the promoters— certainly something understood by theatre producers and wrestling promoters throughout history.[23] The productive labor of wrestlers made money for promoters but had its limits, namely it could not be easily replicated.

Professional wrestling is a deeply laborious endeavor and like other dramatic forms, it operates under its own logic with conventions that are implicitly and explicitly understood by the audience and performers. Most performance conventions in professional wrestling are rooted in the idea that conflict will be resolved through physical fights. Because professional wrestling is largely improvisatory, with some details worked out prior to the match, the act of wrestling itself is based on a prevailing logic meant to elicit an emotional response from the audience. The matches then can be considered as a sort of improvisatory dance or physical storytelling.

Professional wrestlers manipulate emotions for a living and share in the emotional labor of building an in-ring story. Their ability to do so is what makes them productive laborers for promoters. However, the labor of wrestling is not simply affective as wrestlers sweat, bleed, and very obviously exert themselves physically, making their labor exemplary of the concept of "passion work" defined in relation to professional wrestling by R. Tyson Smith as

> jointly performed emotional labor intended to elicit a passionate response from subjects through an impression of extreme states such as joy, agony, or suffering. Ideal performances of passion work such as pro wrestling are situations in which two (or more) performers jointly perform emotional labor in a high-stakes context where there is great risk for pain, injury or death.[24]

Passion work is largely affective, except for the fact that in order to elicit the desired emotional response, in professional wrestling, the potential for injury is greatly heightened. Passion work echoes, perhaps more extremely given the potential for serious injury and death in professional wrestling, acting and performance traditions wherein the calling forth of emotions is as physically involved as any manual labor.[25] The theatrical overlay of professional wrestling doesn't make the work safer for its workers; rather, the move away from sport makes the events safer for producers, allowing them to adapt to new markets and more tightly control the content of the wrestling matches and the wrestlers themselves.

These controls are built into the theatrical form of pro wrestling itself as a set of rules that guide the action. Laurence DeGaris describes the work of performing a wrestling match in "The 'Logic' of Professional Wrestling."[26] DeGaris highlights the physical and affective aspects of working a match in his description of the labor that goes into a maneuver as basic as a headlock: "While mastering the mechanics of a headlock is important, the 'logic' of the headlock is equally important.... Both wrestlers must internalize the logic of the headlock in order to be completely effective."[27] Because pro wrestling moves are largely martially ineffective, both wrestlers must understand what the moves are intended to portray. The physical interaction between the wrestlers must tell a story, in the case of the headlock, of dominance and submission and then escape or defeat as one wrestler clenches the other's head in the crook of an arm and appears to apply pressure, ostensibly cutting off the blood supply to the headlocked wrestler's brain.

The physical logic of wrestling conventions is especially evident in wrestling moves that involve one wrestler jumping or falling on another.

Generally, if the wrestler doing the jumping manages to land on the other wrestler, the pain is theatrically absorbed by the receiving wrestler. However, should the leaping wrestler miss the mark or should the receiving wrestler avoid the impact, the offensive wrestler receives the bulk of the pain contained in the move. It is hard to imagine, in watching such maneuvers, however, that there is such a material difference between landing on or not landing on another wrestler rather than the mat.[28] The dominant position (the one meting out pain and punishment) between the wrestlers is decided in the moment of the fall or the jump before gravity takes hold and pulls the wrestler to the mat. Such maneuvers are intensely dramatic and dynamic for wrestlers who are particularly adept at so-called high-flying moves. Will they land on the prone wrestler or will the prone wrestler move out of the way? Whether the flying wrestler lands on the prone wrestler or not, the moves are not without risk.

Jumping off any structure is physically dangerous, and wrestlers are regularly injured by such moves, but the theatricality of the wrestling logic overlays any actual injuries sustained. The simulation in professional wrestling makes it unclear whether "the simulator is sick [or in this case, injured or in pain] or not given that he produces 'true' symptoms."[29] The wrestlers are not paid to be injured (as independent contractors, it is in their best interest to stay healthy), only to create the illusion of injury. To sustain an actual injury may garner some respect from fans or promoters, but the injury may cause the wrestler to miss performances and thus lose pay. R. Tyson Smith also acknowledges that "from the standpoint of the organization, debilitating injuries are problematic because they remove potential talent from the shows."[30] The problem, therefore, is that much of the immaterial labor that goes into creating such simulations carries with it the possibility of bodily harm.[31]

While wrestling wears some of its worst labor offenses openly, it does so in parallel with theatre proper. Michael McKinnie via Nicholas Ridout reminds us that

> the theatre is an economic sub sector in which work is highly alienated. Picking up on this perception one notes how the employee's time is regulated with rigorous force by bells and curtains, how both the rehearsal process and the nightly routine of performances are dominated by repetitive activity, how wage levels are set in structures of extreme differentiation, how these are maintained by a huge pool of surplus labour which renders effective industrial organization impossible, and how the core activity itself is both a metaphor of alienation and alienation itself: the actor is paid to appear in public speaking words written by someone else and executing physical movement which has at the very least usually been subjected to intense and critical scrutiny by a representative of the management who effectively enjoys the power of hiring and firing.[32]

As another form of productive labor, professional wrestling makes these working conditions explicit. Jamie Lewis Hadley explains the clear connection in terminology between violence and economic exchange with the term "selling," as when a wrestler is selling the pain, which "means reacting to moves and strikes in a particular way so as to give the impression of being injured or in pain."[33] However, even as workers are exploited in the classic Marxist sense that promoters are extracting their labor and the wrestling form clearly stages such alienation, the mechanics and indeed the logic of wrestling may actually rely on in moments of care and camaraderie.

The caring and cooperative nature of professional wrestling has been observed by many scholars who have done ethnographic work and who have trained in the form. And perhaps such cooperative work has developed in light of the alienating theatrical work of wrestling. In Heather Levi's training in lucha libre in Mexico, she notes that "every throw, every lock is a technique of mutuality."[34] Broderick Chow describes the intentionally soft touches that are required as wrestlers attempt to make their work look brutal while caring for each other.[35] R. Tyson Smith explains that rather than the usual negative tolls of emotional labor, "pro wrestlers demonstrate a contrary effect. Intimate, physical work with each other within high-risk, dangerous context has the potential to generate something satisfying—a product that is neither tangible nor financial but social."[36] Even if that social product is productive and financially beneficial for the promoter, Smith claims the labor itself is not necessarily experienced by the workers as "harmful or alienating."[37] Professional wrestling, in Smith's observation and estimation "because of its inherent empathy built upon mutual trust and protection, has the capacity to be connective, intimate, and a means of solidarity."[38] This sense of care is both potentially empowering and similarly part of the logic of the game and thus a form of training.

It is a strange combination of work and theatricality as wrestlers dive and throw each other around the ring even as the give and take of the match benefits the promoter. Sharon Mazer describes the learning process that new wrestlers would go through decades ago in Gleason's gym, where she did her field work for *Professional Wrestling: Sport and Spectacle*. She observes the careful balance of a new wrestler understanding how

> to respect himself while respecting others. He must learn to display hostility and to act violently toward another man without actually damaging him. He must surrender his aggression, his competitiveness, his desire for victory, and his fear of humiliation to the demands of the promoter, the performance, the game. If he refuses to play by the rules, whether in workouts or in matches, he runs the risk of vociferous derision at best and a serious beating at worst. For most, the lesson in respect is learned by testing the limits and tasting the consequences, not by talking or thinking about it or by figuring it out.[39]

As in theatre, while the labored performance of professional wrestling may allow some moments or sense of solidarity between workers, it is at the same time leveraged for the needs of the promoter. Nonetheless, the risks of performing are placed on the individual wrestlers as the profits and often creative control of the wrestling event is considered the realm of the promoter, especially since the fights in wrestling are not actually fights, but predetermined nodes in longer storylines. The rest of this chapter examines the power and profitability that comes with controlling the wrestling narrative through the notion of kayfabe. The term kayfabe stems from the early carnival language of professional wrestling and has come to be the central idea of performing and of watching professional wrestling. So, even as wrestlers might be in control of the logic of individual matches, the overarching narratives are an important element of theatrical control for promoters.

Kayfabe: etymology and practice

It is impossible to consider professional wrestling without thinking through kayfabe. It is the concept from professional wrestling that draws significant scholarly attention, in part because it is both the central analytic and conceit of professional wrestling. At this point, kayfabe is understood as it functions in professional wrestling, as a sort of shared suspension of disbelief or as sort of theatrical shroud or the diegetic world of wrestling storylines and characters; indeed, and as kayfabe is playful engagement between the theatricality of the ring and all that surrounds it, kayfabe also becomes useful outside the not so strict bounds of professional wrestling itself.[40] On the one hand, kayfabe is professional wrestling's core theoretical intervention and the very concept that has driven its success throughout the twentieth century; and on the other hand, like professional wrestling itself, kayfabe is all just a little too obvious. Of course wrestling is theatrical, and of course we know it, and of course we play along. But professional wrestling, through kayfabe, highlights the ways that everything is theatrical, and of course we know it, and of course we play along.

Wrestler and academic Laurence DeGaris believes "kayfabe is pretty straightforward. It's the truth that's slippery."[41] I love this framing for a number of reasons, not the least of which is that it shifts the focus of the discussion away from kayfabe. In many ways it is a classic move to maintain kayfabe. The statement itself is a wonderful bit of truth twisting, turning around the common idea that the truth is clear and the fabrications are complications. The entire made-up world of professional wrestling is the easy part, it's the rest that is problematic. Given the work in the field on kayfabe to this point, I am less concerned here with a close examination of how kayfabe is maintained or how it breaks down.[42] Rather, I hope that this section might help trace a bit of the theatrical history of professional wrestling through the etymology of the term. Understanding that the concept of kayfabe is broadly understood by most who study professional wrestling, I hope that this might also ground such discussions by bringing together the disparate discussions of the term's roots and historic usage, which are closely tied to the theatrical business practices of professional wrestling.

Despite a history of use that spans most of the twentieth century, kayfabe is not yet listed in most standard dictionaries or the expansive *Oxford English Dictionary*. Linguists Carol L. Russell and Thomas E. Murray trace the development of the term to show that professional wrestlers used "carnie talk" until the practice began dropping off in the mid-1980s.[43] Russell and Murray explain the difficulties of tracing the history of a largely undocumented argot in their essay "The Life and Death of Carnie," where they write that carnie, "now nearly dead has left but a dim trail and that trail is rife with dead ends, inconsistencies of fact, and unanswered questions."[44] In other words, the origins of the term kayfabe are as murky as the situation it describes—the path to a definitive history is full of false turns, rumors, and deception.

For most of the twentieth century, kayfabe represented a theatrical overlay and secret understanding that wrestling industry was not actually a competitive endeavor. Those in the know were "smart" to the business and maintained the façade of sportive competition at all costs—their livelihoods depended on it. From the perspective of the wrestlers, who had certainly worked hard to make it to the inside, and had endured the processes of learning the business, why should anyone else get an easy pass? The strict boundary was enforced by wrestlers who were forbidden from giving any indication that they were any different from their in-ring personas. Wrestlers thus maintained character whenever in public. In the carnie argot used among wrestlers and carnival workers, the term kayfabe was alternately a verbal warning (to "kayfabe!" or "keep kayfabe!") or a way of distinguishing the real from the theatrical (one could be kayfabe enemies but actually very close friends).

As an invented language that traveled largely through touring carnivals and circuses, carnie is purposefully flexible and necessarily malleable to maintain its secrecy. For a good part of the twentieth century, the walls of secrecy were particularly harsh. One had to be an insider to understand kayfabe and pro wrestling, and to get in on the business took time, effort, toughness, and a fair amount of pain. Imagine how a theatre might protect itself if spectators expected the actors to have the same traits and personalities as the characters they played. Or think of the ways that magicians guard the secrets of their illusions. In the case of professional wrestling, the illusions are actually the wrestlers' portrayal of their characters. The secrets of the trade are then the differences between wrestler and character.

Wrestling promoters knew that it was not enough to simply maintain character in wrestling: they needed wrestlers who could actually wrestle. Known as "shooters" or "hookers" throughout the twentieth century, some wrestlers were employed by promoters for their legitimate wrestling ability. These skilled wrestlers were hired by wrestling promoters who knew that, at some point, the legitimacy of the matches and thus kayfabe might be challenged. The shooters were supposed to be able to best any challenger and keep the audience (or "marks") believing, paying for, and betting on the performances. The meanest of these wrestlers were referred to as "rippers," and were put to use, especially on the carnival circuit and traveling at-shows (short for athletic shows), "often surprising college standouts and solid technical wrestlers who didn't know enough dirty tricks."[45] Such talent was of use even in the more organized and tightly controlled arenas of regional promoters where "there was always the danger of a double cross, a gambling coup, the use of a ringer, or even a paid-off referee."[46] Kept out of the public view, some shooters were referred to as "policemen," and would wrestle any unknown or unaffiliated challengers as a tryout before the outsider might be allowed to safely face the champion.[47] So while kayfabe was and continues to be maintained through more theatrical methods, for some time it was physically enforced.

Sharon Mazer's ethnographic research from the late 1980s and early 1990s reveals that the term kayfabe was used more rhetorically. She notes that "Professional wrestling is threaded throughout with language of the con game."[48] Mazer reinforces the notion that the term kayfabe is "taken from nineteenth-century carnival, medicine show, and sideshow practice and simply refers to a con or deception."[49] Mazer's research suggests that kayfabe can "refer to participants' self-promotional, rhetorically inflated, and somewhat truth-obfuscating patter that resembles that of the talkers at the traditional sideshow."[50] Those who were particularly adept at such deception and distortion would be called a "kayfabian" or someone practiced in kayfabe—in other words, "a con artist."[51] She notes that "most wrestlers are proud to be called kayfabians because it means they're in on the (con)game."[52] The theatricality of the con game of pro wrestling is thus linked to the theatricality of selling, of carnival barkers trying to get marks in the door to the show. The ability to influence people, to sell them an idea, to help them convince themselves is then a key aspect of professional wrestling business. Not only do wrestlers need to work together, but they need to be able to sell the match, both physically and verbally.

"Kayfabe" appears in *The Routledge Dictionary of Modern American Slang and Unconventional English*, which offers two uses of the word, the first of which is likely the most common understanding today: "The protection of the inside secrets of professional wrestling."[53] It is worth noting that the so-called secrets of professional wrestling have changed over the years from protecting the business and the ruse of the carnival workers to protecting the business and its brand and share price.[54] The idea that the wrestling event was determined might have been the biggest secret for some time throughout wrestling history, but the secrets of wrestling are now more about where the storylines are headed and whose contracts are being renewed and who is out with a legitimate injury versus who has been written off the show. The secrets of wrestling today are perhaps not dissimilar to movie spoilers, with the key difference being that wrestling fans actively seek out that information that would otherwise be considered a spoiler in most other narrative forms.

The entry in *The Routledge Dictionary of Modern American Slang and Unconventional English* also includes what we can assume is the earliest print example the editors could find—a quote from an online message board in 1990: "What is this 'kayfabe'? ★★★ Nowadays it simply refers to insider info."[55] In 1990, as the quote suggests, the term had already shifted from previous understandings, but the focus on insider info is consistent with the idea of keeping secrets. To complicate the meaning, the second example of the term offers a very broad definition: "In professional wrestling, [kayfabe is] used as an all-purpose verb." The example offered echoes the first definition and example of use: "To 'kayfabe' basically means that the wrestler keeps the inner workings of the business to himself and doesn't share them with the fans."[56] Consistent with Mazer's and others' observations, according to the available dictionary definition, kayfabe is an act ("protection") in defense of shared, hidden knowledge ("inside secrets"), or it may be the "insider info" itself.

Similarly, Shaun Assael and Mike Mooneyham, sports writers who cover professional wrestling, point to "a pig-Latin dialect called Carny" that wrestlers would deploy "whenever an outsider was in their midst."[57] While originally a verbal warning that non-wrestlers were around, according to Assael and Mooneyham, "in time *kayfabe* became a metaphor for the wall of silence that wrestlers built around their business."[58] B. Brian Blair, a former wrestler (turned business owner turned author turned Florida politician), published a glossary of wrestling terms in his book *Smarten Up!: Say it Right*, put out by the Kayfabe Publishing Company.[59] Blair's entry for "Carny" describes it as "The official inside language of pro wrestling that is being taught to you in this book; originally used by carnival people to speak to each other without customers knowing what they've said."[60] Whereas kayfabe is defined as "keep secret, tighten your lips, don't tell" (similar to the verbal warning Assael and Mooneyham ascribe to its original meaning), for Blair it is the term "work" that has the meaning of "not real," as in a "worked" storyline or doing the work of performing one's character.[61] In Blair's configuration wrestlers then "keep kayfabe about a work." Indeed, in Blair's glossary and many other sources wrestlers are referred to as "workers" and "Wrestler's Honor" is "a promise made as a joke."[62] The con or the ruse required the participation of all involved—everyone had to be a kayfabian. It was not enough to simply have a few genuinely tough shooters, hookers, rippers, or policemen: the act of keeping up the image of fair fights and sportive ideals was more nuanced and widespread than just roughing up the inquisitive locals.

In an article titled "Professional Wrestling's Clandestine Jargon," journalist John Lister asserts that

> there have been several attempts to explain the term's etymology. The most spurious involve second- or third-hand tales of a wrestler named

Kay Fabian who, depending on the variant, was either mute (and thus a literal inspiration for a code of silence) or an untrustworthy gossip; there is no record of such a man existing.[63]

Lister also provides the most involved explanation for the term:

> It is a variant of the Latin *caveo* (in the sense of "be on guard against" or "look out for"). While tales of upper-class schoolboys using the warning "keep cavey" appear to be literary inventions of the "cripes" and "jeepers" variety, there are accounts of the phrase being used in this fashion among East London Jews between the wars. Many of the leading US wrestling promoters and performers of this period were of Eastern European origin and spoke a broken or heavily accented English, perhaps explaining the term's transformation in pronunciation.[64]

Lister's explanation, while an outlier for its complexity, may be both the most accurate and is perhaps most in the spirit of kayfabe in that it presents plausible ideas that still may be exaggerations of facts.

While the etymology of kayfabe might be complex and/or full of mystery, the definition today is fairly well understood (again, even if the implications of the idea are wide-ranging). It perhaps seems fitting, given the popular origins of the term, to turn to the publicly maintained *Wikipedia*:

> In professional wrestling, kayfabe /ˈkeɪfeɪb/ is the portrayal of staged events within the industry as "real" or "true", specifically the portrayal of competition, rivalries, and relationships between participants as being genuine and not of a staged or predetermined nature of any kind. Kayfabe has also evolved to become a code word of sorts for maintaining this "reality" within the direct or indirect presence of the general public.[65]

Wikipedia also notes that "a wrestler breaking kayfabe during a show would be likened to an actor breaking character on camera."[66] However, "since wrestling is performed in front of a live audience, whose interaction with the show is crucial to its success, kayfabe can be compared to the fourth wall in acting."[67] This comparison between wrestling and theatrical realism is not perfect because the fourth wall of the theatre can be physically placed at the opening of the proscenium arch. Wrestling does not have a fourth wall that remains in place, but it is rather more fluid and flexible.

R. Tyson Smith's ethnographic work, decades after Mazer, places kayfabe in particular relation to the physical performance and exertions of wrestling matches where "Performers follow rules similar to the rules of magicians: make your 'move' appear as real as possible without it actually being real."[68] While he uses the unusual construction "Performing *with* kayfabe," his definition and exploration of the concept are noteworthy in their emphasis on how wrestlers are caught between caring for their partners in the ring while convincing the audience of the opposite.[69] Smith's emphasis on the physical implications of kayfabe highlight the contradictory impulses where "agony and the infliction of pain are enthusiastically celebrated on the stage at the same time they are skillfully avoided backstage."[70] Further, the stage and backstage can share a physical space as wrestlers negotiate and signal using coded language meant not to be understood by outsiders.

Smith uses theatrical language to begin mapping the social, psychological, and physical terrain of wrestling and kayfabe:

> As with most of social life, the onstage performance the audience experiences is dependent on a backstage most cannot see or know. In the case of pro wrestling there is a literal stage (often in the round) and a literal backstage. In addition to these tangible spaces is a figurative backstage, which is concealed—at least until there is a mistake.[71]

Smith marks the difference between the intention or belief behind outward appearance and action. His spatial analysis is noteworthy in that the literal stage and literal backstage both exist physically, but access is prohibited to those buying tickets (to view the stage) or those vetted and invited (into the backstage area). The *figurative* backstage, however, exists at the level of personal intentionality and in the relationships among performers. This figurative backstage can be exposed on the literal stage or the literal backstage when something goes wrong or even when wrestlers reveal their true feelings (intentionally or not). Indeed, the literal stage thrives on this interplay with its unique ontology of representation and performance. For theatre and performance scholar Broderick Chow, "The potential for real violence gives wrestling its unique frisson, but also makes working into an ethical practice."[72] To work as a wrestler is to protect one's partners *and* one's business, both in the ring and well beyond the walls of the stadium.

Eric Weinstein, a mathematician and economist, has suggested that if we were to fully engage kayfabe as a theoretical concept, "we would undoubtedly have an easier time understanding a world in which investigative journalism seems to have vanished and bitter corporate rivals cooperate on everything from joint ventures to lobbying efforts."[73] The production of kayfabe—the narrative world that produces the horizons of possibility (for a company, for an event, or even, say, for an election)—or, per Weinstein, "Kayfabrication," is "the process of transition from reality towards kayfabe" and

> arises out of attempts to deliver a dependably engaging product for a mass audience while removing the unpredictable upheavals that imperil participants. As such Kayfabrication is a dependable feature of many of our most important systems.[74]

Kayfabrication (the fabrication of kayfabe) is not simply deception or performance or a narrative that paves over real events. Rather, it is the process by which corporations, governments, and other organizations produce saleable and predictable and engaging products. It relies as much on those producing it as those who are consuming it. Indeed, in many ways, professional wrestling is far more advanced than many business models. Rather than positing their product as a genuine item (i.e., "the real thing"), the narrative product is intentionally flexible, allowing fans to buy in to the created world through various mechanisms of feedback and critique.[75] Kayfabrication, then, can be seen as the process of making something into theatre in order to make it more productive, more profitable, more controlled. Professional wrestling is an example of taking the unruliness of sport into the contained field of theatre, where managers and producers can manage the bodies of performers.

Conclusion: expanding territories

To consider professional wrestling as theatre is to also consider the ways that professional wrestling and theatre operate economically. Theatre is clearly a productive economic activity that produces profit from the labor of its workers. Professional wrestling operates on the same fundamental principle, even if at times it appears to be an entirely separate endeavor. As a form of live entertainment, professional wrestling is limited in what it can do to sell its product. It relies on the embodied labor of its workers to perform, even as the product of their labor disappears as it is created. Like other forms of live entertainment, the professional wrestling industry has always thrived by expanding to new markets and finding new audiences. Even well before various digital means of circulating the wrestling product, wrestling promoters were actively searching for ways to expand their territories, sometimes through collusion with their supposed business rivals and sometimes relying on routes of commerce established through transnational politics and war. The wrestling industry, with its various agents from promoters to wrestlers to fans, has thus operated for some time as a sort of parallel and shadow theatrical industry—mirroring, relying upon, and at times leading innovations in theatre and performance and its ability to find and develop new markets.

The possibilities for a live performance form to not only take hold but to become incredibly profitable mark the ways, perhaps, that current musical producers and Broadway-based companies consider international markets and the possibilities for expansion. As wrestling territories became saturated in the US, wrestling promoters looked for new areas to expand and adjusted their labor pools accordingly—physically expanding their reach to international markets. John Griffiths suggests that between 1930 and 1945, professional wrestling was one of the best examples of a transnational sport spanning the US and colonial Britain.[76] Following World War II, US promoters expanded significantly into Japan. Lee Austin Thompson's 1986 article "Professional

Wrestling in Japan—Media and Message" provides an overview of the history of Japanese professional wrestling with analysis of "The Role of the Foreign Wrestler."[77] Thompson observes that after Japan increased its connection to and trading with the rest of the world in the 1800s, some Japanese wrestlers traveled to and trained in other countries and some recruited wrestlers while abroad and returned with them to Japan. It seems, however, that there was little interest at the time in such sporting events. Thompson asserts that in the early 1900s, "some wrestlers from abroad came to Japan to challenge *Kōdōkan* Judo, but nothing much came of it."[78] In the US, however, exchanges between US wrestling and Japanese martial arts were met with some level of interest in fitness magazines and other articles in the US in the early 1900s.[79]

By most accounts, wrestling in the US was still largely practiced as a legitimate sport at the beginning of the twentieth century. It was also considered a way of testing national superiority while gesturing towards global unity, not unlike the Olympics. Nonetheless, in Japan, wrestling apparently failed to capture the imagination of most people until 1951. The year marks a tour by former boxing champion Joe Louis and former professional wrestlers, including a former champion and a Japanese-American wrestler, who were invited by a branch of the Shriners Club to perform for US troops stationed in Japan after the war.[80] The first professional wrestling training facility opened in 1953, led by former sumo wrestler Rikidōzan, who also founded the Japan Professional Wrestling Association. By the end of 1954, the first televised matches had appeared on Japanese broadcasts and Rikidōzan had toured in the United States with the National Wrestling Alliance. Rikidōzan's company returned to Japan with the World Tag Team Championship belt and brought US and other foreign wrestlers with him, thus establishing the figure of the foreign wrestler as a recognizable trope in professional wrestling in Japan.[81]

The story is told somewhat differently from the perspective of the US-based National Wrestling Alliance, however. Tim Hornbacker's study of the NWA, subtitled *The Untold Story of the Monopoly that Strangled Pro Wrestling*, credits Rikidōzan as a founding figure of Japanese pro wrestling on the order of Frank Gotch, perhaps one of the most famous wrestlers in the US in the early 1900s.[82] However, for Hornbaker, Rikidōzan is more of a figurehead or sports legend than the impetus behind professional wrestling's expansion to Japan. Rather, Hornbaker's line of reasoning is that the NWA had expanded so quickly across the United States from 1949 to 1952 that international expansion was only logical as the next step:

> Every segment of the United States was controlled by a member, and bookers governed all corners of Canada. [Mexico City's Salvador] Lutteroth's admission accommodated Mexican clubs, and full-time operations in Japan were being considered by [Al] Karasick, working from the Hawaiian islands."[83]

Hornbaker states: "Japan was a market the Alliance yearned to exploit."[84] Karasick not only bragged about his efforts to develop Rikidōzan but also "concentrated on helping Asian wrestlers adapt to an 'American' style" and even worked and practiced with the theatre and entertainment company Yoshimoto Kogyo.[85] The reason, perhaps, for the fascination with foreign wrestlers, as Thompson asserts, may have to do with the fact that the NWA treated the Japan Pro-Wrestling Association as its base in Asia. From the 1950s to the 1970s, the NWA promoted its wrestlers through Japanese companies. Hornbaker describes this in language that echoes empire and missionaries: "The seeds planted by American emissaries created an entertainment brand that has provided Japanese fans decades of thrilling action."[86] Such action, however, has a certain logic to it that cannot be overlooked. And, indeed, the logic of professional wrestling is strikingly similar in many parts of the world—from the US to Japan to Australia to the UK to Central and South America.

Part of the appeal of professional wrestling is the simple fact that the act of wrestling is quite easy to grasp and the performance has an internal logic that is immediately understandable to most spectators. The headlock needs to be legible to everyone from ringside to the cheap seats. The wrestling form also requires a sense of care for the other performers while performing outwardly agonistic actions. The wrestling moves and the way they fit together allow for endless combinations and an immediate sense of storytelling. Ironically, it is the sense of care and shared physicality that makes the wrestlers interchangeable and also valuable commodities and workers for a promoter. A wrestler who can safely work with anyone will make more money and can be sent out to more territories than one that is regularly injured or causing harm to others. This is something that hardcore wrestling, discussed in the third chapter, seems to flout, even as the ability to mete out and receive bloody and gruesome injuries becomes its own sort of currency.

Real competition, real sport, is unruly and doesn't follow neat narrative arcs or tell the stories that sell the most tickets. Kayfabe handles most of those contingencies as both a code of conduct for workers ("Don't give up the business!") and as a theatrical overlay to the affective and physical labor of the wrestlers. The difference between theatre and professional wrestling, it seems, is that professional wrestling often goes a bit too far. Over the past century, it has believed its own theatricality too much, even as it has fervently denied it—professional wrestling has thus profited from theatricality through its own anti-theatricality.

Notes

1 Eero Laine, "Stadium Sized Theatre: WWE and The World of Professional Wrestling," in *Performance and Professional Wrestling*, eds. Broderick Chow, Eero Laine, and Claire Warden (London: Routledge, 2017), 39.

2 See Lawrence W. Levine, *Highbrow/Lowbrow: The Emergence of Cultural Hierarchy in America* (Cambridge, MA: Harvard University Press, 1988); and David Savran, *Highbrow/Lowdown: Theatre, Jazz, and the Making of the New Middle Class* (Ann Arbor: University of Michigan Press, 2010).
3 Marcus Griffin, *Fall Guys: The Barnums of Bounce: The Inside Story of the Wrestling Business, America's Most Profitable and Best Organized Sport* (Chicago: Reilly Lee Company, 1937), 15.
4 Griffin, *Fall Guys*, 15.
5 Griffin, *Fall Guys*, 15.
6 Joe Williams, "The Hippo Hippodrome," *Judge*, reprinted in *The Literary Digest*, February 6, 1932, 41.
7 "Wrestling Placed Under New Status," *New York Times*, April 9, 1930, www.nytimes.com/1930/04/09/archives/wrestling-placed-under-new-status-commission-rules-clubs-must-list.html?searchResultPosition=1.
8 "Wrestling Placed Under New Status."
9 "Muldoon Denounces Bouts in Civic Centre," *New York Times*, May 15, 1931, www.nytimes.com/1931/05/15/archives/muldoon-denounces-bouts-in-civic-centre-sees-desecration-in-staging.html?searchResultPosition=1.
10 Christopher Balme, "Selling the Bird: Richard Walton Tully's 'The Bird of Paradise' and the Dynamics of Theatrical Commodification," *Theatre Journal* 57, no. 1 (2005): 3–4.
11 Balme "Selling the Bird," 4.
12 "Arts and Cultural Production Satellite Account, U.S. and States 2016," Arts and Culture, Bureau of Economic Analysis, bea.gov, March 19, 2019, www.bea.gov/data/special-topics/arts-and-culture.
13 "Broadway Season Statistics," Research & Statistics, The Broadway League, accessed April 19, 2019, www.broadwayleague.com/research/statistics-broadway-nyc/.
14 "World Wrestling Entertainment Inc. Cl A," *Wall Street Journal*, https://quotes.wsj.com/WWE/financials/annual/income-statement. For further economic analysis and statistics related to WWE's financials, Wrestlenomics, provides the most in-depth analysis of wrestling industry financials: Wrestlenomics, wrestlenomics.com, https://sites.google.com/view/wrestlenomics/home.
15 Michael Shane Boyle, "Performance and Value: The Work of Theatre in Karl Marx's Critique of Political Economy," *Theatre Survey* 58, no. 1 (January 2017): 3–23. Here, my summary of Marx's and Smith's arguments is largely drawn from my 2016 dissertation and echoes the section of Boyle's article subtitled "Performance and Productive Labor."
16 Adam Smith, *Wealth of Nations*, edited by Jim Manis (Old Main, PA: Electronic Classics Series Publication, 2005): 270, https://web.archive.org/web/20150218062802/www2.hn.psu.edu/faculty/jmanis/adam-smith/Wealth-Nations.pdf.
17 Smith, *Wealth of Nations*, 270.
18 Smith, *Wealth of Nations*, 271.
19 Boyle, "Performance and Value," 13.
20 Karl Marx, *Grundrisse: Foundations of the Critique of Political* Economy, translated by Martin Nicolaus (New York: Penguin Classics, 1993), 328–329.
21 Karl Marx, "Chapter IV: Theories of Productive and Unproductive Labour," *Theories of Surplus Value*, www.marxists.org/archive/marx/works/1863/theories-surplus-value/ch04.htm.
22 Marx, "Chapter IV.
23 Not-for-profit, state-sponsored, and various forms of community-based theatre have, of course, operated at times under different assumptions.

24 R. Tyson Smith, "Passion Work: The Joint Production of Emotional Labor in Professional Wrestling," *Social Psychology Quarterly* 71, no. 2 (2008): 159.
25 See Joseph Roach, *The Player's Passion: Studies in the Science of Acting* (Newark: University of Delaware Press, 1985). For example: Roach cites Aaron Hill's *Prompter* from the 1700s wherein he signed his writing "'B' for 'Broomstick' because he meant to sweep the stage clean of worn-out conventions" (79): "Embodying a passion demands physical labor as exhausting in its way as threshing grain, and Broomstick savaged those overly elegant players who thought that sweat should be left to the stagehands (*Prompter*, no. 66, 85)" (82).
26 Laurence DeGaris, "The Logic of Professional Wrestling," in *Steel Chair to the Head: The Pleasure and Pain of Professional Wrestling*, ed. Nicholas Sammond (Durham: Duke University Press, 2005), 192.
27 De Garis, "The Logic of Professional Wrestling, 203.
28 Indeed, being initially "ignorant of the rules of the art form," Lawrence B. McBride describes a sense of confusion during his ethnographic research with an independent wrestling company in Illinois. Without a more comprehensive understanding of the logic of the maneuvers, it was unclear to him who was actually being hurt during some wrestling moves. (Lawrence B. McBride, "Professional Wrestling, Embodied Morality, and Altered States of Consciousness" (MA Thesis, University of South Florida, 2005), 4.)
29 Jean Baudrillard, *Simulation and Simulacra* (Ann Arbor: University of Michigan Press, 2008), 3.
30 Smith, *Fighting for Recognition*, 129.
31 The physical toll of professional wrestling will be explored further below, but the injuries seem to be endemic to the form itself rather than correlated to payscale (wherein wrestlers taking more risks might be better compensated). The *Wall Street Journal* reporting on an independent wrestling league in the Bronx: "Like in World Wrestling Entertainment—pro wrestling's grandest stage—outcomes of [the independent wrestling league] BWF matches are predetermined, rivalries and storylines manufactured. But the physical toll is real: wrestlers describe painful injuries such as concussions and bone fractures." (Louie Lazar, "Bronx Wrestlers Punch, Body-Slam for Glory," Culture, Metropolis, *The Wall Street Journal*, 19 March 2014, http://blogs.wsj.com/metropolis/2014/03/19/bronx-wrestlers-punch-body-slam-for-glory/)
32 Nicholas Ridout, "Animal Labour in the Theatrical Economy," *Theatre Research International* 29, no. 1 (2004): 60.
33 Jamie Lewis Hadley, "The Hard Sell: The Performance of Pain in Professional Wrestling," in *Performance and Professional Wrestling*, eds. Broderick Chow, Eero Laine, and Claire Warden (New York: Routledge, 2017), 155.
34 Heather Levi, *The World of Lucha Libre: Secrets, Revelations, and Mexican National Identity* (Durham, NC: Duke University Press, 2008), 36.
35 Broderick Chow, "Work and Shoot: Professional Wrestling and Embodied Politics," *TDR: The Drama Review* 58, no. 2, T222 (Summer 2014): 73.
36 Smith, *Fighting for Recognition*, 87.
37 Smith, *Fighting for Recognition*, 87.
38 Smith, *Fighting for Recognition*, 87.
39 Mazer, *Professional Wrestling*, 91.
40 Nearly every publication on professional wrestling considers kayfabe in one way or another. My own work on kayfabe and the fictional worlds that it sustains can be found in the following articles: Eero Laine, "Professional Wrestling: Creating America's Fight Culture," in *Sports at the Center of Popular Culture: The Television Age*. Vol. 2 of *American History Through American Sports: From Colonial Lacrosse to Extreme Sports*, eds. Daniel Coombs and Bob Batchelor (Santa Barbara: Praeger,

2013), 219–236; Broderick Chow and Eero Laine, "Audience Affirmation and the Labour of Professional Wrestling," *Performance Research* 19, no. 2 (June 2014): 44–53; Eero Laine, "Professional Wrestling Scholarship: Legitimacy and Kayfabe," *The Popular Culture Studies Journal* 6, no. 1 (2018): 82–99; Eero Laine, "World Building in the WWE Universe," in *#WWE: Professional Wrestling in the Digital Age*, ed. Dru Jeffries (Bloomington, IN: Indiana University Press, forthcoming).
41 Laurence DeGaris, "The Money and the Miles," in *Professional Wrestling: Politics and Populism*, eds. Nell Haynes, Eero Laine, Heather Levi, Sharon Mazer, Enactments, Richard Schechner, series editor (Calcutta: Seagull Books/University of Chicago Press, forthcoming).
42 See for instance: Benjamin Litherland, "Breaking Kayfabe is Easy, Cheap and Never Entertaining: Twitter Rivalries in Professional Wrestling," *Celebrity Studies* 5, no. 4 (2014): 531–533; and CarrieLynn D. Reinhard, "Kayfabe as Convergence: Content Interactivity and Prosumption in the Squared Circle," in *Convergent Wrestling: Participatory Culture, Transmedia Storytelling and Intertextuality in the Squared Circle*, eds. CarrieLynn D. Reinhard and Christopher J. Olson (London: Routledge, 2019), 31–44; Marion Wrenn, "Managing Doubt: Professional Wrestling Jargon & the Carnival Roots of Consumer Culture," in *Practicing Culture*, eds. Craig Calhoun and Richard Sennett (London: Routledge, 2007), 149–170.
43 Carol L. Russell and Thomas E. Murray, "The Life and Death of Carnie," *American Speech* 79, no. 4 (Winter 2004), 408.
44 Russell and Murray, "The Life and Death of Carnie," 401.
45 Jonathan Snowden, *Shooters: The Toughest Men in Professional Wrestling* (Toronto: ECW Press, 2012), 111.
46 Mark S. Hewitt, *Catch Wrestling: A Wild and Wooly Look at the Early Days of Pro Wrestling in America* (Boulder, CO: Paladin Press, 2005), 151.
47 Mark S. Hewitt, *Catch Wrestling*, 152.
48 Mazer, *Professional Wrestling*, 22.
49 Mazer, *Professional Wrestling*, 22.
50 Mazer, *Professional Wrestling*, 22–23.
51 Mazer, *Professional Wrestling*, 23.
52 Mazer, *Professional Wrestling*, 23.
53 Tom Dalzell, ed., *The Routledge Dictionary of Modern American Slang and Unconventional English* (New York, Routledge: 2008), 586.
54 See, for instance, Fiona A. E. McQuarrie's article on how kayfabe is used in corporate settings: Fiona A. E. McQuarrie, "Breaking Kayfabe: 'The History of a History' of World Wrestling Entertainment," *Management & Organizational History* 1, no. 3 (2006): 227–250.
55 Dalzell, *The Routledge Dictionary of Modern American Slang*, 586.
56 Dalzell, *The Routledge Dictionary of Modern American* Slang, 586.
57 Shaun Assael and Mike Mooneyham, *Sex, Lies, and Headlocks: The Real Story of Vince McMahon and World Wrestling Entertainment* (New York: Three Rivers Press, 2004), 11.
58 Assael and Mooneyham, *Sex, Lies, and Headlocks*, 11.
59 B. Brian Blair, *Smarten Up!: Say it Right* (St. Petersburg, FL: Kayfabe Publishing Company), 2001. Brian Blair, "About," www.brianblair.com/about.html. Note: *Say it Right!* is the only manuscript published by the Kayfabe Publishing Company.
60 Blair, *Smarten Up!*, 13.
61 Blair, *Smarten Up!*, 46.
62 Blair, *Smarten Up!*, 47.
63 John Lister, "Professional Wrestling's Clandestine Jargon," *Verbatim* 31, no. 2 (Summer 2006): 7.

64 Lister, "Professional Wrestling's Clandestine Jargon," 7.
65 "Kayfabe," *Wikipedia*, accessed April 6, 2019, *Wikipedia*, http://en.wikipedia.org/wiki/Kayfabe.
66 "Kayfabe," *Wikipedia*.
67 "Kayfabe," *Wikipedia*.
68 Smith, *Fighting for Recognition*, 68.
69 Smith, *Fighting for Recognition*, 69. Emphasis mine.
70 Smith, *Fighting for Recognition*, 69.
71 Smith, *Fighting for Recognition*, 5.
72 Chow, "Work and Shoot," 74.
73 Eric Weinstein, "Kayfabe," World Question Center, *Edge*, 2011, http://edge.org/q2011/q11_16.html#weinstein.
74 Eric Weinstein, "Kayfabe."
75 See Eero Laine. "Kayfabe: Optimism, Cynicism, Critique," in *Professional Wrestling: Politics and Populism*, eds. Nell Haynes, Eero Laine, Heather Levi, Sharon Mazer, Enactments, Richard Schechner, series editor (Calcutta: Seagull Books/University of Chicago Press, forthcoming).
76 John Griffiths, "All the World's a Stage: Transnationalism and Adaptation in Professional Wrestling Style *c.*1930–45," *Social History* 40, no. 1 (2015): 38–57.
77 Lee Austin Thompson, "Professional Wrestling in Japan—Media and Message," *International Review for the Sociology of Sport* 21, no. 1 (1986): 74.
78 Thompson, "Professional Wrestling in Japan," 69.
79 For instance, the May 1905 issue of *The Cosmopolitan* featured a cover story entitled "American Wrestling vs. Jujitsu." The article was co-written by a New York wrestling instructor and a jujitsu instructor. It opens with a quote from each of them speaking condescendingly about the other's martial art and continues with an extended interview on the purpose of each form. The article also includes a number of photographs of various wrestling and jujitsu holds with captions that describe what bone might be broken or what joint dislocated. (H.F. Leonard and K. Higashi, "American Wrestling vs. Jujitsu," *The Cosmopolitan*, May 1905.)
80 Thompson, "Professional Wrestling in Japan," 69.
81 Thompson, "Professional Wrestling in Japan," 69–70.
82 Tim Hornbaker, *National Wrestling Alliance: The Untold Story of the Monopoly That Strangled Wrestling* (Toronto: ECW Press, 2007), 41.
83 Hornbaker, *National Wrestling Alliance*, 24.
84 Hornbaker, *National Wrestling Alliance*, 27.
85 Hornbaker, *National Wrestling Alliance*, 27.
86 Hornbaker, *National Wrestling Alliance*, 28.

Chapter 2

Form and content
Professional wrestling's troubling theatrics

Why is professional wrestling so terrible? Why are so many of its significant events, notable figures, and memorable narratives so often overshadowed by nationalism, racism, sexism, homophobia, and a generally cringeworthy sense of acceptable or sociable behavior? The history of professional wrestling is littered with troubling representations and puerile displays of unchecked belligerence and senselessness. What's to like? Why would anybody watch or participate in this rotten thing? Indeed, the question of whether or not professional wrestling has any redeeming value, both in itself and as an object of study, is an evergreen topic. And it is hard to deny that this does stem from the material itself.

Professional wrestling, like other representational arts, has a long history of regressive characters and storylines. And the situation is, perhaps, made more troubling by the fact that these characters persist due in large part to the fact that professional wrestling and its performers do not simply put something on and take it off again. The representations and actions of the performers themselves fold into their legacy and cultural spaces in which professional wrestling operates. The wrestlers and their characters are recognized in retrospectives and in wrestler biographies; they are called back through contemporary tropes and characters. A common refrain is that wrestling promoters are just giving the audience what they want to see—professional wrestling is entertainment, not edifying. But can professional wrestling do better? Or is such a possibility beyond the pale, as some might suggest, because professional wrestling, ontologically and as a form, creates, sustains, and relies on these terrible representations?

Going back to Sharon Mazer's field-defining study, at the core of many of these considerations are questions about the connections between wrestling and masculinity. Throughout *Professional Wrestling Sport and Spectacle*, many interactions observed by Mazer, in and out of the ring, are marked as acts of overt and troubling masculinity—Mazer notes that even "the way in which the appearance of women in wrestling—as wrestlers, as managers/consorts, and as spectators—serves to legitimate wrestling's masculine discourse."[1] Mazer found such issues "most problematic and consequently most

40 Form and content

intriguing" as she observed the action in the ring.[2] Much more recently, Mazer has asserted that these actions can only ape a sort of masculine way of being that is ultimately only sexualized by spectators and must be exorcised in order for the action to proceed.[3] Patrice A. Oppliger's *Wrestling and Hypermasculinity* centers such a reading and makes obvious a number of links between viewing professional wrestling and masculinist behavior such as verbal and physical aggression and violence.[4] Oppliger's sociological research from the late 1990s and early 2000s on gender norms and wrestling storylines that address race and class points to the implications of wrestling violence as a highly gendered activity. In the hypermasculine, theatrical world of pro wrestling, every interaction leads to conflict and every conflict ends in violence, leading to further violence. Oppliger's analysis of such a violent worldview embeds such practices within larger cultural norms surrounding masculinity and gender performance. Similarly, Danielle M. Soulliere analyzed hundreds of hours of WWE programming between 2001 and 2002, and found six "messages about manhood" that recurred throughout: "(1) Real men are aggressive and violent, (2) men settle things physically, (3) a man confronts his adversaries and problems, (4) real men take responsibility for their actions, (5) men are not whiners, and (6) men are winners."[5] Echoing such ideas, after watching a live performance of WWE's touring show in Edmonton during the so-called Attitude Era of the late 1990s, Darrin Hagan writes:

> Its symbols of masculinity—brute force, fake violence, bravado, posturing, drawing your power from the disempowerment of others—are tried and traditional. It's a brilliant symbol of the last bastion of the old guard clinging to the tattered shreds of its former glory and power.[6]

Would that it were true that the Attitude Era signaled a broader decline of the old guard.

Rather, two decades later, it seems that the Attitude Era has found its way out of the ring and into the political arena. The performances of WWE's Attitude Era of the late 1990s and even in the early 2000s seem relatively tame when compared to the behavior of some elected officials and political actors. This, even as pro wrestling itself has rather dramatically changed as WWE and other companies do not seem to be competing for the bottom of the cultural barrel or trade as openly in crude sexuality while chasing viewers through shock value. However, the claims of toxic masculinity do stem, in no small part, from the basic format of professional wrestling wherein opponents attempt to physically manipulate and dominate each other, quite literally trying to hold each other down against their will. Such a reading might implicate more than just wrestling. And many of the problems with professional wrestling stem not from the aspects that resemble sport, but what is laid on top of the sports format.

In the performance of professional wrestling, emotions are heightened and the moral universe is simplistic and clear-cut, leading Heather Levi to describe professional wrestling as "sport in the melodramatic mode."[7] The melodramatic mode of professional wrestling fits well within a contemporary political context. It recalls proclamations of being either "with us or against us" and an "axis of evil" used by political leaders to justify military interventions and wars.[8] Defined by its clear-cut moral universe, melodrama melts into these and other political narratives of fighting the allegedly "good fight" against "evil."

Henry Jenkins perhaps bridges the apparent central problems of professional wrestling, calling it "masculine melodrama."[9] His reading of wrestling is taken one step further when Jenkins suggests that "The core myth of [WWE] wrestling is a fascistic one: ultimately, might makes right; moral authority is linked directly to the possession of physical strength."[10] Going further, Jenkins suggests that "The appeal of such a myth to a working-class audience should be obvious" since in their day-to-day lives physical strength is alienated through their labor but in pro wrestling "physical strength reemerges as a tool for personal empowerment, a means of striking back against personal and moral injustices."[11] Certainly, the reading is compelling and more than a few scholars have taken up the theoretical and rhetorical tack. Maybe pro wrestling is simply fascist and allows the working classes a convenient fantasy based in their *ressentiment* and declining social mobility in the post-industrial, late-capitalist hell-scape of the past forty years.

I'm less inclined to take up this argument, however.[12] I think other readings are necessary, in part because Jenkins' argument works perhaps a bit too well. Placed in relief to the actual fascists in the streets and on social media today, as opposed to when the article was written, wrestling might even be considered liberal or progressive or maybe could even find anti-fascist manifestations. Just to remind us here: Roland Barthes, certainly no fascist, found something useful in the performance form of pro wrestling.[13] And Bertolt Brecht admired those sporting events with thousands of cheering fans gathered to watch the competitive action play out.[14] To see such work in practice, we can look to R. Tyson Smith's ethnographic study of an independent wrestling promotion, which dissects the performance of masculinity at the core of the wrestling spectacle. Smith observes the differences between those who play the characters and the characters themselves, observing that the wrestlers are "men completely preoccupied with preparing to be men they are generally not … men prepping to play the part of intimidating, invulnerable men."[15] That is to say, the characters of wrestling are more the problem than any particular wrestling maneuver. Or, as Carrie Dunn reminds us:

> Men and women in professional wrestling are not different because of the training they do or the moves they can do in the ring; instead, they

are different because of the ways in which they perform and behave in character in the ring, and the ways in which they are perceived by their audience.[16]

The performance of wrestling itself is thus considered as a blank slate of sorts, an empty stage and set of gestures onto which gendered activity is projected, inscribed, exaggerated, and reified.

Many of the presumed motivations for such performances are called into question by Smith's ethnographic research as he pushes against what he refers to as the "compensation" theory exemplified in Jenkins' quote above that reads pro wrestling as "a reclamation project in which men enact a version of manhood that they have lost or never successfully found in other realms of life."[17] In order to be successful as a wrestler among Smith's subjects, who are for the most part white, working class, heterosexual men,

> performers must unlearn the rugged individualistic habitus they have spent their lives being groomed into. While they may have been drawn to pro wrestling because of its masculine symbolism, these young men end up in a pursuit in which doing masculinity can be self-conscious, soft, and counterintuitive (not to mention painful).[18]

Smith helpfully points out that "paradoxically, performing violent masculinity is a nuanced, self-conscious, and collaborative activity."[19] It might be worth considering a shift in the assertion only so slightly from professional wrestling as "masculine melodrama" to the performance of professional wrestling as a "melodramatic masculinity." At least in the ring, as performed by wrestlers who are decidedly not the characters they play, masculinity is made melodramatic. Put another way: understanding masculinity in a wider sense than macho, heterosexual aggressiveness, it is perhaps the melodramatic mode that shapes and alters masculinity and not the other way around.

I admit to being fairly ambivalent to professional wrestling when I started thinking about it some time ago. It was seemingly irredeemable, even if interesting conceptually. The more I looked at professional wrestling, however, and the more I considered my own relationship to theatre (broadly), I came to understand that the problems of professional wrestling, as in the real problems of representation and oppressive reification, were problems of theatre. And like recent campaigns in theatre, it seems that wrestling is trying to right what might be called without hyperbole, I think, centuries-old problems of representation and equity. That is, professional wrestling might be any number of terrible things, but it learned all of those terrible things from the theatre. This is surely not surprising to most theatre scholars. Without the theatrical overlay, the costumes, the sets, the climactic plot structures based in conflict, a melodramatic sense of ethics and justice, not to mention the over-the-top, often caricatured characters, wrestling would just be a fixed sporting event.

In response to such horrible content, Matt Foy suggests delving deeper—critiquing and troubling such matters "at the micro level of individual characters and storylines as they unfold on an episodic basis."[20] This is appealing on a number of levels, not least of which that it will keep wrestling scholars busy for a long time, but also because such content does need a response. I am curious, however, in light of the many critiques leveled against professional wrestling, if there might be something wrong with the form itself or if professional wrestling, like the broad category of theatre that it often imitates, might rather just need new writers. So, instead of drilling down into characters and minute plot twists, here I step back to consider the form of professional wrestling itself in relation to its content.

In order to follow this inquiry, this chapter attempts to peel apart the notions of form and content in professional wrestling. I look at pro wrestling theatrically, through two key plays that make evident the ways that form and content are not stable categories in professional wrestling. In Kristoffer Diaz's *The Elaborate Entrance of Chad Deity*, nominated for the 2010 Pulitzer Prize, we find a clear distinction between professional wrestling and theatrical stage combat that is linked to the ways that the characters in the play navigate the violent stereotypes they are made to inhabit in order to keep their jobs. The play is a critique of pro wrestling but also a critique of much more than that, situating the form as deeply embedded in US capitalism. I don't want to ascribe sentiments to the playwright, but to me it seems clear that *Chad Deity* is written from the perspective of someone who knows that wrestling can do better. Roughly thirty years before *The Elaborate Entrance of Chad Diety* and before even the astounding growth in the pro wrestling industry, Claire Luckham's *Trafford Tanzi* explored the form and took up the possibilities of pro wrestling as a decidedly feminist endeavor. The play was developed in the late 1970s and early 1980s and deploys a number of Brechtian techniques that make use of the wrestling form and trouble neat ideas about what content might fit into that form.

By juxtaposing these two theatrical representations of professional wrestling, we invert the relationship between wrestling and theatre. Whereas much of professional wrestling might be seen as a sort of example of the worst kinds of theatre—offensive and regressive stereotypes in brutally oversimplified and jingoistic narratives—to see it reflected back at itself through theatre has the perhaps counterintuitive effect of seeing what wrestling could be. Indeed, the critiques leveled by both *The Elaborate Entrance of Chad Deity* and *Trafford Tanzi* show the critical possibilities of pro wrestling itself through the exploration of professional wrestling form as physical theatre and its content, which is revealed to be highly malleable. Even as the critique of both of these plays is turned inward, both on wrestling and on theatre, because both theatre and wrestling are deeply social, the critique also points outward in potentially radical directions.

The Elaborate Entrance of Chad Deity

Kristoffer Diaz's play *The Elaborate Entrance of Chad Deity* explains and dissects the backstage details and physical nuance of professional wrestling. The play offers up the form's long history of racist stereotypes as comic fodder for theatre audiences, and it does so in a surprisingly endearing fashion. The play is narrated by Macedonia Guerra, described by Diaz as "A Puerto Rican professional wrestler. Good at what he does, undersized, our hero."[21] Referred to by his ring name, Mace, because his white boss cannot pronounce his full name, he is a wrestler employed as a "jobber" or enhancement talent, hired to lose to the more popular wrestlers in order to make them look good and appeal to the fans.

The play begins with a long monologue wherein Mace describes his early life growing up in the Bronx and watching pro wrestling on Saturday mornings with his brothers. Mace explains that he always liked the wrestlers who were not hulking monsters like those favored by THE Wrestling (a fictional wrestling company that perhaps is meant to stand in for WWE). The play progresses with a primer on the basics of wrestling for those unfamiliar, and the introduction of two of the play's three other characters: EKO or Everett K. Olson, the racist, exploitative, capitalist boss who owns THE Wrestling (and may or may not be based on Vince McMahon), and Chad Deity, "The African-American Champion of THE Wrestling," who is "confident, handsome, not a very good wrestler."[22]

The play eventually finds Mace on a team with the fourth character, Vigneshwar Paduar or VP, ("A young Indian-American Brooklynite") and they are promptly cast as regressive stereotypes Che Chavez Castro and The Fundamentalist, respectively.[23] Mace is drawn in to the troubling world of portraying a stereotype that garners him the most attention and acclaim he's ever received as a wrestler. The play mostly occurs in the backstage spaces as Mace and VP attempt to bargain with their employer and make sense of their roles as racist caricatures. Mace is an agile narrator, switching between speaking to EKO and directly addressing the audience—saying one thing to keep his job and another to explain the conventions of wrestling and its long history of stereotypes and racial impersonation.

The crudely stereotyped and racist caricatures evince what Kimberly Ramirez describes in her essay "Let's Get Ready to Rhumba: Wrestling with Stereotypes in Kristoffer Diaz's *The Elaborate Entrance of Chad Deity*" as the all-too-common pro wrestling "narratives often spin[ing] jingoistic, xenophobic scenarios packaged as patriotism."[24] Indeed, Ramirez suggests that some in the theatre might consider some of the play's content "too parodic to be plausible" but notes that it is "difficult to distinguish Diaz's seemingly overblown characters with popular wrestling counterparts."[25] Diaz even includes a primer in the Author's Notes at the beginning of the script, presumably because many who might be producing, acting, directing, or designing a production may not be as familiar with wrestling history, noting that "Most of the classic and truly offensive ones are from the WWF/WWE, largely in the eighties and nineties."[26] He includes the names of some to particularly look out for, including Mohammad Hassan, whom, during the play, Mace encourages the audience to google during the intermission as an example of a truly egregious character and storyline. In all of this, Diaz confronts the problems of wrestling head on, often through Mace, who code switches quickly between his boss (and the world of the play) and the audience in the theatre. Thus the regressive characters are also tied to the regime of wage labor that finds Mace trying to keep his head down and his paychecks coming.

Interviewed in the *New York Times*, Diaz acknowledges the political work of the play, even while explaining that the politics relies on the embodied work of the actors:

> There's clearly an agenda in the play that goes far, far beyond a look at the world of wrestling, but the play will succeed or fail partly on audience members' believing that these characters are professional wrestlers and not simply political symbols[27]

Indeed, part of the reason the play might be considered effective is the fact that audiences are allowed to laugh at the absurd violence of the representations, which point to the structural forces that sustain such representations. Mace's asides, when juxtaposed with the racist caricatures presented in the play, serve two purposes. They provide a theatrical and satirical critique of the wrestling industry and its long history of racism and nationalism, and they offer a comfortable way to enter the world of wrestling for an off-Broadway or regional theatre audience.

One does not have to like wrestling to like *The Elaborate Entrance of Chad Deity* or to understand its political message. Noe Montez notes the effectiveness of the play, explaining how the lead character, Mace, "gives voice to an understanding of how the American dream was built upon the exploitation of bodies of color."[28] Montez notes Diaz's use of the wrestling form and the ways that wrestling, theatre, and other cultural forms overlap and interact:

> In sum, Diaz uses his satirical agency as a theatrical tool of political resistance. Mace and VP initially fall into the trap of the culture industry by allowing themselves to be framed as passive objects in EKO's fictionalized representation of the American dream, but as the play concludes, Diaz acknowledges the multiple powers who own wrestling, theatre, and popular culture.[29]

And cast member Michael T. Weiss, who played Everett K. Olson, "said he viewed the play as less about wrestling than about the frustrations of men who are pitted against one another by a system that seeks to profit from antagonism and conflict."[30] Thus, Diaz, through the character of Mace, both praises the form and disparages the content of professional wrestling in ways that should be appealing to a theatergoing audience that may or may not have had much experience with professional wrestling.

The play also highlights the work of wrestling. Diaz explains the importance of the physicality in a note to directors and producers of the play when he states that "it is vitally important—VITALLY—that any wrestling or wrestling moves that are used in the course of the play are indeed wrestling moves and not stage combat."[31] Actors must perform as wrestlers, they must wrestle. This is not without consequence, however. Diaz also warns that the powerbomb, a wrestling move that features prominently in the play and involves lifting a wrestler to shoulder height before dropping them down on the mat, is "difficult and dangerous even for professionals … for real. Take it seriously."[32] This attention to the physicality of professional wrestling is essential to the production. The labor of the workers (here, both the actors and the characters they play) is highlighted and put on display for the audience. So, even as Mace moves between the diegetic world of the play and the theatre, critiquing and commenting upon the often vicious content and characters of wrestling, the wrestling itself is properly and directly staged.

Diaz makes the distinction between wrestling form and content especially clear in their relation to the United States. For instance, Mace suggests:

> Not the storylines, not the competition, not the dazzling physiques or the pretty colors or the elaborate entrance of Chad Deity is the reason that professional wrestling is the most uniquely profound artistic expression of the ideals of the United States: [Chad Deity continues:] In wrestling, you can't kick a guy's ass without the help of the guy whose ass you're kicking.[33]

This passage neatly encapsulates the message of the play. Professional wrestling and especially its backstage politics and disturbing labor practices stands in as a site to examine US politics, where one must beat oneself up in order to collect a paycheck or to make it in America.

The play also, however, points to the camaraderie of wrestling, and the pleasures of laboring in performance. Getting beat is a cooperative effort, yes, but the physical performance of pro wrestling perhaps surpasses any regressive characters and narrative. As Broderick Chow suggests in his 2014 *TDR* article "Work and Shoot: Professional Wrestling and Embodied Politics," wrestling is

> a kind of "language," an embodied shibboleth: "A wrestler from Japan will be able to wrestle a guy from Mexico, even if they don't speak the same language and've [sic] never touched each other before" ([Wrestling Trainer] G.V., 25 August 2011).[34]

He suggests that one may certainly "read the history of wrestling ... as a compendium of the most offensive stereotypes" but provocatively indicates that the form also offers a more progressive reading through wrestling praxis and the shared labor of theatrical performance.[35] This shift from plots and characters based in stereotypes to mutual labor and support perhaps allows a reading of wrestling as Chow suggests "as a place where the marginal, the excluded, and the immigrant have found friendship with others though a shared practice."[36] Thus, the wrestling form, the actual physical practice of wrestling, is less the problem than its theatrical overlay.

It is hard to ignore the offensive theatrical tropes, however. In a perhaps counterintuitive reading, Warren Kluber sees some positive possibilities for the regressive stereotypes that Mace and VP must take up, asserting that

> embracing the unambiguous roles of Islamic terrorist and illegal immigrant brings a soothing clarity, even as it misrepresents their real identities. Within their false forms they can radiate an anger that is real and for once recognized by its objects.[37]

But even this reading does not address the underlying form of professional wrestling. Kluber cites Chris Hedges who pegs the downfall of civilization on professional wrestling in the opening to his book, *Empire of Illusions*.[38] Hedges serves as an easy reference that explains the dangerous and troubling spectacle of wrestling, but critics like Hedges rarely go beyond the diegetic world of wrestling plots and characters to consider the form of wrestling itself. In doing so, these readings ignore the physical world in which Diaz locates his characters and indeed his performers. *The Elaborate Entrance of Chad Deity*, like wrestling itself, highlights the physical world of the wrestling ring and the labor of wrestling. As Mace constantly reminds us through his monologues and asides, there is a person behind the character and that person is working, laboring to live.

Through such a reading, we might begin to extricate theatrical content from theatrical form and its praxis. It's a possibly troubling gambit, however, wherein bringing professional wrestling into the theatrical fold reveals and makes explicit the perhaps well-known dangers of theatrical representation. Wrestling is a shared physical vocabulary and way of working, overlaid with theatricality—those things that make wrestling so offensive and truly troubling are indeed the most theatrical.

Trafford Tanzi

Roughly three decades before *The Elaborate Entrance of Chad Deity*, another wrestling play highlighted the potential of the theatrical form of wrestling. *Trafford Tanzi* by Claire Luckham is not produced quite as much as it once was, but it had a number of productions in the late 1970s and early 1980s and eventually transferred to Broadway for a short run. In 2014, there was a revival in London under the title *Tanzi Libre* and it is still produced, especially as interest in professional wrestling has again increased, likely driven by the Netflix show *GLOW* and WWE's continued appeal. Luckham's play centers on Tanzi, who is from the neighborhood of Trafford in Manchester. The play has a few names, such as *Tuebrook Tanzi, The Venus Fly Trap*, with names changing to reflect the neighborhood or city that the play is performed in.[39] (Tuebrook is a neighborhood in Liverpool.) The name changes function to make Tanzi the hometown hero, the local who is clearly marked as the one to cheer for. This is, of course, a time-tested strategy in live performance and professional wrestling in particular, where the heroes will compliment or show some connection to the performance site while the villain will actively insult it.

The play is presented as a series of matches, and the wrestling is interspersed with dialogue and songs and takes place entirely in and around a wrestling ring. The play is also particularly noteworthy for its many musical interludes and for the ways that the dialogue of the play is incorporated into the rounds of wrestling that structure the play. The main characters are Tanzi; her husband, a wrestler named Dean; the Referee; a not-so-friendly friend, Platinum Sue; the school psychologist, Dr. Grobe; and Tanzi's Mum and Dad. The play proceeds episodically, and each of the ten rounds of the play is an episode from Tanzi's life—from childhood (Mum sings about how she wanted a boy and submits Tanzi with a "step-over leglock"[40]) to the final bout where Tanzi wrestles her husband Dean with the stipulation that the loser "quit the wrestling ring and become a housewife."[41] Over the course of the play, Tanzi battles each of her parents twice, Platinum Sue twice, the school psychologist once, and Dean three times.[42] Michelene Wandor calls the play "A little agitprop fable" and notes that

> its storyline recalls the simple agitprop lessons of the early 1970s feminist theatre work: the baby girl brought up to be feminine and pretty and clean, resists and fights back, and is labeled a tomboy and told off by everyone, from her Mum to her teacher.[43]

The play thus leverages the obvious spectacle of professional wrestling for a particular form of feminist politics. While some have raised questions regarding the effectiveness of the presentation and the implications for the political message, the play itself fairly neatly answers the question of what the professional wrestling form might look like if the content was explicitly feminist. There are, of course, other ways that the form might be politically leveraged, but, unlike much of the wrestling that academics were responding to from the 1980s and 1990s, *Trafford Tanzi* shows us what wrestling might be when it is made by a feminist theatre company with attention to the working class.

The play opens with a wonderful piece of stage directions: "The wrestling ring. The audience should be able to purchase drinks at reasonable prices."[44] The ring is as important as the drinks and their reasonable prices. This bit of instruction from the playwright is rooted in the play's production history as it was designed and written to be performed in pubs. The play premiered at Eric's, a punk and hardcore club in Liverpool, on April 18, 1978 and was produced by the Everyman Theatre Company.[45] That incarnation of the production is listed on a poster for Eric's as *Venus Flytrap* and was a double bill with a "Rock and Roll Disco."[46] Other acts that spring at Eric's included the Buzzcocks, Siouxsie & the Banshees, X-Ray Spex, Reggae with The Gladiators, and The Young Ones.[47] The play was thus developed, in a way, outside of the theatre proper, even as it relied on a script and director and actors who were trained in theatre, singing, and, yes, professional wrestling.

The Everyman Theatre in Liverpool was closed in the 1970s while the building was being improved and the company toured pubs with various shows—*Tanzi* was "specifically conceived to survive the pub atmosphere."[48] The play received a number of other productions, including a July 6 to August 29 run at the Theatre of the Half Moon in London in 1980,[49] a Manchester production in October 1980 (which the published script was finalized for), and a subsequent tour of Birmingham, Belfast, and London that began with a production at the Edinburgh Festival in 1981.[50] Wandor considers the play's route, from Liverpool and Manchester to London, as important in "explaining the way it took hold of and subverted the popular working-class sport of wrestling."[51] The play ran at the Mermaid Theatre in London in 1983,[52] but when it moved to Broadway at the Nederlander Theatre with the title *Teaneck Tanzi: The Venus Flytrap* and starring Andy Kaufman as the Ref and Deborah Harry of Blondie as Tanzi, it had twenty preview performances and then closed immediately after opening night.[53]

Almost presciently, in a review in *Theatre Journal*, Joel G. Fink wrote:

> The strength of *Trafford Tanzi* clearly lies in its power to rip through theatre conventions and speak to a non-theatre audience with the immediacy of a local pub brawl. In the East End production, the same ring used for *Tanzi* is also used for Sunday wrestling matches presented by the Olympic Wrestling Association. This is both a skillful publicity move and a realistic attempt to move theatre out to a broader audience. The danger exists, however, that with the move towards a mainstream middle-class audience, *Trafford Tanzi* could become a precious, clever theatre piece, safe from the audience-actor connection that gave it vitality and life.[54]

The connection between audience and performers in the play is precisely like the connection in professional wrestling. Prefiguring *Chad Deity*, characters regularly talk to the audience through asides, the Referee narrates the story to the audience, and a number of songs break up the action and reveal the characters' past and inner thoughts. Wandor notes that "the wit of the play lies in the way the form and content match" explaining that the ten round structure makes the theatrical audience into the wrestling audience as we witness Tanzi's life from childhood to the faceoff with her husband, where the spectators are "incited (encouraged?) to cheer either for Tanzi or Dean—in other words, the audience is drawn into participation and into taking sides."[55] This is what professional wrestling demands of its audience. Playwright Claire Luckham was drawn to this aspect of professional wrestling in particular, noting that "there aren't a lot of places that you can shout straightforward abuse, particularly if you are a woman."[56] Even as the space of the play is coded as masculinist, Luckham apparently saw the potential for liberating opportunities for the audience. In the case of *Trafford Tanzi* the play sides with Tanzi, but it is also important to remember that the audience might not cheer for the "good guy." The seeming freedom of shouting abuse means that such heckling can go any number of ways. The audience could, for instance, cheer for Dean. This is the gamble of professional wrestling, however. While face and heel characters are fairly clearly delineated, one does not know if the audience is full of heels until the match begins.

For Janelle Reinelt, the play can be read as a sort simplistic morality play, but the larger issue is the very public debate and performance of what would otherwise be assigned to the private sphere. Working through considerations of Brecht and Barthes, Reinelt writes:

> Within the context of the working class already colored with socialist ideology, the debate about the relationship of work in the home to work in the public sector is recognizable. But it is the wrestling match itself, the perfect Brechtian "gest" for the struggle of women to free themselves from male oppression both economic and sexual, which is the central feature of the play. This struggle must be conducted in the open, in the public arena, where the audience can participate in it and identify its political as well as its personal character. The transformation of traditionally private experience into public spectacle helps transform conceptions of individual problems into social ones. As Barthes points out, both wrestling and theatre give "intelligible representations of moral situations which are usually private."[57]

Even as the private space is made public, the ring and the pub that surrounds it are shaped by the first lines of the Referee: "Gentlemen, gentlemen; ladies and gentlemen."[58] The Ref then goes on to introduce all of the characters in the play, promising that in the end they will witness "a man and a woman fighting to the finish."[59] The woman here, of course, is Trafford Tanzi, the "reigning European Ladies Champion," and the man is "the ever-popular Dean Rebel."[60] Through the character of the Ref, who in sports is the objective figure who maintains the rules, Luckham sets the wrestling ring and the audience as a particularly male space. The women are addressed as an afterthought sandwiched between the initial double address of "gentlemen, gentlemen" and a final "gentlemen." In this gesture, Luckham both marks the space as masculine and indicates that the men in the audience are the loud ones who need quieting. Indeed, the Ref's opening lines acknowledge the Ref's allegiances and priorities, and as the audience we see, from the outset, that the match is fixed against Tanzi, who is notable in her introduction for her accomplishments ("reigning European Ladies Champion"), as opposed to Dean who is simply popular. In wrestling, it is a fairly common heel tactic to try to control the audience by telling them to shut up or to listen quietly as wrestling audiences (and I imagine pub audiences in the late 1970s and early 1980s) don't like to be told what to do. Thus, from the beginning, the odds are against Tanzi as she literally fights her way through the play.

Amidst this male-dominated labor, Wandor notes, "Tanzi is shown to be able not only to do the job that men do, but—in this one instance—to do it better."[61] Wandor believes this reveals

> a solid bourgeois feminist dynamic at work, in showing a woman taking a "top" place on traditionally male-held territory. The bourgeois feminist dynamic is reinforced because Tanzi accepts the terms of male-defined territory: housework is reckoned as work fit for the loser.[62]

Reinelt acknowledges the apparently personal aspects of the production, writing: "The songs, the referee, and the wrestling ring can all be perceived as Brechtian elements. The content of the play, however, seems to privilege a personal struggle for equality more than the specifically socialist issues outlined above."[63] It is noteworthy that the wrestling structure or the act of pro wrestling is less the problem than the particular storyline of the play. Reinelt ultimately questions Wandor's claims about bourgeois feminism:

> Considering the audience for whom the play was originally conceived, Wandor's critique of the play as "bourgeois" seems a bit ironic. The play takes certain relationships for granted—all of the characters are working class, making it an in-house discussion. Actually, the co-option of women's work for capitalist profiteering is vividly portrayed when Tanzi's father attempts to become her manager and take a 50% cut of her wrestling profits.... In addition, her arguments with husband Dean Rebel over the division of labor are named in terms of the discussion of women's work as reproducing labor power mentioned above.[64]

The wrestling form is especially useful for this. Even if wrestlers do have individual identities, they are often reduced to their embodied positions. Especially considering the ways that wrestling bodies are bared and staged, stretched and displayed, it is difficult to conceal the battles of identity that often play out in the ring.

This is heightened in professional wrestling by an apparent violent physicality. *Trafford Tanzi* trades in this violent physical vocabulary throughout the production, providing a physical (sub)text that supports the spoken word and, at times, tells the story and explains the relationships between characters even more clearly than the text. Fink, writing about the London production, notes the importance of the wrestling to the production: "the central metaphor and the constant excitement of *Trafford Tanzi* are centered squarely in the wrestling ring."[65] In the printed script, wrestling moves appear in parentheses and punctuate most of the dialogue. For instance, in the ninth scene (mentioned in the quote above by Reinelt), Tanzi has achieved success with her wrestling career and her father attempts to capitalize on her achievements by literally selling her and her labor while planning to take fifty percent:

DAD: Tanzi, be reasonable. After all, you're only a slip of a girl, slip of a woman. And this isn't a picnic in the park you know. This is cut-throat world of commerce. You need someone behind you can trust. Otherwise there'll be blood all over the place. And anyway, I've already fixed up you next fight. Mud wrestling. In Hamburg. Naked. We'll make a fortune.
TANZI: Right!
("Ref's hold." TANZI gets DAD in a "backhammer." She takes the contract and "head mare" DAD with his arm still in the "backhammer.")
(Ripping up the contract.)
This is what I think of your contract, Dad.
(She scatters the pieces of the contract on him.)
(TANZI ropes DAD and "flying tackle." Bell)
DAD: But, Tanzi … please … I'm your old dad. I'm family. And what about your mum? I've got to support her.
TANZI: Tough bananas, Dad.
(TANZI "dropkicks" DAD out of the ring.)[66]

The stage directions rather neatly incorporate professional wrestling as a performance form into what otherwise might be considered a domestic dispute. Professional wrestling as a form escalates the drama, making the characters archetypical, while rooted in feminist class-consciousness. More than instruction related to physical violence such as slaps or punches, the stage directions perform a physical vocabulary that demands professional wrestling and its attendant pleasures and slippages. There is something significantly more satisfying in seeing Tanzi dropkick Dad out of the ring than whatever stage combat might be conceived of for a living room drama with similar dialogue. Thus, in the pairing of domestic drama with professional wrestling, the ostensible premise of the play, that a woman can defeat a man in the wrestling ring, is not the biggest take away from the production but is leveraged as useful dramaturgy.

The way the play relies on actual wrestling is central to its success as a rowdy pub play, but it also means that the performers must be in wrestling shape and properly trained for the potentially dangerous moves that wrestling entails. Indeed, this was notable for Fink in his review of the London production: "The performance, two hours of flips, falls, holds and realistic combat, is executed flawlessly by actors working with complete physical control, merging text and action to create the illusion of spontaneity and unexpected violence."[67] The intense action of the play seems to be its enduring legacy. A 2014 revival in London by the Southwark Playhouse was the first in London in thirty years and embraced the physicality of the play, updating it with fast-paced and high-flying lucha libre moves and costumes and calling it *Tanzi Libre*.

The production was described by Dominic Cavendish of the *Telegraph* as "sweatily committed."[68] Cavendish, however, like Michael Billington at the *Guardian*, found the play outdated in its message. Billington described the production as "big, bold, and Brechtian" but repeated some of the longstanding critiques of the play with his concern that wrestling might not be the best form for such matters, writing "I'm not sure it greatly advances the cause of women to show them turning into a more sophisticated version of [wrestler] Giant Haystacks."[69] Andrzej Lukowski of *Time Out* complained about the simple plot, writing "If it were a kitchen sink drama it'd be awful, basically."[70] He went on to complement the technical elements and the spectacle of the entire event, but seemed to otherwise consider it a bit of empty fun. Nathan Brooker of *Exeunt Magazine* enjoyed the spectacle of it all and noted that the crowd warmed up quite a bit after a few trips to the bar, but seemed to want something more sophisticated than wrestling and feminism: "it's about as subtle as being battered around the head by someone in a wrestling mask screaming 'This is a feminist play! This is a feminist play!' over and over again."[71] It is noteworthy that the apparent complaints about the play are actually its features—amplifying domestic disputes through wrestling matches, cheap drinks, action-fueled Brecht. It is also unclear why the theme seemed to simultaneously bore and irritate so many of the male critics, while critic Hannah Elsy's only real complaint about the production was that some of the singing wasn't as strong as the other aspects of the production. She was also particularly impressed with the wrestling itself for its "dance-like fluidity, with the actors bouncing off the ring's elastics, performing flips, lifts and engaging in extremely complex fight sequences."[72] Unfortunately, that same physicality is what brought the production to an early end when lead actor Olivia Onyehara was hospitalized after an in-ring injury during a production of the play. The play was subsequently canceled "due to the complex nature of the role and the lack of time and resources to train someone new."[73] Injuries in professional wrestling are not particularly rare and are a fairly regular reminder that wrestling may be highly theatrical, but is at its core an extremely physical performance form. The injury only highlights the difference between *Trafford Tanzi* and a piece of domestic realism. By placing the action of the play in a wrestling ring, surrounded by an audience that may or may not cheer for Tanzi, the play actually enacts the politics of the play. That is, the performer playing Tanzi must not only win each match through submission or dropkick but also has to win over the audience using the words and actions afforded by the script.

Conclusion

To return to some of the questions that opened the chapter: rather than asking why we might deal with such rotten stuff as professional wrestling, we might inquire after what has made it so bad in various parts of its history. I think the question needs to be applied more broadly. Nearly all of the claims that are leveraged against professional wrestling, from nationalism to causal and overt misogyny to the most insidious forms of racism are just as easily lobbed against theatre itself. Neil LaBute and David Mamet still write plays, The Metropolitan Opera only stopped performing *Otello* in blackface a few years ago, *On the Town* opens with the Pledge of Allegiance, *In the Heights* and *West Side Story* are regularly cast with white casts, and most classic plays do not pass the Bechdel test. Should we then, as we are often wont to do with professional wrestling, dismiss the entire field of the performing arts? Perhaps. The various bans on theatrical representation stemming from Plato can seem tempting in light of such work. However, the reason to study wrestling as theatre, for me, is not to somehow redeem some terrible art form, but rather to show its malleability and its possibilities. Theatre can be as awful as professional wrestling on its worst days and is often even more troubling as it panders to an "enlightened" liberal audience. Neither need to be that way and the wrestling form, as a form of theatre, can accommodate many disparate viewpoints and political stances.

In *The Elaborate Entrance of Chad Deity* and *Trafford Tanzi*, we see the characters struggle with the roles they are assigned. In *Chad Deity*, these characters are wrestling characters themselves that differ from but rely on the people the wrestlers are outside of the ring. In *Trafford Tanzi*, the characters (Tanzi in particular) negotiate their social roles through wrestling and their performances in the ring. In both there is a particular attention to the physical details of the performance, and the wrestling form is championed even as the content of professional wrestling is offered up for mockery or critique. Through both plays, we see that the troubling stereotypes on display are a direct result of the theatricality of the performances. That is, there would be little room for such disconcerting representations without the conceits of theatre.

In *Chad Deity*, the racist and crudely stereotyped characters that Mace, VP, and Chad Deity must put on in order to do their job are read as sitting aside from and on top of the physical collaboration of professional wrestling. In

Trafford Tanzi, the singular narrative of Tanzi and her familial problems are what led some commentators to deem the play bourgeois in its aims, through a focus on individual rather than collective struggle, but it is the wrestling form that saves the play from such simplifications.

While both of these plays rely on a sort of backstage or fourth-wall-breaking reveal of the characters and the performers, *Trafford Tanzi*, utilizes the professional wrestling frame itself and Brechtian staging techniques in order to deploy professional wrestling as a storytelling genre in its own right. That is, *Tanzi* does not set out to reveal the "truth" about professional wrestling by upending its representational structure—a structure that should be well known to any who watch professional wrestling—rather, Tanzi inverts the relationship of theatre to wrestling and uses wrestling itself to provide analysis and to alienate the spectator from the otherwise sordid and familial plot. Taken together, these two plays, through their theatrical staging and representation of professional wrestling, show professional wrestling's potential for critique and even something approaching progressive, left, feminist, and maybe even socialist politics. It seems that while the major problems of professional wrestling do seem to stem from its regressive deployment of theatrical tropes, its real use and revitalization might also be found in the theatre.

Notes

1 Sharon Mazer, *Professional Wrestling: Sport and Spectacle* (Jackson, MS: University Press of Mississippi, 1998), 122.
2 Mazer, *Professional Wrestling*, 122.
3 Sharon Mazer, "Donald Trump Shoots the Match," *TDR/The Drama Review* 62, no. 2, T238 (Summer 2018): 191–192. Such claims have been questioned: Claire Warden, Broderick Chow, and Eero Laine, "Working Loose: A Response to 'Donald Trump Shoots the Match' by Sharon Mazer," *TDR: The Drama Review* 62, no. 2, T238 (Summer 2018): 201–215. In addition, quite a bit of recent wrestling scholarship has managed to complicate and also celebrate the roles of women in professional wrestling: Keiko Aiba, "Transformed Bodies and Gender Norms: Gender Identity of Japanese Women Pro Wrestlers," in *Identity and Professional Wrestling: Essays on Nationality, Race and Gender*, ed. Aaron D. Horton (Jefferson, NC: McFarland, 2018), 120–136; Christina Molldrem Harkulich, "Sasha Banks, the Boss of NXT: Media, Gender, and the Evolution of Women's Wrestling in WWE," in *Identity and Professional Wrestling: Essays on Nationality, Race and Gender*, ed. Aaron D. Horton (Jefferson, NC: McFarland, 2018), 148–161; Rachel Wood and Benjamin Litherland, "Critical Feminist Hope: The Encounter of Neoliberalism and Popular Feminism in *WWE 24: Women's Evolution*," *Feminist Media Studies* 18, no. 5 (2018): 905–922.
4 Patrice A. Oppliger, *Wrestling and Hypermasculinity* (Jefferson, NC: McFarland and Company, 2004).
5 Danielle M Soulliere, "Wrestling with Masculinity: Messages about Manhood in the WWE," *Sex Roles* 55 (2006): 8.
6 Darrin Hagan, "Why I Hate Wrestling (the Sport, Not the Foreplay!)," *torquere: Journal of the Canadian Lesbian and Gay Studies Association/Revue de Ia Societe canadienne des etudes lesbiennes et gaies* 1 (1999): 119.

7 Heather Levi, "Sport and Melodrama: The Case of Mexican Professional Wrestling." *Social Text* 50 (Spring 1997): 61.
8 Lucy Nevitt, for instance, has claimed professional wrestling, at least as it manifested in WWE performances in the early parts of the 2000s, as emblematic of the US "War on Terror" (Lucy Nevitt, "'The Spirit of America Lives Here': US Pro-Wrestling and the Post-9/11 'War on Terror.'" *Journal of War and Culture Studies* 3, no. 3 (2010): 319–334.)
9 Henry Jenkins III, "'Never Trust a Snake': WWF Wrestling as Masculine Melodrama," in *Steel Chair to the Head: The Pleasure and Pain of Professional Wrestling*, ed. Nicholas Sammond (Durham, NC: Duke University Press, 2005), 33–66.
10 Jenkins, "'Never Trust a Snake,'" 41.
11 Jenkins, "'Never Trust a Snake,'" 41.
12 See Warden, Chow, and Laine, "Working Loose."
13 Roland Barthes, *Mythologies*, Trans. Annette Lavers (New York: Hill and Wang, 1972.
14 Again, for more along this line of argumentation, see Warden, Chow, and Laine, "Working Loose." Also see Bertolt Brecht, "Emphasis on Sport," *Brecht on Theatre: The Development of an Aesthetic*, trans. John Willet, 6–9. (New York: Hill and Wang, [1926] 1964).
15 R. Tyson Smith, *Fighting for Recognition: Identity, Masculinity, and the Act of Violence in Professional Wrestling* (Durham, NC: Duke University Press, 2014), 92–93.
16 Carrie Dunn, "'Most Women Train with Men, so Why Not Wrestle Them?': The Performance and Experience of Intergender Wrestling in Britain," in *Performance and Professional Wrestling*, eds. Broderick Chow, Eero Laine, and Claire Warden (London: Routledge, 2017), 96.
17 Smith, *Fighting for Recognition*, 94.
18 Smith, *Fighting for Recognition*, 96.
19 Smith, *Fighting for Recognition*, 113.
20 Matt Foy, "The Ballad of the Real American: A Call for Cultural Critique of Pro-Wrestling Storylines," *The Popular Culture Studies Journal* 6, no. 1 (2018): 173–188.
21 Kristoffer Diaz, *The Elaborate Entrance of Chad Deity* (New York: Samuel French, 2011), front matter.
22 Diaz, *The Elaborate Entrance of Chad Deity*, 5.
23 Diaz, *The Elaborate Entrance of Chad Deity*, 5.
24 Kimberly Ramirez, "Let's Get Ready to Rumba: Wrestling with Stereotypes in Kristoffer Diaz's *The Elaborate Entrance of Chad Deity*," *Label Me Latina/o* 3 (Fall 2013): 2.
25 Ramirez, "Let's Get Ready to Rumba," 3.
26 Diaz, *The Elaborate Entrance of Chad Deity*, 6.
27 Patrick Healy, "Here, a Careful Body Slam Is as Vital as Deft Dialogue, *New York Times*, May 16, 2010, accessed May 5, 2019, www.nytimes.com/2010/05/17/theater/17wrestle.html.
28 Noe Montez, "The Heavy Lifting: Resisting the Obama Presidency's Neoliberalist Conceptions of the American Dream in Kristoffer Diaz's *The Elaborate Entrance of Chad Deity*," *Theatre History Studies* 37 (2018): 312.
29 Montez, "The Heavy Lifting," 312.
30 Healy, "Here, a Careful Body Slam."
31 Diaz, *The Elaborate Entrance*, 6.
32 Diaz, *The Elaborate Entrance*, 6.
33 Diaz, *The Elaborate Entrance*, 15.
34 Broderick Chow, "Work and Shoot: Professional Wrestling and Embodied Politics," *TDR* 58, no. 2 (Summer 2014): 83.
35 Chow, "Work and Shoot," 83.

36 Chow, "Work and Shoot," 83.
37 Warren Kluber, "Character-World Dialectics on the Contemporary American Stage: Gaming, Role-Playing, and Wrestling with Idioculture," *Theatre Journal* 70, no. 2 (June 2018): 218.
38 Kluber, "Character-World Dialectics," 218. Kluber is citing Chris Hedges, *Empire of Illusion: The End of Literacy and the Triumph of Spectacle* (New York: Nation Books, 2009), 7.
39 "Tuebrook Tanzi, The Venus Fly Trap," Digital Collections, Liverpool John Moores University, accessed May 5, 2019, http://digitool.jmu.ac.uk:8881/R/GS V45LA611RKNXRK8J2S1PLLMT9STHPXETA8N4SFG5TGH7YUA9-00292?func=dbin-jump-full&object_id=16464&local_base=GEN01&pds_handle=GUEST and the record itself: digitool.jmu.ac.uk:1801/webclient/DeliveryManager?pid=16464&custom_att_2=direct
40 Claire Luckham, *Plays* (London: Oberon, 1999), 19.
41 Luckham, *Plays*, 41.
42 The episodes move quickly into the next with some overlap as characters come and go and linger at ringside and proceed as follows: (1) Tanzi vs. Mum (Mum wins by submission); (2) Tanzi vs. Platinum Sue; (3) Tanzi vs. Dr. Grobe, the school psychologist, (4) Tanzi vs. Dad; (5) Tanzi vs. Dean Rebel; INTERMISSION; (6) Tanzi vs. Dean Rebel (no contest—the first that Tanzi doesn't lose); (7) Tanzi vs. Platinum Sue (Ref calls the bell before Tanzi wins); (8) Tanzi vs. Mum (Tanzi wins by submission and discovers her finishing move, the Venus Flytrap); (9) Tanzi vs. Dad (Tanzi wins and dropkicks Dad out of the ring); (10) Tanzi vs. Dean Rebel (Tanizi wins and Dean immediately demands a rematch).
43 Michelene Wandor, *Carry On, Understudies: Theatre & Sexual Politics* (London: Routledge & Keegan Paul, 1981), 177.
44 Luckham, *Plays*, 15.
45 "Eric's – April 1978," *Liverpool Eric's*, May 30, 2016, Accessed May 4, 2019, http://liverpoolerics.blogspot.com/2016/03/erics-april-1978.html.
46 "Eric's – April 1978."
47 "Eric's – April 1978."
48 Luckham, *Plays*, 7.
49 "Trafford Tanzi (1980)," Productions, *Stages of Half Moon*, Accessed May 4, 2019, www.stagesofhalfmoon.org.uk/productions/trafford-tanzi/.
50 Luckham, *Plays*, 14.
51 Wandor, *Carry On, Understudies*, 177.
52 "Trafford Tanzi by Claire Luckham," Past Productions, *Theatricalia*, accessed May 5, 2019, https://theatricalia.com/play/980/trafford-tanzi-by-claire-luckham.
53 "Teaneck Tanzi: The Venus Flytrap," *Playbill*, accessed May 5, 2019, www.playbill.com/production/teaneck-tanzi-the-venus-flytrap-nederlander-theatre-vault-0000013345.
54 Joel G. Fink, "*Trafford Tanzi* by Claire Luckham. Half Moon Theatre, London. August 9, 1982," production review, *Theatre Journal* 35, no. 1 (March 1983): 118.
55 Wandor, *Carry On, Understudies*, 177.
56 Claire Luckham, *Trafford Tanzi: Her Hopes, Her Fears, Her Early Years* (London: Quartet Books, 1983), [6]. Luckham follows this assertion with a note about the offensive stereotypes often at play in wrestling matches, a matter her play does well in not reproducing.
57 Janelle Reinelt, "Beyond Brecht: Britain's New Feminist Drama," *Theatre Journal* 38, no. 2 (May 1986): 159–160. Citing Roland Barthes, "The World of Wrestling," *Mythologies*, trans. Annette Lavers (New York: Hill and Wang, 1972), 18.
58 Luckham, *Plays*, 15

59 Luckham, *Plays*, 15.
60 Luckham, *Plays*, 15.
61 Wandor, *Carry On, Understudies*, 177.
62 Wandor, *Carry On, Understudies*, 177–178.
63 Reinelt, "Beyond Brecht," 159.
64 Reinelt, "Beyond Brecht," 159.
65 Fink, "*Trafford Tanzi*," 118.
66 Luckham, *Plays*, 39
67 Fink, "*Trafford Tanzi*," 118.
68 Dominic Cavendish, "Tanzi Libre, Southwark Playhouse, Review," Theatre, *Telegraph*, May 22, 2013, accessed January 15, 2019, www.telegraph.co.uk/culture/theatre/10073756/Tanzi-Libre-Southwark-Playhouse-review.html.
69 Michael Billington, "Tanzi Libre—Review," Theatre, *Guardian*, May 22, 2013, accessed January 15, 2019, www.theguardian.com/stage/2013/may/22/tanzi-libre-review.
70 Andrzej Lukowski, "Tanzi Libre," *Time Out: London*, May 29, 2013, accessed January 15, 2019, www.timeout.com/london/theatre/tanzi-libre-southwark-playhouse-29-may-2013.
71 Nathan Brooker, "Tanzi Libre," *Exeunt Magazine* May 22, 2013, accessed January 15, 2019, http://exeuntmagazine.com/reviews/tanzi-libre/.
72 Hannah Elsy, "Review: Tanzi Libre," Off-West End, *A Younger Theatre*, May 27, 2013, accessed January 15, 2019, www.ayoungertheatre.com/review-tanzi-libre-southwark-playhouse/.
73 Nicola Merrifield, "*Tanzi Libre* Cancelled After Lead Actor Suffers Injury," News, *The Stage*, May 28, 2013, accessed January 15, 2019, www.thestage.co.uk/news/2013/tanzi-libre-cancelled-after-lead-actor-suffers-injury/.

Chapter 3

Hardcore wrestling
Deregulation and theatrical danger

The sound of two heads colliding is a sickening sound. The fact that I was easily thirty feet away and could still hear the impact made me queasy. Two wrestlers, bleeding from their heads and torsos, were head-butting each other—forcefully slamming their heads together, separating, and then repeating the action. Sometimes they would fall down after a strike, sometimes they would just stand in place, dazed. A person seated behind me told their friend: "It sounds awful! Like a nail clipper?" Indeed, the hollow cluck of two skulls colliding with enough force to generate such an awful sound *was* awful. Their heads were colliding. There were no stage tricks or special effects, just two men headbutting each other, repeatedly, and apparently cooperatively and consensually.

Hardcore wrestling is determined, the outcome of matches scripted, much like other forms of professional wrestling, but hardcore wrestling distinguishes itself in that the wrestlers, the promoters, and the audience all know that there will be blood. Real blood. Real wounds. And presumably, the wrestlers will suffer real pain. The conventions of hardcore wrestling are similar to those of other incarnations of professional wrestling with the additional focus on extreme stunts that involve falling from often dangerous heights onto household and industrial furniture and finding ever more creative ways to produce wounds. For some wrestling fans, to watch hardcore wrestling is to watch "the real thing," while for others the style is dismissed as garbage wrestling.[1] It is often hard to watch and stunningly gory. And yet, if like other forms of professional wrestling it is scripted, determined, and bound to conventions, one wonders how extreme or hardcore it can really be. Hardcore wrestling strains credibility because who would possibly agree to do such things? On the other hand, there is often little doubt that the violent acts occur, even if they are staged.

Hardcore wrestling is a distinct style of professional wrestling that emphasizes bodily harm through stunts that create bleeding wounds. It also frequently involves falls from dangerous heights onto and through various materials such as tables, folding chairs, and panes of glass. The sportive struggle is reduced to its gruesome symptoms of blood and other various markers of pain: anguished looks, cries, and writhing, convulsing bodies. The form pushes to the extreme the fan belief that "wrestlers suffered and sacrificed, some even died 'for the love of the fans.'"[2] Of course, such configurations are not so uncommon outside of professional wrestling. Marla Carlson notes that "We do at times see an actor actually suffer on stage, due to an accidental injury or intentional performance design … and we see this as a sort of heroic self-sacrifice for art."[3] The pain in hardcore wrestling, however, is rarely accidental. Hardcore wrestling emphasizes agony and the suffering of participants through the visible display of the bloodied, bleeding body. It is sometimes quite serious, but it can also play on its own gruesome absurdity and shocking actions. In any case, hardcore wrestling brings the bodies of the wrestlers even further to the fore, emphasizing their sacrifice for fans, for their art, and yes, for their paycheck. As I've noted before with Broderick Chow, hardcore wrestling

> aestheticizes (however brutally) spectacular displays of pain, suffering, and humiliation. Rather than being a symptom of competition or the narrative, real pain and blood become fetishized commodities. Wrestlers are compensated for their willingness and ability to perform bodily destruction—they are paid to bleed (and jump through tables and get hit with chairs and fall off of ladders and land on thumbtacks and cut each other with kitchen utensils and puncture themselves with staple guns and dive onto fluorescent tubes, cacti, and barbed wire and light each other on fire).[4]

Performers are recognized and rewarded—through cheers, adoration, and money—for their ability to perform stunts that place them in apparent and actual danger. Hardcore wrestling is touted as a violent rebuff to the charge that pro wrestling is fake. Accusations of fakeness are difficult claim to maintain when someone is bleeding profusely.

The bloody spectacle of pro wrestling thus cuts to the quick of any such debates. It is hard to argue in the face of blood. Lawrence B. McBride's ethnographic work from the early 2000s in the suburbs of Chicago describes altered states of consciousness in the act of professional wrestling.[5] He spent time observing the Lunatic Wrestling Federation (LWF), an independent wrestling company not unlike many other independent wrestling companies found dotting the suburbs and the post-industrial and rural areas of the US. One moment stands out for the fact that it involves CM Punk, a now famous (legendary, perhaps) wrestler, whose career was only beginning, and for its description of the astounding power of the spontaneous appearance of blood in a performance. During a match that involved a number of weapons and household items, CM Punk was struck on the head with a toaster and started bleeding. An initial moment of wondering whether the blood was real or not gave way to an astonishing sort of reckoning:

The question of fake or real had been dissolved into a zone of uncertainty, and the change in the crowd's attitude was like a charge of static electricity suffusing the room. Even the audience members who recognized performers from school or work or even their own family were beginning to achieve a suspension of reality as they sensed not so much the staged nature of the spectacle, but rather the panic that follows the loss of situational certainty. The blood signaled the audience that here, in a void between real and unreal stood something dangerous, obeying rules alien to the laws of everyday reality.[6]

It is an odd constellation of objects and events that bring such a profound sense of being outside of the everyday. To strike someone or to be struck with such an ordinary object—one that many use every day to make toast, itself one of the most mundane foods—is to reshape the object. That it caused a bleeding wound sets the action even further from any sense of the ordinary. That wrestlers might do such things intentionally only confounds the situation further.

The performance of hardcore wrestling thus must not simply be a representation of violence—the performers must feel pain and blood is one of the most readily available markers of such painful performances. Lucy Nevitt writes:

> The authenticity of bleeding in pro-wrestling rests on the shedding of actual blood. To use a capsule or a blood bag would be seen as cheating. While it is fundamentally important to much of theatre that the act of simulation remains uninterrupted, wrestling is built on a spectatorial understanding of the physical actuality of performed action. At the heart of this performance form is the undisputed and crucial fact that wrestling *hurts*.[7]

Indeed, Nevitt's succinct observation that "pain is the authentic core of wrestling" is taken to its furthest logical conclusion in hardcore wrestling where the wrestlers' blood is the outward sign of suffering, produced in order to make pain legible.[8] It is possible to execute some wrestling moves without experiencing serious pain, but it is usually difficult to bleed without pain, so blood stands in as proof of the suffering body. Blood provides a performative short circuit to the fact that "pain comes unsharably into our midst as at once that which cannot be denied and that which cannot be confirmed."[9] The equation and argument of hardcore wrestling thus appears to be: blood = pain = authenticity. The fans show up to see the instruments of pain and they pay tickets to see real blood flowing from real bodies.

Like blood in other forms of performance, blood in wrestling gives the performance an air of authenticity. The ostensible differences between hardcore wrestling and pain art likely have more to do with audience, taste, and location (art galleries vs. sporting arenas). Like pain artists, hardcore wrestling also draws authenticity from blood and the performed, painful labor of the performers. However, the authenticity gained from the bloody performances in hardcore wrestling might rather be called "extreme authenticity." The irony, of course, is if something is truly authentic then it needs no qualifier or descriptive adjective, "extreme" or otherwise. Anything that is actually authentic (and even that phrasing—"actually authentic"—might call authenticity into question) need not be anything other than "authentic." Extreme authenticity is thus either a tautology or an oxymoron (or more likely, both). Extreme authenticity describes the peculiar fact that professional wrestling is widely acknowledged to be "predetermined, not fake" in that even though the event is scripted, it is still actually violent. The violence in hardcore wrestling functions in an over-the-top, exaggeratedly bloody style wherein wrestlers embellish their conflicts through overblown displays of bloodletting. In order to be "not fake," hardcore wrestling must assert its utmost authenticity, which ironically only calls those assertions into question. While there is generally no doubt that the wrestlers are really bleeding, in doing so (and in such an over-the-top manner) hardcore wrestling confirms all doubts regarding the legitimacy of the sporting event. Blood becomes the sign of both an authentic performance and the presumed inauthenticity of theatricality. Hardcore wrestling, then, maintains its own sort of kayfabe, through a kind of bloody theatricality. It is quite similar to the idea of kayfabe developed throughout the 1900s from the carnivals to contemporary wrestling in that everything is determined and the bloody performances are leveraged as a way of keeping the performance from slipping into real competition.

It is strange to watch hardcore wrestling in person. There is a sense of absurd nihilism that perhaps stems from the mix of the pedestrian and the precarious that attends hardcore wrestling matches. For instance, Combat Zone Wrestling's (CZW) annual *Tournament of Death*, which has been produced in partnership with Big Japan Pro-Wrestling (BJW) takes place during the day, lit only by daylight and with few, if any, of the special effects that sometimes make violence palatable in film and on television.[10] Even as the matches are determined, the headbutts described at the outset of this chapter were far from the most graphic or bloody stunt performed the late afternoon I watched hardcore wrestling in a field empty except for a wrestling ring just outside of the sleepy town of Townsend, Maryland.

Combat Zone Wrestling earned its reputation as a hardcore wrestling promotion in part because of its institutional connections to Extreme Championship Wrestling (ECW), which is considered by many the standard bearer of hardcore wrestling and the subject of many popular histories.[11] For instance, in 2001, CZW held its third annual Cage of Death match in the arena that had previously been used by ECW. A number of former ECW wrestlers made appearances in front of a sold-out crowd.[12] CZW also appeared at a time when hardcore wrestling was reaching the height of its popularity in the larger wrestling promotions and as those promotions were beginning to be consolidated. An account of CZW promotional material from the late 1990s advertised "a wrestling show that promised the employment of chairs, tables, barbed wire, and thumbtacks, known in shorthand as, 'The Mick Foley Diet.'"[13] While invoking Mick Foley would certainly give potential audience members an idea of the nature of the matches, the account also notes that the weapons for the matches were more prominently featured than the names of the wrestlers.[14]

CZW's Tournament of Death is the event where wrestler Nick Gage almost died when glass from a shattered florescent light tube severed an artery in his arm.[15] At the same event, among other many other terrible incidents, DJ Hyde thrust syringes through the cheeks of Thumbtack Jack.[16] At Tournament of Death 4, one wrestler landed on a stack of florescent light tubes that had been arranged on top of a metal grocery cart, resulting in injuries that took months to recover from and required nearly 200 stitches.[17] These stories and many like it are well chronicled on blogs and in biographies, and played and replayed on DVDs and streaming videos. The stories sit, oddly perhaps, between the commonplace and the legendary. The stunts are the everyday grist of hardcore wrestling, and yet are still almost too extreme to be believed—did they really do that?

From what can be observed in watching hardcore wrestling matches, however, the actual brushes with death are less common than hardcore wrestling lore might indicate. That is not to downplay the repeated rending of flesh or the inherent risks associated with the style. Indeed, hardcore wrestling favors the bloody and the spectacularly violent. Florescent light tubes make a popping sound and produce a small cloud of powdered chemicals when they are smashed over wrestlers' heads and bodies, stepped on, or even bitten. Barbed wire, strung up around the ring and wrapped around baseball bats, punctures and leaves jagged scrapes on exposed skin. Razorblades attached to any number of objects make already brutal strikes bloody and are cruel cushions for body slams. Panes of glass shatter, cut, and grind into backs, legs, heads, ears, and scalps as they are run into, landed on, and thrown from the ring onto wrestlers standing on the ground. It is incredibly violent, and, at the same time, it is all wrapped in the theatricality of the determined wrestling event. The excess blood and gory performances, while real, feel staged precisely because it is all so excessive.

More than just an aberration, the form is an outgrowth of international market forces and deregulation efforts that emerged in the late 1980s and early 1990s. After tracing the development of hardcore style, this chapter examines the form and its deployment in two parts. The first looks at Darren Aronofsky's *The Wrestler* and the theatrical methods of staging a hardcore match for film and the clashing modes of disbelief of both film critics and wrestling fans alike. Whereas the film critics do not believe such things would ever happen outside of a film made by Darren Aronofsky, the wrestling fans cannot believe that stage combat or anything other than hardcore wrestling practice might be filmed. The second part takes up two examples: Jamie Lewis Hadley's performance art and a much-discussed moment from a CZW Tournament of Death involving construction tools. When read alongside each other, they provide the possibility of parsing the act of intentionally bleeding in front of an audience. Hardcore wrestling, perhaps more than any other wrestling form, emphasizes the toll of wrestling on performers, and even as wrestlers are rewarded by fans, they are rarely compensated financially in a way that seems to match those efforts. All of the examples highlight a particular kind of theatrical labor that surrounds such actions, from the sleight of hand of stage combat to the austere staging of performance art to the unrestrained, screaming and distressed reaction of a wrestler whose head is being cut open with a reciprocating power saw.

Deregulation and great spectacles of suffering

Hardcore wrestling is, perhaps, as far as one might be able to take Roland Barthes's description of wrestling as, among other things, a "great spectacle of suffering."[18] However, the spectacle of suffering of hardcore wrestling as developed in the 1990s is quite different from the spectacle of suffering found in Parisian wrestling of the 1950s. While the description holds in many ways, the different practices indicate historical and spatial distinctions in the form itself. For Barthes:

> wrestling is the only sport which gives such an externalized image of torture. But here again, only the image is involved in the game, and the spectator does not wish for the actual suffering of the contestant; he only enjoys the perfection of an iconography. It is not true that wrestling is a sadistic spectacle: it is only an intelligible spectacle.[19]

Hardcore wrestling may appear sadistic, but the highly intelligible spectacle of bleeding bodies, like other forms of wrestling and theatre, is mutually constructed. In Barthes' analysis, wrestling holds ("any figure which allows one to immobilize the adversary indefinitely and to have him at one's mercy") and the "forearm smash" ("with which one clouts the chest of one's adversary, and which is accompanied by a dull noise and the exaggerated sagging of a vanquished body") are the outer limits of wrestling's iconography.[20] Barthes' audience exclaims its distaste for the obvious spectacle of these moves "not because it regrets the absence of real suffering, but because it condemns artifice: as in the theatre, one fails to put the part across as much by an excess of sincerity as by an excess of formalism."[21] In short, the wrestling audience for Barthes was not complaining about the moves because they were not violent enough, rather because they betrayed the theatrical spectacle of wrestling in his time.

Today, the spectacle of suffering goes far beyond painful-looking holds and actual slaps to the chest in order to be intelligible, and the audience, it seems, does want to witness something that appears as suffering. For many, that is a clearly bleeding body. Hardcore wrestling fans are eager to complain to the performers should they pull any punches or exhibit what most would consider a sense of self-preservation. As Jodi Enders asserts, violence in a theatrical setting "might well present the same ontological and phenomenological problems but assaulting as opposed to pretending to assault is subject to both moral and legal intervention,"[22] yet hardcore wrestling presents this experiment and generally shows neither legal nor moral interventions.[23]

The type of wrestling that is regularly featured at Combat Zone Wrestling draws on a number of traditions that congealed into a rather cohesive style in the 1990s under the name of hardcore wrestling. Hardcore wrestling is very much an international style with roots tracing back to Mexico, Japan, Puerto Rico, and the US. However, it was not until the wrestling industry was deregulated and no longer classified as sport, but rather as an exhibition or an art form, that hardcore was able to really develop in the US. Thus, making wrestling more like theatre had the effect of making it bloodier and more dangerous. Contact sports are safer than theatre, it turns out.

One of the forms of wrestling that contributed significantly to the hardcore style in the US was lucha libre from Mexico. Lucha libre is a quick-moving form of wrestling and many wrestlers are trained for high spots, wherein they jump off the ring ropes or turnbuckles and dropkick or otherwise land on their opponents. The history of lucha libre itself is not necessarily hardcore, but the lucha form, with its fast and high-flying work pace, fit neatly into many of the hardcore programs of the 1990s that often eschewed the bodybuilder aesthetic and slower matches of WWE and its rivals.

For most of its history, lucha libre has been a live performance form, despite brief stints on television and luchadores playing popular roles in film.[24] However, this changed in the early 1990s when the wrestling promotion AAA began broadcasting lucha libre matches in Mexico. According to Heather Levi, who participated in lucha libre training, there was concern among luchadores that television and televisual circulation might have the possibility of ruining lucha libre as a performance form. Levi notes that when she began her training she "wondered what it could possibly mean for *professional wrestling to be vulgarized*, even by television."[25] She recalls a speech given to her on one of the first days of lucha libre training, one which expressed sentiments that were frequently articulated during her year and half training as a luchadora:

> Lucha libre is not the clown show you see on television, with the ones from the AAA. If you want to learn *real* lucha libre, you have to learn it step by step. First falling, tumbling, then Olympic wrestling,

Greco-Roman wrestling, intercollegiate wrestling, locks from jiujitsu, strikes from karate. Only then can you learn *professional* wrestling. If you're willing to learn real lucha libre, then I will teach you. I am a great teacher, many people know and respect me, but I had a greater teacher behind me and had had others behind him.[26]

As explained by Levi's teacher, lucha libre is treated as a performance form that is passed from generation to generation. It is not considered a televised entertainment, but rather more closely resembles an oral and embodied tradition, often rooted in a particular neighborhood or locale.

However, US promoters were mostly interested in lucha libre for its potentially dangerous and spectacular stunts and the crowds they might attract. Luchador Rey Mysterio writes: "And I also knew, from my trips with ECW [Extreme Championship Wrestling], that America was ready for a *lucha libre* style. Fans wanted high-flying action, and I could deliver it."[27] In sections of his co-written book entitled "Day Laborer" and "Problems in Mexico" Mysterio describes the working conditions for luchadores in the 1990s. Despite not receiving a contract from World Championship Wrestling (WCW), Mysterio claimed he was happy because "The pay for one night was a lot more than what I got in Mexico."[28] He also characterizes his work in the US as "a future with one of the two biggest wrestling franchises in the US, *and therefore the world.*"[29] Mysterio also notes that in the midst of the ratings wars of the 1990s between WWE and WCW, wrestlers may have benefitted as the major promotions began to search for talent in Mexico. However, these arrangements were not without their problems, as Mysterio recalls an event where there "was a dispute over how the wrestlers from Mexico should be paid: whether the money should go to AAA, who would then pay them, or to them directly."[30] Mysterio was able to sidestep being directly involved in the issue of payment: "Since I was an American citizen living in San Diego, I was paid directly and the issue never came up."[31] The precarious arrangement for Mexican wrestlers is highlighted here in the hardcore working conditions. Despite the potential for higher pay, they were physically and financially in danger for their work—precarious workers performing precarious roles in the ring as they were hired to jump from heights onto the mat or fellow wrestlers or the concrete below. Mexico was not the only country to contribute to the style as it developed in the US.

Wrestling in Japan would enter global trade in the 1990s with the innovation of a form of wrestling centered around an event called the "death match." It was not actually a fight to the death, but death certainly seemed to be a possibility given the many dangerous stunts and materials. While the elements—barbed wire, steel chairs, brass knuckles, and other weapons—of death matches had been part of wrestling for some time, Frontier Martial-Arts Wrestling in Japan would take the form to new heights and, surprisingly for some, new popularity.

Japanese wrestler Atsushi Onita began wrestling in the 1970s and in the early 1980s began touring in the US and Puerto Rico, where he was exposed to barbed-wire matches and sprawling brawls that spilled out of the ring into the audience.[32] At the time, wrestlers such as Abdullah the Butcher and Terry Funk had made careers out of bloody brawling matches throughout the 1970s and 1980s. Many credit the introduction of barbed wire to wrestling promotions in Puerto Rico in the early 1980s, specifically Capitol Sports. Wrestlers Carlos Colon and Abdullah the Butcher gained notoriety in the 1970s and 1980s for their often bloody and intentionally brutal displays of violence, which involved barbed-wire matches, chain matches, "Puerto Rican Death Matches," and "traditional steel cage" matches.[33]

The narrative of the death match is that after retiring due to an injury, Onita returned to wrestling in 1989 and began applying his global experience with extreme matches by founding Frontier Martial-Arts Wrestling in Japan. Originally meant to be a one-off event, pitting wrestlers against legitimate fighters trained in karate, the success of the event led Onita to develop an ongoing promotion. The idea was to take the wild brawls of the southern US promotions and combine them with the violence of the barbed-wire matches from Puerto Rico and the excited and overblown interviews of televised US wrestling.[34] The promotion would eventually bring in a number of famous wrestlers from the US including Terry Funk, The Sheik, his nephew Sabu (who would go on to ECW fame), and Mick Foley. The death matches would become increasingly absurd and legitimately dangerous:

> A barbed wire match for a big show became an Exploding Barbed Wire Death Match, the first of its kind on August 4th, 1990.... Exploding Barbed wire became an Exploding Barbed wire Cage Death Match in front of over 33,000 fans at Kawasaki Stadium on September 23rd, 1991.[35]

These matches gained attention in the US as wrestling magazines printed images and fans began to circulate copies of videos. Many of the US wrestlers who performed in the death matches would find employment in the US, where the style was re-branded as "hardcore" and developed as a separate style throughout the 1990s.

The US had been primed for such wrestling styles in large part due to efforts of deregulation in the 1980s. The fast-paced matches of lucha libre and especially the maneuvers involving jumps from dangerous heights and the bloody use of weapons on a scale like that seen in death matches would not have been possible in the US when wrestling was deemed a sport, rather than an exhibition or even art. While the wrestling industry maintained a front as legitimate sport for most of the last century, the financial benefits of deregulation encouraged some promoters, notably Vince McMahon, to claim wrestling to be entertainment or "sports entertainment." This in turn pushed many others to find ways to perform, as graphically as possible, just how real professional wrestling could be. This move was hastened by a series of deregulatory measures advanced throughout state legislatures beginning in 1989 in New Jersey.[36] The campaign for deregulation was advanced by former presidential candidate and then US senator Rick Santorum in Pennsylvania. The law firm that Santorum was working for represented Titan Sports (the parent company for what was then Vince McMahon's World Wrestling Federation, what would become WWE) in various attempts to deregulate the pro wrestling industry. Santorum's goal was to:

> Get the Pennsylvania State Athletic Commission out of the ring. There was no need for state officials to act as referees, because wrestling was a spectacle, not a sport. Nor did it need the state to supply timekeepers, announcers, and doctors—the promoters could take care of that. The new legislation, backed by Santorum and the WWF, would also reduce state taxes on wrestling events, from 5 percent to 2 percent.[37]

The arguments that both Santorum and Linda McMahon pushed in order to gain the necessary vote in Pennsylvania appealed to the free market and the apparent benevolence of wrestling promoters as business owners and capitalists. McMahon testified to the Pennsylvania Legislature: "I don't think I have to tell you how much prestige and money it would cost Titan Sports if Hulk Hogan or Andre the Giant or any number of our wrestlers were seriously injured and unable to perform."[38] McMahon was implying, of course, that state regulations and oversight were not necessary because the company had a vested interest in protecting its workers from harm. If its workers could not work, the company could not generate a profit. The argument is somewhat disingenuous, however, because wrestlers were only contractual employees, not full-time, salaried personnel. And, of course, the wrestling promoters weren't going to encourage Hulk Hogan or Andre the Giant to set themselves on fire in a barbed-wire ring or jump off balconies through tables or take direct hits to the head with steel chairs. Promoters knew they could hire any number of less established wrestling talents from Mexico and Japan and the US. And they knew they could hire them on contract and that anything the wrestler did in the ring, they did at their own risk. Imagine the already precarious life of the actor, but without a union and with every play involving stage combat and the theatre audiences expecting the actors to bleed.[39]

Santorum made the matter incredibly clear: "these people are their income."[40] In other words: wrestlers are promoters' revenue, literally. Santorum and Marx may not agree every day, but we should note when it happens. ("The worker has become a commodity, and it is a bit of luck for him if he can find a buyer. And the demand on which the life of the worker depends, depends on the whim of the rich and the capitalists."[41]) The lobbying efforts were successful and lifted many of the health restrictions and much of the state oversight of wrestling as an industry. As part of the agreement, however, the events were still taxed.[42] The state maintained a part of its revenue and wrestling promoters were given quite a bit of leeway in the manner they managed and handled their employees and events. With success in Pennsylvania, many other states followed suit, allowing for WWE's expansion.[43] Jim Cornette writes:

> Wrestling entered a sort of "deregulation" that would make Wall Street shudder, where the experienced promoters who controlled all wrestling in their territories and would protect the credibility of the business to their fans were gone. Anyone with enough money to book a building and hire some wrestlers could be a promoter. Anyone with enough money to buy boots and tights (and these days, even those are not needed) could be a wrestler.[44]

Even assuming that a company such as WWE might have an interest in maintaining the health of its employees (an assumption that has been disproven in many other arenas), deregulation allowed for unchecked drug use and opened the door for more and more extreme stunts. In a way, hardcore wrestling is a perfect theatrical performance of this market-based reasoning. By removing the elements of wrestling that might make it sportive and leaving only those elements that might be dangerous, state legislatures applied a logic of neoliberalism that assumed the forward progress of the free market while ignoring the human costs.

Hardcore wrestling is not a real sporting event or even a real fight, but the material effects on the bodies of the performers are the same, or often worse, than if it was a sport. Many of the wrestlers are heavily scarred from careers made of such matches. Jun Kasai from Big Japan Pro-Wrestling has a back that appears to be more scar tissue than skin. It's an aesthetic marking that indicates his previous work, but it's also functional. Thomas Hackett describes this extreme level of scarring as both a symptom of the profession and a practicality, which reduces the need for stitches and acts "like armor."[45] The ability to perform painful maneuvers is a skill, and one that the body must adapt to. Thus, the workers' bodies are (dis)figured by their labor, alienated from their bodies as they become better wrestling commodities—not necessarily through the usual routes of body building and tanning and developing technique, but through use and literal wear and tear. And the promoter will sell you a ticket to watch it happen. It is a front-row seat to contingent physical labor.

Hardcore wrestling can thus be read as a violent application of the market economy with low-wage workers taking on often extreme risks. It also vividly and disturbingly stages and lays bare the effects of wage labor on the body. Lucia Rahilly, for instance, reads the turn to more extreme or hardcore wrestling forms of the late 1980s, 1990s, and 2000s as an extension of post-industrial logic, which echoes the pre-industrial period in which the body has little utility as labor power or commercial value and thus is open to overt torture and destruction.[46] Even as the body commodity withers away, the wrestler is made productive for the promoter. The hardcore wrestling form asserts the unobtainability of the body through bloody physicality while performing the economic logic of laboring without a social safety net. Despite or perhaps because of its very baldness of message and effects, it is treated with incredulity.

The Wrestler and disbelief

Hardcore wrestler Necro Butcher (or Dylan Keith Summers) is probably best known for playing himself in Darren Aronofsky's 2008 film *The Wrestler*. The film tells the story of a once successful professional wrestler, Randy "The Ram" Robinson (played by Micky Rourke) who is now wrestling small matches on the weekends, working hourly jobs that don't pay enough to cover his rent. In his attempt to get into shape for one last big match, he starts booking more matches and he finds himself wrestling in a hardcore match with Necro Butcher, after which he has a heart attack. The hardcore wrestling scene, like the matches Necro Butcher frequently wrestled in real life, involved florescent light tubes, panes of glass, ladders, barbed wire, thumbtacks, kitchen utensils, a garbage can, a prosthetic leg, and, famously, a staple gun, which Necro Butcher uses to attach a dollar bill to his own forehead. While Micky Rourke utilized a stunt double and his bleeding prosthetic forehead that facilitated a shot of Rourke having his face gouged with a fork is on display at the Museum of the Moving Image in Queens, it seems Necro Butcher performed the scene in the film like he might any other hardcore wrestling match.[47]

Aronofsky shot the scene in between other matches at a live Combat Zone Wrestling (CZW) event. There are a number of online videos posted by audience members, and one in particular indicates the difference between the illusion of violence created by film (and often strived for in theatrical stage violence) and the violence in live performances of professional wrestling.[48] The video shows Necro Butcher and Mickey Rourke sitting down on folding chairs opposite each other in a wrestling ring strewn with hardcore wrestling implements. A man with a shoulder-mounted camera crouches behind Necro Butcher, his camera aimed at Rourke. Necro Butcher winds up and throws an open-hand slap, which, in fine theatrical stage combat style, misses Rourke's face by at least a foot.

Rourke reacts as if the slap had made contact—throwing his head to the side, sweaty hair flying, his posture slumping—before returning upright, at which point Necro Butcher repeats the gesture and Rourke his reaction. From the vantage point of Wilt Chamberlin, the YouTube handle for the person who posted the video and presumably also recorded it, there is no illusion of violence. The empty space between Necro Butcher's hand and Rourke's face makes it abundantly clear that no one is being slapped.

However, after the second feigned slap, Rourke rolls out of the ring and the man with the shoulder-mounted camera follows. Another man, wearing the same ring attire as Rourke and with a physique and hair resembling Rourke, enters the ring and seats himself across from Necro Butcher. The slap gesture is repeated by Necro Butcher—this time making physical contact across the other man's face. The man resembling Rourke, presumably Rourke's stunt double, slaps back, making contact with the side of Necro Butchers head. The two men trade slaps until Necro Butcher sprays the contents of an aerosol can in the face of Rourke's stunt double, sending him sprawling out of the chair and onto the mat, where Necro Butcher grapples with him until the video ends.

Even if the slaps between Necro Butcher and Rourke's stunt double were not full force, the difference between a theatrical (or filmic, in this case) strike, with a wide space for safety between the participants, and a wrestling strike, where contact is made, indicates the difference between stage combat and wrestling. Yet, in wrestling the premise is as staged as in theatre, and in hardcore wrestling any possible ambiguity of violence is eliminated. While it is not evident on the YouTube video, watching hardcore wrestling live, there is no question of the physical pain. One can hear the impact of the slaps, one can see the blood pouring from puncture wounds, one can see someone fall from the top of a steel cage through two panes of glass, a folding table, and onto a small pile of steel chairs. There is no question that it happened—and there is little question that all of those items were available and arranged as they were because the spot was planned in advance. It is both not fake and "not fake."

Spectators are very aware of this fact and hold it up as a quality that makes the form worth watching. It does not matter that wrestling is predetermined, precisely because it is not fake. The injuries are not accidental or an unfortunate byproduct of competition. Indeed, it appears at times that the predetermined nature of the events makes them even more "hardcore." One can argue about whether it is stupid or brave to willingly enter a situation that will be physically painful, but the conscious choice to do so does indicate a certain, almost fanatical, commitment to the performance.

And fans expect such fanaticism. The disappointment of seeing even a simple wrestling move made theatrical for a film shoot is palpable for YouTube commenter DingusStudley:

> I'm sure it'll look real on screen, but I don't understand why they have to fake it, just let a couple wrestlers actually do it for real. They're faking pro wrestling, kinda funny, given all the talk about how "fake" pro wrestling is to begin wtih [sic].[49]

It does not seem to matter for this fan who performs the violent acts, as long as they are actually performed.

The match in the film closely resembles actual hardcore matches in performance. And like hardcore wrestling matches, the scene was described variously in reviews of *The Wrestler* as "horrifying,"[50] "gruesome,"[51] and "hard to watch."[52] It's a bloody, pained sequence made even more disturbing by unflinching close-ups, handheld camera work, and documentary-style framing that places the viewer perhaps too close to the action. It is a sequence so disturbing and realistic that Kenneth Turan of *The Los Angeles Times* thought the film was

> yearning for the excessive until it feels like Aronofsky and company are making a fetish of audience discomfort. When a wrestler is introduced whose trademark is using a staple gun on opponents, it becomes clear that these scenes are not about realism, they are about making us squirm for squirming's sake.[53]

A question and answer section about the film on *About.com* presents a similar level of incredulity at the scene: "They don't use staple guns. Do they?"[54] Like Turan, the fact that this might happen in performance somewhere is seemingly too absurd to believe. The answer to the question, however, only hints at the violent limits of the form: "If you felt that this scene of the movie was particularly gruesome, just be glad that the Necro Butcher didn't pull out a weed whacker."[55] In fact the answer to the question might go even further—yes, be glad that he did not use a weed whacker … or razor blades, gusset plates, meat hooks, a tank of piranhas, hermit crabs, scorpions, cacti, syringes, explosives, or power tools.[56] This list, surely not exhaustive, is both macabre and, indeed, cartoonish. Turan notes that wrestling was "a subculture that was into performance art well before the high culture world heard of it."[57] However, when presented outside the walls of a downtown gallery, even if it is packaged in a filmic veneer, the disturbing subculture of hardcore wrestling is too much to face let alone believe. For such sentiments, it seems, hardcore wrestling is too theatrical to be real and simply too extreme to not be fake.

Staple gun art and power tool theatrics

Of course, most wrestling fans know the wounds are real and that the staples are not some trick of the stage—they are most likely just purchased at a hardware store. Hardcore wrestling is both the most grotesque style of professional wrestling and the one that shares the most with other forms of performance art. Reducing the spectacle to bodily destruction with little reference to competition places the focus on the (however gruesome) aesthetic of blood and wounds. This connection has been made by Daniel Schulze, who points to the "common ground of physical pain in performance art and wrestling" through analysis of the communicative aspects of pain in the work of Marina Abramović and pro wrestling.[58] However, there is a vast social difference between the highbrow suffering of bodies in an art gallery and what is seen by many as simply self-mutilation in a cinder-blocked community hockey rink.

Jamie Lewis Hadley, a London-based performance artist, has made the connection through his practice, which highlights

> his career as a former professional wrestler and uses it as a departure point to create live art performances that explore, both aesthetically and thematically: blood, deterioration, endurance, pain and violence. The materials he uses can often be found in hardcore a wrestling match; fluorescent light tubes, razor blades, staple guns and steel chairs. He attempts to subvert the use of these objects, transforming their original uses (from both wrestling and daily) into images that are affective, challenging and beautiful.[59]

Indeed, Hadley's art performances often embrace many of the tropes of hardcore professional wrestling, but his performances take place in galleries and at art festivals, in front of often quiet, reserved patrons (i.e., not wrestling fans).

One such performance, *We Will Outlive the Blood You Bleed*, performed most prominently as part of the 2014 Spill Festival of Performance in London, involved a white flag, a staple gun, an industrial fan, and Hadley's arm. In the performance, Hadley uses the staple gun to attach the white flag to his forearm. He then turns on the fan and holds his arm up, allowing the breeze to move the flag. He then removes the staples from his arm, which opens the wounds that had until that point actually been stopped up by the staples. The white flag is used to dry the bleeding wounds and the flag is then attached to the fan, which is then turned on. The performance ends with a bloody, white flag blowing towards the audience.

In Hadley's description of the work, he suggests "Not everybody bleeds in the same way, but every-body bleeds."[60] Throughout the performance his face is passive, void of emotion save for a slight grimace as he removes some of the staples from his arm. Perhaps surprisingly, he has very little reaction as the staples are applied. This is quite different from the yelling and hyped-up agony of the wrestling ring.[61] The audience sits quietly. There are no gasps, it seems, let alone cheers or chants. The work might be read as meditative in its tone, inviting the audience to consider their own relationship to blood, the body, and industry.

The white fabric transitions from rag to flag and back again. It is only legible as a flag once it has been attached to Hadley's arm. In order to wave the white flag, Hadley must first join it to himself using a machine most often deployed in construction and other manual labor. Once removed from his arm, the flag is used to clean the wounds that made it intelligible as a flag—it is returned to a rag or a piece of medical equipment. Stained with blood, and hung on the fan, the bloody white flag is further transformed, blowing at the audience. All of the materials rely on Hadley's bleeding body to make them apparent. His blood literally and figuratively marks the performance. There is no question as to whether the blood is his or what is happening is real or fake.

In this context, the various props of hardcore wrestling take on a seriousness that cannot be attained in the wrestling ring, despite the gruesomeness and even morbid nature of some hardcore wrestling matches. Even as the sight of blood can hold an audience transfixed, the effect does not linger. The theatrical overlay of the wrestling match, with two people seemingly trying to injure each other for one reason or another, always betrays itself as fabricated. Thus, the motivation and the violent action are actually held separately by the wrestling ring, but that separation begins to break down if the action is so extreme that the theatrical frame falls off entirely.

While there is no doubt that the risks of hardcore wrestling are real and certainly it is not possible to perform such maneuvers without experiencing pain, there is an element of theatricality to the anguished grimaces and tortured screams. One such example, Jon Moxley's infamous match with Brain Damage in 2009 at CZW's Tournament of Death 8, ended with Moxley's head being cut open with a handheld electric saw.[62] The match is grisly throughout, involving tables, chairs, a set of dinner plates, barbed wire, and other weapons commonly found in hardcore matches. Near the end of the match Moxley is kneeling in the center of the ring, apparently dazed and swinging his arms. Brain Damage approaches him from behind, grabs Moxley by the hair with one hand, pulling his head back. In his other hand he is holding a reciprocal saw and in a deliberate move cuts a clear line straight across Moxley's forehead. Moxley breaks free and writhes in pain on the ropes of the ring. The crowd chants "Hol-y shit!, Hol-y shit! Hol-y shit!" One of the announcers on the video says: "I've never seen anything like that." And the other exclaims: "That's human flesh under a knife!" A moment later, Brain Damage has caught up with Moxley and has grabbed him again by the hair holding the saw in the air. He cuts Moxley across the forehead again, perhaps less assertively or convincingly this time, but there is still the fact of a power saw making contact with John Moxley's face.

Well before such videos were widely available, the spot was frequently debated because it is both incredibly brutal and highly theatrical. Some were not sure if it really happened or if it was all a bit of theatre. Video of Moxley discussing the match is available online, wherein he calls the spot entirely fake.[63] He notes that he had received criticism for doing such a dangerous spot and that people had frequently asked him about it and called him a "dumbass" for doing such a thing. He says:

Alright, let me put this to fucking bed, if you think that I took a skilsaw to the head, and survived, and I'm sitting here talking to you today, then you're an idiot. Because there's no middle ground, either it was complete Hollywood bullshit fake, like, John Cena falling off the fucking, like, stage, and the packing peanuts flying everywhere and the sparks, or it was real and I'm dead. It was totally like fake.[64]

Moxley also states that he didn't believe the audience would accept the spot, thinking it was "too over the top."[65] He also asserts that the blade was not sharp, he already had blood on his forehead, and the saw simply moved it around. And yet, video of the match appears to rather clearly show the saw opening a wound across Moxley's forehead. It is true, however, that if Brain Damage had really attacked Moxley with an electric saw with the intention to kill him (perhaps the most likely intention for someone wielding a motorized saw to harm someone else), the damage to Moxley's head would have been significantly greater than breaking the skin on his forehead. As Moxley notes, he would be dead. The wound is real, but the situation is worked, set up, determined, theatricalized. The events are generally agreed upon before time, but the question in performance is one of degrees. The extreme nature of the electric saw attack, even for a hardcore wrestling match, makes the theatricality of the event fall away. Moxley is adamant that the saw did not cut him, but the video at least appears to tell a different story.

Conclusion: Necro Butcher's medical bills

Hardcore wrestling takes the notion of "predetermined, not fake" to its furthest ends and in doing so stages the bloody labor of wrestling. Indeed, to see Necro Butcher or another wrestler perform is not just to watch him assault his own body and his performance partner's, it is to watch a contingent performer slowly expire in front of you. In an interview with the *Village Voice*, Necro Butcher describes the appeal of being witness to a clearly injurious performance:

> The simple fact is that blood draws people into the match more. Nothing makes a crowd sympathize with someone more than if that someone is a bloody mess. In the same regard, when the crowd wants to see someone injured, nothing satisfies them more than if that person is busted open. I find it thrilling to satisfy the crowd, so the blood has been a constant thing throughout my career, both me and my opponents.[66]

However, the real effects of such matches reveal the working conditions of many wrestlers and many other contingent and hourly employees. After one particularly difficult match, Necro Butcher was forced to raise money to pay for his hospital bills as his insurance likely would not cover many of the expenses. His wife at the time wrote:

> Dylan has the crappiest insurance known to man and we are looking at physical therapy, another doctor's visit on top of the ambulance ride, the transfer to two hospitals out of state (so insurance won't cover it) and the time he is going to have to take off of work.[67]

Thanks to many of the fans, it appears that the fundraiser reached its goal of $2500.[68] This situation should be familiar to many workers who have limited or no health insurance and are an accident away from bankruptcy and limited employment options.

While it is easy, perhaps, to dismiss Necro Butcher and other hardcore wrestlers, their fans, and even the act of hardcore wrestling itself, it is hard to ignore the way it stages wage labor so clearly and bluntly. While the theatrical frame of professional wrestling contains it to a point, the labor of the wrestlers bleeds through and reminds us what unregulated capital looks like. In its extreme and often disgusting destruction of the human body, hardcore wrestling remains almost beyond belief for many commentators writing for middle- and upper-class readers. However, it is perhaps almost too real for spectators who daily experience the dangers and contingency of low paying wage labor. Watching hardcore wrestling as it performs labor relations is to watch the bodies of workers be literally torn apart for pay.

Notes

1. Garbage wrestling is a term of derision adopted by hardcore fans as a point of pride and gestures to the fact that the matches can literally involve garbage and everything but the kitchen sink.
2. Thomas Hackett, *Slaphappy: Pride, Prejudice & Professional Wrestling* (New York: Ecco, 2006), 20.
3. Marla Carlson, *Performing Bodies in Pain: Medieval and Post-Modern Martyrs, Mystics, and Artists* (New York: Palgrave Macmillan, 2010), 159.
4. Broderick Chow and Eero Laine, "Audience Affirmation and the Labour of Professional Wrestling," *Performance Research* 19, no. 2 (June 2014): 49.
5. Lawrence B. McBride, "Professional Wrestling, Embodied Morality, and Altered States of Consciousness" (MA Thesis, University of South Florida, 2005).
6. McBride, "Professional Wrestling," 5.
7. Lucy Nevitt, "Popular Entertainments and the Spectacle of Bleeding," *Popular Entertainment Studies* 1 no. 2 (2010): 83
8. Nevitt, "Popular Entertainments," 84.
9. Elaine Scarry, *The Body in Pain: The Making and Unmaking of the World* (New York: Oxford University Press USA, 1987), 4.
10. I attended the 13th annual Tournament of Death in 2014.
11. ECW emerged in the early 1990s and attracted a rabid subcultural following. Many of the wrestlers who started with ECW ended up working for one of the larger promotions. Indeed, ECW founder Paul Heyman is currently employed by WWE. See Thom Loverro, *The Rise and Fall of ECW: Extreme Championship*

Wrestling (New York: Gallery Books, 2007); Scott E. Williams, *Hardcore History: The Extremely Unauthorized Story of ECW* (New York: Sports Publishing, 2011).

12 Bob Magee, "As I See It 12/27: Arena History, Part 2.... The Post-ECW Era," As I See It, Pro-Wrestling Between the Sheets, *Gerweck.net*, 27 December 2013, www.gerweck.net/2013/12/27/as-i-see-it-1227-arena-history-part-2-the-post-ecw-era/.

13 Justin Henry, "Real By Nature: Combat Zone Wrestling Celebrate 15 Years of Signature Anarchy," *CCB*, 29 January 2014, http://camelclutchblog.com/combat-zone-wrestling-15-years/.

14 Henry, "Real By Nature."

15 Jason Nark, "Nick Gage, Jailed Icon of Violent Wrestling, Speaks of Drugs & Bank Heist," Collections, *Philly.com*, 8 January 2011, http://articles.philly.com/2011-01-08/news/27017192_1_addictions-facebook-fans-heist.

16 Bob Magee, 'As I See It 6/8," *Pro-Wrestling Between the Sheets, pwbts.com*, www.pwbts.com/columns/2009/b060809.html.

17 Pro Wrestling Doctor, "Blood's Arm and Leg are Severely Gashed by Light Tubes," *Pro Wrestling Doctor*, June 2, 2011, 2019, www.pro-wrestling-doctor.robtencer.com/wrestling-injuries/bloods-arm-and-leg-are-severely-gashed-by-light-tubes.

18 Roland Barthes, *Mythologies*, Trans. Annette Lavers, (New York: Hill and Wang, 1972), 17.

19 Barthes, *Mythologies*, 18.

20 Barthes, *Mythologies*, 18.

21 Barthes, *Mythologies*, 18.

22 Jodi Enders, *Murder by Accident: Medieval Theater, Modern Media, Critical Intentions* (Chicago: University of Chicago Press, 2009), xviii.

23 There are a few notable exceptions to this, of course. Perhaps the most notorious incident is often referred to as the "Mass Transit Incident" wherein a seventeen-year-old named Erich Kulas claimed to be older than he was and properly trained as a wrestler. He had never cut himself in a match and asked New Jack, another wrestler to do the cutting. Another wrestler who was at the event stated: "What New Jack and Mustafa did to him was criminal; it really was. I was just inches away from him, and I swear, in all my years in wrestling, I never saw blood shooting out like that. The kid's dad was yelling, 'Stop!'" (Scott E. Williams, *Hardcore History: The Extremely Unauthorized Story of ECW* (Champaign, IL: Sports Publishing, 2006), 108.) The incident caused ECW to lose a number of their booked shows and resulted in a lawsuit on the part of Kulas that was unresolved by the time ECW was sold and was dropped when Kulas died at the age of twenty-two from an unrelated surgical procedure. (Williams, *Hardcore History*, 111.)

24 Heather Levi, *The World of Lucha Libre: Secrete, Revelations, and Mexican National Identity* (Durham: Duke University Press, 2008), 23.

25 Levi, *The World of Lucha Libre*, 178. Italics in original.

26 Levi, *The World of Lucha Libre*, 178.

27 Rey Mysterio with Jeremy Roberts, *Behind the Mask* (New York: Pocket Books, 2009), 140.

28 Mysterio, *Behind the Mask*, 140.

29 Mysterio, *Behind the Mask*, 148. (italics mine)

30 Mysterio, *Behind the Mask*, 148.

31 Mysterio, *Behind the Mask*, 148.

32 FMWWrestling.us, accessed May 19, 2019, http://fmwwrestling.us/FMWHistory.html.

33 Steve Slagle, "Carlos Colon," *The Professional Wrestling Hall of Fame Presented by The Ring Chronicle*, accessed May 25, 2019, www.wrestlingmuseum.com/pages/wrestlers/carloscolon2.html.

34 Bahu, "FMW History," *Poruresu Central*, 2007, www.puroresucentral.com/FMW.html.
35 Bahu, "FMW History." Punctuation and capitalization retained from original.
36 Peter Kerr, "Now It Can Be Told: Those Pro Wrestlers Are Just Having Fun," *New York Times*, February 10, 1989, www.nytimes.com/1989/02/10/nyregion/now-it-can-be-told-those-pro-wrestlers-are-just-having-fun.html. Also see Eero Laine. "Professional Wrestling: Creating America's Fight Culture," in *Sports at the Center of Popular Culture: The Television Age*. Vol. 2 of *American History Through American Sports: From Colonial Lacrosse to Extreme Sports*, eds. Daniel Coombs and Bob Batchelor (Santa Barbara: Praeger, 2013), 219–236.
37 Tim Murphy, "Hate Wrestling? Blame Rick Santorum," Politics, *Mother Jones*, March 16, 2012, www.motherjones.com/politics/2012/03/rick-santorum-wwf-pro-wresting.
38 Murphy, "Hate Wrestling?"
39 Andrew Zolides, "The Work of Wrestling: Struggles for Creative and Industrial Power in WWE Labor," in *#WWE Professional Wrestling in the Digital Age*, ed. Dru Jeffries (Bloomington, IN: Indiana University Press, forthcoming).
40 Murphy, "Hate Wrestling?"
41 Karl Marx, "Wages of Labor," *The Economic Manuscripts of 1844*, marxists.org, www.marxists.org/archive/marx/works/1844/manuscripts/wages.htm.
42 Eric Boehm, "In Pennsylvania, Pro-Wrestling is Taxation Without Regulation," Features, *Pennsylvania Independent*, 22 July 2013, http://paindependent.com/2013/07/in-pennsyvania-wrestling-is-taxation-without-regulation/.
43 Boehm, "In Pennsylvania."
44 Jim Cornette, "The Slippery Slope of Hardcore Wrestling, *jimcornette.com*, accessed January 15, 2019, http://jimcornette.com/cornettes-commentary/slippery-slope-hardcore-wrestling.
45 Thomas Hackett, *Slaphappy: Pride, Prejudice, and Professional Wrestling* (New York: Ecco, 2006), 219.
46 Lucia Rahilly, "Is *RAW* War?: Professional Wrestling as Popular S/M Narrative," in *Steel Chair to the Head: The Pleasure and Pain of Professional Wresting*, ed. Nicholas Sammond (Durham: Duke University Press, 2005), 224–225.
47 Quint, "Wanna see Mickey Rourke and Darren Aronofsky in the Ring? Footage From the Shooting of *The Wrestler* is Here!," February 12, 2008, www.aintitcool.com/node/35591; and Wally Gobetz, "NYC – Queens – Astoria: Museum of the Moving Image – forehead wound from The Wrestler," April 2, 2011, www.flickr.com/photos/wallyg/6456719717/.
48 Wilt Chamberlin, "The Wrestler – Mickey Rourke – Stunt Double," *Youtube.com*, February 15, 2008, www.youtube.com/watch?v=5n9UeLiCUrk.
49 DingusStudley, comment on Chamberlin, "The Wrestler."
50 A.O. Scott, "Hard Knocks, Both Given and Gotten," Movie Review, *NYTimes.com*, December 16, 2008, www.nytimes.com/2008/12/17/movies/17wres.html.
51 J. Hoberman, "Mickey Rourke and Darren Aronofsky Both Make Visceral Comebacks in *The Wrestler*," Movies, *The Village Voice*, December 17, 2008, www.villagevoice.com/2008–12–17/film/mickey-rourke-and-darren-aronofsky-both-make-visceral-comebacks-in-the-wrestler/.
52 Joe Morgenstern, "Takedown!: Rourke Reigns as Failed 'Wrestler,'" Film Review, *Wall Street Journal*, December 19, 2008, http://online.wsj.com/news/articles/SB122963414294619431.
53 Kenneth Turan, "As Fake as Wrestling," Movie Review, *Los Angeles Times*, December 17, 2008, http://articles.latimes.com/2008/dec/17/entertainment/et-wrestler17.

54 Eric Cohen, "Secrets of the Wrestler," Professional Wrestling, *About.com* via Internet Archive Wayback Machine, accessed January 22, 2019, https://web.archive.org/web/20090211151910/http://prowrestling.about.com/od/beginnersguide/tp/secretsofthewrestler.htm.
55 Cohen, "Secrets of the Wrestler." In another article, Mick Foley commented on the scene:

> And a few people have suggested that I inspired that grisly wrestling scene. But I can claim with a clear conscience that I never used a staple gun on an opponent. Thumbtacks, yes; barbed wire, definitely; but never a staple gun.
> (Mick Foley, "The Wrestler is Good," Life and Art, *Slate.com*, December 18, 2008, www.slate.com/articles/news_and_politics/life_and_art/2008/12/the_wrestler_is_good.2.html.)

56 It is worth noting here that John Zandig, the promoter of CZW when *The Wrestler* was filmed, was under the impression that the exposure provided by the film would somehow elevate hardcore wrestling to new heights of popularity. While certainly one of the more memorable scenes in the film, it is unlikely that many of the viewers of *The Wrestler* were turned from independent film to hardcore wrestling. (A.D. Amorosi, "There Will Be Blood … And Weed Whackers," Naked City, *Philadelphia CityPaper*, February 13, 2008, http://archive.today/orGG#selection-359.463-363.147.)
57 Turan, "As Fake as Wrestling."
58 Daniel Schulze, "Blood, Guts, and Suffering: The Body as Communicative Agent in Professional Wrestling and Performance Art," *Contemporary Drama in English* 1, no. 1 (2013): 113–25.
59 "Jamie Lewis Hadley," Supported Artists, Arts Admin, accessed May 22, 2019, www.artsadmin.co.uk/artists/supported/jamie-lewis-hadley.
60 Jamie Lewis Hadley, *We Will Outlive the Blood You Bleed*, Spill Festival of Performance, October 29, 2014, accessed May 22, 2019, http://spillfestival.com/show/we-will-outlive-the-blood-you-bleed/.
61 Hadley considers the performance of pain in professional wrestling, its indications and connections between theatrical performance and medical knowledge, in Jamie Lewis Hadley, "The Hard Sell: The Performance of Pain in Professional Wrestling," in *Performance and Professional Wrestling*, eds. Broderick Chow, Eero Laine, and Claire Warden (London: Routledge, 2017), 154–162.
62 CZW, "[FREE MATCH] CZW Tournament Of Death 8: Jon Moxley Vs Brain Damage," YouTube, December 31, 2018, www.youtube.com/watch?v=Z_ZJZ-r9t8E.
63 MadManAmbrose, "Jon Moxley (Dean Ambrose) talks about his first Tournament of Death," YouTube, June 9, 2015, www.youtube.com/watch?v=eQhjUz5LLMc
64 MadManAmbrose, "Jon Moxley."
65 MadManAmbrose, "Jon Moxley."
66 Sharyn Jackson, "Interview: Five Questions for *The Wrestler*'s Necro Butcher," Blogs, *The Village Voice*, March 20, 2009, http://blogs.villagevoice.com/music/2009/03/interview_five.php.
67 "Fundraiser Launched for Injured Wrestler Necro Butcher," *prowrestling.net*, August 15, 2013, www.prowrestling.net/artman/publish/miscnews/article10032888.shtml.
68 "'Necro Butcher' Dylan Summers' Medical Expenses," *giveforward.com*, September 11, 2013, www.giveforward.com/fundraiser/sfw2/dylan-summers-medical-expenses.

Chapter 4

Trading likenesses
Wrestling labor and the branded body

Mick Foley believes he has suffered permanent brain damage from his career as a professional wrestler.[1] And brain damage is certainly not the only injury he sustained. The back cover of his *New York Times* best-selling memoir, *Have a Nice Day: A Tale of Blood and Sweatsocks*, provides a handy illustration. The image takes up the entirety of the back of the book and shows Foley dressed as his most famous gimmick: Mankind. In the kayfabe world of wrestling storylines of the late 1990s and 2000s, Mankind was an apparently deranged character who wore sweatpants, a rag-like shirt, and a patchwork leather mask. The figure on the back of the book is surrounded by small white boxes that detail his injuries. Like a dissection specimen in a biology textbook, thin white lines connect the boxes of text to the affected parts of his body. While some of the injuries might be similar to other professional athletes—from torn muscles to bruised organs to dislocated joints—many others are not. For instance, listed among the many injuries are eight concussions, four lost teeth, a severed ear, broken bones (ribs, thumb, toe, and cheekbone), close to 400 stitches, and second-degree burns.[2] In addition, unlike other athletes, for whom injuries are an unfortunate outcome of playing the game, for Foley the injuries appear to be central to what he does as a performer. Where other publications might have a synopsis or endorsements intended to help sell the book, Foley has an illustrated list of injuries. His injuries are his identity, his brand—here, both a means of marketing and permanent marks on his body.

This chapter investigates the branded wrestling body in performance. While previous chapters have examined the productive labor of performers, the wrestling form itself, and the material effects on the wrestling body when taken to its logical, hardcore ends, this chapter considers the ways that the bodies of professional wrestlers are made saleable apart from the moment of live performance. Professional wrestling, in almost every instance, relies on a live event with an audience as its core activity; however, wrestling is not limited to this. While other studies have examined the WWE network and pay-per-view events,[3] social media,[4] transmedia,[5] and other profit-making projects peripheral to the live event, I am interested here in one of the key legal and philosophical ideas that make such ventures possible: likeness.

Legally, likeness and the right to trademark and otherwise protect one's likeness stems from a celebrity's rights to have some control over their identity and image. Putting a celebrity's face on a product might sell more product, but you have to ask (and very likely pay) the celebrity for the opportunity to use their image and the celebrity clout that goes with it. This seems easy enough to understand; however, it begins to unwind a bit when likenesses are treated as discrete commodities to be bought and sold. If an individual celebrity can sell, rent, or trade their likeness to a company for a definite or indefinite period of time, why can't a company pay an individual for use of their likeness as a condition of their employment? What is stopping a company from owning the visage of a person as a vendible object (however ephemeral) apart from that person? Remember: to trademark a likeness is not to trademark a particular image, but every image that is like the likeness.

These inquiries proceed from two separate but interlocking problems found at the root of professional wrestling as a form of productive theatre: 1) wrestlers perform immaterial labor in that they produce no physical good, yet this immaterial labor relies on a spectacularly embodied, violent physicality; 2) the bodies of the wrestlers are clearly not replicable, but in order to be productive (i.e., to produce capital) they must be circulated and consumed globally, or as broadly as possible. This labor and the labor performed in the wrestling ring benefit wrestling promoters as they trademark, market, and sell the wrestlers' likenesses and images. The bodies of professional wrestlers perform doubly as themselves and as the corporately owned likeness that bears an almost identical resemblance to them. Indeed, wrestlers' bodies are constantly laboring in order to be profitable for the company, often as a likeness that is trademarked, replicated, re-packaged, and resold. This arrangement places the risk and the work on the individual laborer often under the guise of entrepreneurialism. Images of the wrestlers become tangible goods owned by the promoter—a perhaps troublesome development considering the idea of physical goods as merely disposable icons for the company. Unlike other performers, who can more readily take off their costumes after a performance, professional wrestlers inhabit a visage every day that is more often than not owned by someone other than themselves. That is, the wrestlers' bodies stand in for corporate identity and are used up and consumed (like any other consumer good) through their often (self-)destructive performances. Performing their labor to create an immaterial product, but bared except for a pair of wrestling trunks or a singlet, wrestlers play characters that share their own likeness.

This is similar to but distinct from the performer who puts on a Mickey Mouse costume at Disneyland, or even, say, Sutton Foster, who played Fiona in DreamWorks's *Shrek the Musical*, and can rather easily change out of their costumes.[6] Disney, DreamWorks, The Blue Man Group, Cirque du Soleil, and other performing companies can tour shows in many locations at the same time because the actors hired for such performances are paid only to inhabit the costumes and characters that are performed. On the other hand, WWE and other wrestling companies rely solely on their workers as singular performer/characters, who cannot be replicated and must be physically present at each event whether it is televised or not. Wrestling promoters cannot clone their performers, and they are not digital or animated creations—they must exist corporeally and then be digitally and legally reproduced.

WWE, in particular, maneuvers around this issue in its leveraging of trademark law and likenesses, which can be replicated, repackaged, and altered. This arrangement alienates the wrestlers from their visage and character, even as the legal mechanisms of likeness are intended to offer some level of control. This chapter illustrates this point with key legal examples ranging from a foundational case involving Vanna White to the threat of legal action from Apple regarding the likeness of Steve Jobs, and a lawsuit involving the NFL that reinforced the idea of likeness beyond one's image to one's achievements and statistics. Professional wrestling takes such legal understandings as foundational to its business model, trademarking and copyrighting wrestlers' images, names, and even gestures. Once signed to a contract, a wrestler is thus tasked with maintaining and enhancing the likeness that is owned by the company. They may own their own body, but they do not own what it looks like (or really anything that might be construed to resemble it). Like other performers, wrestlers exercise, rehearse, and perform, and this labor contributes directly to the immaterial and material construction of the promoter's brand. The wrestlers become analogous to the promotion, even though they are employed on temporary contracts. Their bodies are placeholders laminated with the corporately owned likeness—a costume they can never actually remove.

Living gimmicks

Given his many injuries, it might be evident that Foley, the "Hardcore Legend," consistently put his body in dangerous positions throughout his career. Foley's career and the careers of many who wrestle in a similar hardcore style are more akin to that of a stunt performer or even a pain artist. Indeed, Foley's wrestling performances have involved stunts such as strikes to the head with steel chairs, being thrown through tables and onto ladders (both of which were at times on fire), leaping and being thrown onto piles of thumbtacks, having florescent tubes broken over various parts of his body, and other dangerous and bloody stunts. Foley sums up his wrestling career on his website:

> As Cactus Jack, Foley won the 1995 "King of the Deathmatch" tournament in Yokohama, Japan, and continued wrestling, despite the amputation of his right ear, in a match against Vader in Munich, Germany in

1994. As Mankind, Foley was a 3-time WWE Champion, but is best known for his epic and brutal battle with The Undertaker in 1998's "Hell in a Cell" match, during which he was knocked unconscious after falls both off of and through the 16 foot Cell structure. Despite the injury, Foley finished the match—with one of his front teeth lodged in his nose.[7]

As noted, Foley wrestled as a number of characters throughout his career, which are referred to as the "Three Faces of Foley" in the title of a DVD by the same name: Cactus Jack (outlaw bad guy), Dude Love (tie-dyed, pseudo-hippy free love guru), and Mankind (deranged recluse).[8] Foley is thus notable for wrestling in one of the most extreme and physically grueling styles of wrestling, while also maintaining not one theatrical gimmick, but three. While the characters are hypothetically interchangeable (certainly someone else could put on the Mankind mask and costume) his wrestling style emphasized his performance and the labor of such under the costumes.

In 1998, Foley portrayed all three characters in a single match.[9] Some fans suggest that Foley's success in the late 1990s was the final indication of the end of the kayfabe era, where wrestling was presented as real, including its often almost cartoonlike gimmicks:

> Instead of focusing on Mankind, Dude Love and Cactus Jack as the *characters* portrayed by Mick Foley, the WWF instead chose to focus on *Mick Foley*, the performer who happened [to] portray Mankind, Dude Love and Cactus Jack. Suddenly, the spotlight wasn't shining on what was happening in *front* of the kayfabe curtain, it was shining on what had, in the past, been hidden *behind* it.[10]

In other words, the focus shifted to the performers, the wrestlers who inhabited the gimmicks. Ironically, this shift in focus only further entangled the wrestlers with the companies they worked for, as the wrestling body, wrapped in various gimmicks, is always both the property of the wrestler and the wrestling promotion.

The recent collapse of the professional wall of silence known as kayfabe was significant (having begun well before Mick Foley's widespread popularity) and opened a number of possibilities for wrestling promoters to write storylines for characters that are nearly indistinguishable from the wrestlers themselves. This may sound familiar given the time period and the rise of reality television and other such programing, but the move stands in contradistinction from other live entertainments of the time, notably Broadway musicals, which saw the rapid rise of Disney Theatricals and other costume dependent productions.

Indeed, the financial benefits for producers were explained by Richard E. Caves, writing in 2000, when he noted the trend in Broadway theatre to "depend mainly on concept and special effects, and not the charisma of star performers. This property facilitates setting up road companies that replicate the initial show, and it also eases the adaptation of the shows for non-anglophone audiences around the world."[11] The live event can then be staged anywhere without having to rely on (and pay) any one performer. Thus, the move away from star performers has a twofold impact on live performance: (1) it reduces the importance of any one performer/employee and (2) it makes the production more easily replicable. Further, as Dan Rebellato explains, such maneuvers make productions into franchises, earning them the monikers of "McTheatre" and "megamusical" wherein "the sets are the stars, and the actors are endlessly replaceable."[12] By shifting focus from a star performer to a star concept and star special effects, the specific bodies onstage become interchangeable.

While this may obscure or deemphasize the labor of these performers, the move does not erase the performers. Rather, as David Savran reminds us in his critique of the idea of McTheatre: "The laboring bodies onstage produce not a thing to be ingested but an experience as elusive and polyvalent as it is ephemeral."[13] Setting aside for now whether such labor is grossly alienated and like a hamburger assembly line or potentially mysterious and open to interpretation, I do follow Savran in his proposition "that multinational corporations are well aware of the dangers of standardization and have responded to audiences' anxieties about mass-produced live entertainment."[14] Professional wrestling, then, despite its increasing global footprint in the live entertainment industry, is practically a boutique and custom operation compared to Broadway-style musicals. One can imagine a form of pro wrestling where, like other entertainment companies, wrestling promoters employ wrestlers cast through cattle call auditions to wear the costume of a famous character in one of its many tours, but the industry is far away from operating in such a way.

Professional wrestling promoters, rather, perhaps understanding the thick necessity of the laboring body in professional wrestling, have generally moved not to further obscure the wrestlers, but rather to enmesh them and overlap them with the characters that they play. In contrast to the megamusicals and other spectacular global touring performances, where "because the show is not star-dependent, its rents stick to the entrepreneurial producer or creative team and do not pass to the performer," in wrestling, the show *is* star dependent, *yet* "its rents stick to the entrepreneurial producer or creative team and do not pass to the performer."[15] While character and performer have always been intricately linked in professional wrestling, monetization and legal protections only further highlight the ways that wrestling gimmicks are so neatly sutured to those who perform them.

While gimmicks have long been a central part of professional wrestling performance, the promoters and wrestlers have not always held gimmicks as trademarked properties. David Shoemaker explains that while it was common practice to steal gimmicks before the advent of national television contracts, the practice became significantly more uncouth when done on broadcast television.[16] Indeed, prior to the wide circulation of live wrestling matches via cable television, masked wrestlers might be played by any number of wrestlers. There are accounts of fans recognizing the wrestler under the mask as someone other than who was advertised on television. In 1990, for instance, *The Wrestling Observer* featured a story about fans chanting the name of the wrestler who was supposed to be playing the masked character but was not. Bruce Mitchell writes:

> Fans know many more different wrestlers because of cable…. If promotions can't get away with some tricks that used to work in the past because fans don't fall for them anymore, in the long run that is better for wrestling.[17]

For much of its history, then, professional wrestling promoters considered stealing or "borrowing" gimmicks on the potential for profitability weighed against the possibility of being caught or called out by the originators of a gimmick or by fans.

Sharon Mazer reported rumors from the late 1980s that the Undertaker gimmick was purchased from a wrestler by Vince McMahon's company for around $75,000.[18] While the details of the possible exchange are only a rumor, it is notable that wrestlers were discussing their characters (or the characters of other wrestlers, as this case may be) as vendible commodities, distinct property that might be taken off and put on by others. Today, after a decades-long career, the Undertaker gimmick is intricately linked to wrestler Mark Calaway. The gimmick is notable today as it stands out significantly from the rest of the roster as a (beloved) relic of an earlier time in wrestling. Since the late 1990s, the WWE has largely (but not entirely) transitioned away from characters such as the Undertaker, instead promoting gimmicks that were linked to the wrestlers themselves or at least didn't have supernatural powers, as was the case for the Undertaker. The characters seem to emerge from the wrestler and are not quite so, well, gimmicky. However, this means that in many cases, today, the bodies of the wrestlers themselves are the gimmick.

Like many other performers, wrestlers spend hours every day at the gym and salon, enhancing muscles, skin, and hair with special diets, supplements, chemicals, and quite a bit of physical effort. But even those wrestlers without such toned physiques as, say, Charlotte Flair or John Cena, must take up the labor of maintenance and care for their bodies in order to be profitable.[19] Broderick Chow notes the theatricality of large and well-defined muscles of many wrestlers and the way that they appear as a kind of gimmick:

> The built body, as part of a quite obviously constructed and performative persona, seems to try too little—consider the denigration of wrestlers as

mere "body guys"—and work too hard for the audiences' attention. But it also works too hard in the sense that built bodies wear evidence of thousands of hours of labour in the flesh.[20]

The argument, I think, easily transfers to other aspects of the wrestling physique and style, beyond the strained physical labor of lifting and putting down weights. The labor that both tries too hard and too little, described by Chow, extends to the daily maintenance of hair and skin through tanning and grooming to considering, undergoing, and recovering from procedures such as implants, liposuction, and other body modification. Wrestling has always traded on the extraordinary appearance and physicality of performers, but the demands of such physicality go beyond appearance and also impact training and other forms of bodily maintenance.

Thus, maintenance of the wrestling body is not just building it, bulking it, and augmenting it, but can also involve a sort of toughening process. In the 1970s, wrestler Johnny Valentine summarized the "toughness" required for professional wrestling:

> I don't take long vacations because it takes too long to get back into condition. Condition here isn't just having good wind and muscle tone. Condition in wrestling is taking punishment so your skin won't get tender, and so you won't go mentally soft. If I took two months off, all the hide would come off my knees in the first round. It would get tender, and I'd get mat burns. You'd be nothing but a mass of sores from being pushed around the ring. The body is a strange thing. It can absorb so much punishment. It can get accustomed to it, taking progressively more punishment until it's almost indestructible. Like these karate guys, they start out breaking something soft with their hand, then they progressively break harder things, until they can split bricks without hurting their hand. The whole body is like that. The body just builds up resistance to pain. It's partly physical and partly mental.[21]

This level of abuse and the adjustment to abuse is, perhaps, similar to the potential dangers of or wear and tear of other performers, but, here, the emphasis is actually on enhancing resistance to pain through constant exposure. Like other performers that perform physically difficult and potentially painful performances (from ballet dancers to acrobats), wrestlers practice pain. Unlike many other performing laborers, however, for professional wrestlers the pain (or its simulation through cries, grunts, grimaces, sweat, and blood) is the purpose of the performance, not an unfortunate symptom. Calling back to the opening example of Mick Foley's book, imagine promoting a ballet with pictures of the taped and deformed feet of the dancers, or a football game with images from CT scans. (And, indeed, why stop there? Try selling cell phones with photos from the factory floor or university educations with portraits of sleep-deprived and underpaid adjuncts.) In professional wrestling, painful injuries are highlighted and celebrated and trained for—falling down for a living takes daily practice and maintenance. Wrestling companies complete this transition from wrestler to product by controlling the names of the wrestlers, often giving them names that are not necessarily character names but are actually quite similar to their birth names.

The sports news site *Bleacher Report* suggests that the WWE frequently assigns wrestlers new names in order to more easily control the trademark and copyright over wrestling personas. Some wrestlers, notably Chyna and Warrior (better known as The Ultimate Warrior), legally changed their names to their character names after leaving the WWE, in order to prevent the WWE from continuing to use the character they played while under contract.[22] This marks a historic difference from when wrestlers performed as a gimmick to actually living as a gimmick—making the gimmick indistinguishable from themselves, their bodies.

In the case of Warrior, James Hellwig opened litigation against WWE, which created a number of unique legal problems related to character, celebrity, and performer. Eric Lee notes:

> The Warrior is a character in a performance; yet, he is also the person performing. Where do the rights to protect a character and to exploit one's own image and name meet? Can the WWF prevent Hellwig from appearing as himself?[23]

Lee continues: "Hellwig and Warrior can be argued to have become indistinguishable to the extent that Hellwig is now named Warrior."[24] But how is this possible? Wrestling companies certainly don't own their employees (who are not actually employees, but more often independent contractors). Wrestling companies do, however, own the likeness of these characters that share a visage and personality with the wrestlers themselves.

Legal likeness

The legal category of likeness is usually restricted to something that quite literally looks like an individual (or an object) and can also encompass a series of traits that, when combined, form a likeness. The *Oxford English Dictionary* definition of likeness employs ideas of perception and semblance:

1. The quality or fact of being like; resemblance, similarity; an instance of this.
2. That which resembles an object; a like shape or form, a semblance.
3. The representation of an object; a copy, counterpart, image, portrait.[25]

By definition, then, likeness is: (1) a state of being like something else; (2) an object that bears a resemblance to something else; and (3) a copy or representation. All posit likeness as a thing or condition in relation to another, separate thing or condition.

This connection between one and another is central to the idea of likeness. Sometimes a likeness is very close, almost indistinguishable, and at other times it can be quite distant. Brian Massumi, in *Semblance and Event*, opens the concept of likeness as the discreet doubling that is in excess to something. Massumi writes:

> We live out the perception, rather than living in it. We forget that a chair, for example, isn't just a chair. In addition to being one it looks *like* one. The "likeness" of an object to itself, its immediate doubleness, gives every perception a hint of déjà vu. That's the uncanniness. The "likeness" of things is a qualitative fringe, or aura to use a totally unpopular word, that betokens a moreness to life. It stands in the perception for perception's passing. It is the feeling in this chair of past and future chairs "like" it.[26]

Massumi's definition points to the idea of the sameness or doubleness of the ephemeral body with itself. Likeness is a sort of moreness that spills over from the body in performance. It is this moreness that legal structures cannot fully account for in attempts to define, restrict, and monetize. Likeness has thus been a difficult concept to define and contain legally. Under US law, a person's likeness is separate from but dependent on the performing body. Likenesses are frequently treated as tradable and replicable objects protected by copyright and trademark law and also ephemeral and fleeting. A likeness need not be tangible, it might only be in one's mind.

The case of Steve Jobs presents a useful illustration of how a performance can be considered separate from a likeness.[27] After Jobs' death, a company called In Icons began production on a line of Steve Jobs action figures that were photorealistic representations of Jobs, complete with closely cropped hair, glasses, and black turtleneck. The figurines never made it to market, however, due to threats of legal action from Apple, Inc. The company claimed that the figurines imposed on and stole Jobs' likeness. This is particularly noteworthy here because Apple was not claiming ownership of a particular picture, image, or recording of Jobs, but rather the commonly held idea of what Steve Jobs looked like.[28] The case did not go to court, but production of the figurines was stopped. The president of In Icons explained:

> We respect copyright and trade mark rights and therefore indicated on our site that we were not providing any Mac, iPhone and iPad models with the figurine. Further, we haven't used any Apple related brands. Unfortunately we have received immense pressure from the lawyers of Apple and Steve Jobs family.... Though we still believe that we have not overstepped any legal boundaries, we have decided to completely stop the offer, production and sale of the Steve Jobs figurine.[29]

Again, Apple was appealing to their rights to maintain control over the ability to conjure Jobs' likeness itself, here as a figurine. None of the trademarked brands or logos were used, the action figures were not mapped or copied directly from a single copyrighted image. In short, the Steve Jobs likeness exists as a potential legal entity posthumously separate from his performing body. There was not a particular performance or moment that had been captured and was now being copied or infringed upon, rather Apple was claiming rights over the Jobs' likeness *as such*.

The laws and cases that define likeness fall under the broad category of celebrity rights—the right of publicity, which, "as defined by state courts, is limited to using a celebrity's name, voice, face, or signature" and copyright.[30] In 1993, such rights were greatly expanded when a panel awarded *Wheel of Fortune* host Vanna White $400,000 after she sued Samsung Electronics over an advertisement that featured a robot that turned letters on a set resembling *Wheel of Fortune*.[31] The advertisement features a gold-colored robot, perhaps in the style of C-3PO from *Star Wars*, with golden hair, in a pink strapless gown, turning the letter "T" on what appears to be the *Wheel of Fortune* set. The caption under the image reads: "Longest-running game show. 2012 A.D."[32] The year mentioned in the ad would have been roughly twenty years in the future when the ads were published. In 2018, Vanna White signed a contract to extend her contract until 2022, twenty years even after the futuristic robot supposedly took her job.[33] In any case, White is not featured in the ad, but the case was made that the robot was a likeness of White and thus imposing on her rights to publicity. David E. Wellowitz and Tyler T. Ochea point out that after the *White v. Samsung* case: "A copyright holder can generally avoid using any of these tangible elements [name voice, face, signature] in exploiting copyright. *White* exploded the right of publicity to include anything that brings the celebrity to mind."[34] The case raised questions about the implications of a legal "right to evoke."

Stacey L. Dogan, writing in the *Boston College Law Review*, states that the right to evoke, as it is currently understood, is "a right to prevent others from calling to mind a particular piece of intellectual property even if they have not replicated the intellectual property or deceived the public in any way."[35] The legal ruling of *White* opens the space for the threat of legal action as is seen in the Apple case above, where merely evoking the idea of a likeness (not copying or imitating an already existing object) is grounds for a lawsuit (or the threat of a lawsuit). The right to evoke thus becomes a very real right for copyright and trademark holders. However, the right to evoke raises the question of just what exactly is being evoked.

The dissenting judge in *White v. Samsung*, Alex Kozinski, argued that

> Instead of having an exclusive right in her name, likeness, signature or voice, every famous person now has an exclusive right to *anything that*

reminds the viewer of her: After all, that's all Samsung did: It used an inanimate object to remind people of White, to evoke [her identity].[36]

In effect, the right to use a likeness is no longer bound by copying or otherwise infringing upon a physical or reproducible likeness such as a recording of a performer's voice or a photograph.

White v. Samsung is considered a landmark because it did away with the photographic definition of likeness—again from the dissenting judge, Alex Kozinski: "The panel majority holds that the right of publicity must extend beyond name and likeness, to any 'appropriation' of White's 'identity'—anything that 'evoke[s]' her personality."[37] While the court seems to settle on the ideas of "identity" and "personality" to regard what is at stake rather than shifting the focus of what can and cannot be trademarked, the ruling does expand the definition of likeness. Indeed, later in the dissent, Kozinski returns to the idea of the evoked likeness: "Finally, I can't see how giving White the power to keep others from evoking her image in the public's mind can be squared with the First Amendment. Where does White get this right to control our thoughts?"[38] The ability to control the evocation of one's likeness (which now includes the nebulous concepts of identity and personality) turns likenesses into products.

However, that product is not always so clearly defined, especially as it concerns athletes who not only perform in the sense that their images can be replicated, but through performances that create statistics, metrics, and other measures of what might be encompassed by a likeness. Not only is a likeness what one sees, but it can also be considered what one has done (the statistical representation of one's performance). In an essay titled "Defining Liability for Likeness of Athlete Avatars in Video Games," James J.S. Holmes and Kanika D. Corley write:

> Courts and legislatures have struggled to define the likeness of a person. A likeness has been found to include one's name and biographical information, persona, and voice. The essential aspect of any part of one's likeness is that it makes the person identifiable. The identifiability of the image or other aspect of the plaintiff is an essential element of a claim for misappropriation.[39]

In 2007 the video game company Electronic Arts settled a legal dispute with the National Football League Players Association (NFLPA) for more than $35 million dollars for the use of the names and likenesses of NFL players. This transaction quite literally puts a price tag on the fully intangible objects of the likenesses of the players, or rather the price is put on the right to evoke those objects. Interestingly, just a year later, retired football players sued the NFLPA for nearly as much when it was revealed that "the NFLPA sold rights to use the likenesses of retired players."[40] Not only were the likenesses sold to EA

Sports (a branch of Electronic Arts), but a former executive of the NFLPA indicated that jersey numbers were to be changed and faces altered in order to not be recognizable. The retired players won out.

> Lead plaintiff Herb Adderley said, "If you look at the 1967 Green Bay Packers, you'll know that the only left cornerback that year had to be [me], but they scrambled my face and took the number off of my jersey. Yet, they had my correct height, weight, and years of experience."[41]

Here, despite the lack of any tangible property, likenesses are literally traded back and forth between groups. The collection of pixels on the screen evoked the retired players through their historic positions and statistics without even relying on photogenic likenesses.

The likeness of the player, even an imagistic resemblance, remains as a tradable entity separate from the performing body. As is alluded to in the legal cases above, the likeness is more than just an image, but carries with it accomplishments and identity, accrued labor of creating the body which the likeness is like. There must be something for the likeness to resemble and that something, in order to find its way into the market as a likeness, must have value. Here the labor that is accumulated sticks to the body of the worker, even as capital attempts to peel it off and package and sell it as a likeness.

Wrestling likenesses

The body of the wrestler, like the body of the performer in a Broadway musical, inhabits two identities—itself and the character. Just as Disney owns the trademark to Simba of the *Lion King* and Belle of *Beauty and the Beast*, WWE holds as its exclusive trademarked property all "programming, talent names, images, likenesses, slogans, wrestling moves, trademarks, logos and copyrights" related to its programming.[42] WWE also acknowledges the work that wrestlers perform and their relation to the company:

> Superstars are highly trained and motivated independent contractors, whose compensation is tied to the revenue that they help generate. We own the rights of substantially all of our characters and exclusively license the rights we do not own through agreements with our Superstars.[43]

WWE's rights to its characters are extensive. According to *Forbes*, the contract a wrestler signs with WWE distinguishes clearly between "Wrestler IP" and "New IP," or the wrestler's or employee's intellectual property and new or WWE-generated intellectual property.[44] The contracts designate New IP as almost every aspect of the wrestler and the contract "specifically entitles WWE to the rights to a wrestler's ring name, likeness, personality, character, caricatures, costumes, gestures and even legal name during the term of a booking contract."[45] Except for some special cases involving other stipulations where the wrestler uses their legal name in the ring (such as Brock Lesnar), upon the termination of the contract, the wrestler's legal name reverts back to the wrestler.[46]

While under contract, everything the wrestlers say, do, and look like is considered the intellectual property of WWE. The trademarked likenesses and images and wrestling moves are seemingly one and the same with those people who perform those gestures and embody those likenesses and images. Thus, even though professional wrestling relies on performers that can't be easily replaced or replicated, any power the star performers may have is signed away as part of their contract when the promoter takes over ownership of the wrestler's likeness. Indeed, wrestling companies control and profit from the image of the wrestler, which can circulate separately as a trademarked copy of the living (and sometimes deceased) body of the wrestler.

Wrestling companies thus see great value in trademarking the likenesses of their employees upon signing a contract to work. Other than video and images, action figures are perhaps only the most obvious use of trademarked likenesses. A likeness can be used to sell just about anything, and infringement on likenesses is easily policed with cease and desist orders. Like In Icon and Apple, few businesses want to face what could be a very costly lawsuit from a wealthy company.

The images of the wrestlers are thus tightly controlled and begin to bleed into the identity of the company itself. Wrestler John Cena, one of the highest-profile Superstars on the WWE roster for some time now, is exemplary of WWE's use of trademark. Registered trademarks indicate the various uses of Cena's image and name including clothing (t-shirts, hats, ties, etc.), toys (action figures, masks, puzzles, video games, etc.), and many other miscellaneous items that might come emblazoned with Cena's name or likeness, cited here at length from the US Patent and Trademark Office, largely for effect:

> Paper hangtags; packaging, namely blister cards, paper for wrapping and packaging, paper pouches for packaging, plastic bags for merchandise packaging, plastic bubble packs for wrapping or packaging; collector albums, namely, albums for sticker collectable cards, photo albums for photo collectables, photo collectables, namely, photographs; labels, namely, printed paper labels, printed shipping labels; folders; general purpose plastic bags; paper tableware, namely, paper place mats, paper table mats, paper table linens; stickers; framed pictures; pens; pencils; posters; notebooks; trading cards; calendars; paper tablecloths; photographs; chalk; brochures, magazines, and newspapers all concerning sports entertainment; photographic prints; postcards; greeting cards; pictures; decals; temporary tattoo transfers; coloring books; children's activity books; souvenir programs concerning sports entertainment; books

featuring pictorial biographies; comic books; book covers; paper book markers; bookplates; paper lunch bags; paper napkins; picture books; sticker albums; memo pads; date books; address books; agenda books; pencil sharpeners; rubber stamps; stamp pads; collectible prepaid telephone cards not magnetically encoded; collector stamps, namely, commemorative stamp sheets; customized personal bank checks; checkbook covers and return address labels not of textile; paper banners; printed paper signs for doors; pencil cases; drawing rulers; erasers, namely, rubber erasers, chalk erasers, blackboard erasers; scribble note pads; photo albums; bumper stickers; window decals; lithographs; paper party bags; paper party favors, namely, paper party hats; stencils for tracing designs onto paper; paper gift wrap; paper cake decorations;[47]

and

toy action figures and accessories therefor; cases for action figures; toy vehicles; board games; playing cards; toy spinning tops; stand alone video output game machines featuring wrestling; arcade games related to wrestling; pinball games related to wrestling; hand-held units for playing electronic game; tabletop action skill games related to wrestling; jigsaw puzzles; kites; toy wrestling rings; dolls; bobble-head dolls; puppets; stuffed toy animals; card games; toy guitars; water guns; vinyl pool products for playing, namely, pillow back lounge chair; Christmas tree decorations; costume masks; toy belts, doll furniture; party favors in the nature of crackers and noisemakers; skateboards; bowling balls and accessories, namely, bowling gloves, wrist supports, bowling ball bags; windup toys; toy scooters; bowling pins; knee and elbow pads for athletic use; yo-yo's; plastic model kits for making toy vehicles; pool cues; novelty toys, namely, toy banks made of tin; toy gum machines; toy candy bowl mechanical dispensers; toy stick gum dispensers; toy gum figure makers; confetti;[48]

and

Clothing, namely, tank tops, t-shirts, shirts, sport shirts, dress shirts, polo shirts, undershirts, sweatshirts, sweaters, pullovers, blouses, jackets, raincoats, overcoats, topcoats, trousers, pants, jean pants, jogging suits, exercise pants, exercise suits, sweatpants, shorts, underwear, boxer shorts, socks, clothing ties, pajamas, belts, gloves, Halloween and masquerade costumes, wrist bands, bandannas; footwear, namely, shoes, sneakers, boots, slippers; headgear, namely, hats, caps.[49]

This long list of largely disposable items highlights the relation between wrestler and likeness. None of the items in particular make up the WWE brand;

94 Trading likenesses

indeed, WWE is not in the business of "collectible prepaid telephone cards" or "general purpose plastic bags" or chalk for that matter. And neither is John Cena.

The items themselves may serve a specific function (making a long-distance call, holding items, or writing on a chalk board), but their greater function is to cash in on the legal possession of Cena's likeness, to distribute it as broadly as possible, to overcome the limitations of Cena's ephemeral and embodied performance as a wrestler. Cena—his muscles, his smile, his gestures, indeed everything about him—is as vendible as Mickey Mouse. And WWE is doing its best to be as widely consumed as Mickey. Licensing is one of the cornerstones of the WWE business model, and WWE

> builds partnerships with companies around the globe to create products featuring our marks and logos, copyrighted works and characters in diverse categories, including: toys, video games, apparel, housewares, collectibles, sporting goods, books and more. WWE licensed products, created by our more than 175 licensees in more than 100 categories worldwide, are available at all major retailers, including Walmart, Target, Amazon, GameStop, Walgreens, Barnes & Noble, Hot Topic, ASDA & Smyth's. WWE is a nearly $1 billion global brand at retail annually.[50]

Across all of these venues and markets, WWE, because it employs Cena, is entangled with his physicality and image, and vice versa. He is as much himself as he is WWE. And he is profitable—in an interview with Fox Business reporter Neil Cavuto, "Cena revealed that his character generates about 100 million dollars for WWE yearly."[51] A parallel trademark indicates Cena's image and name as the property of WWE in relation to "Entertainment services, namely, wrestling exhibits and performances by a professional wrestler and entertainer; providing wrestling news and information via a global computer network."[52] Among all of their wrestlers and employees, Cena and his likeness are likely the most profitable for WWE. Cena must attend to the maintenance of himself on a daily basis—a constant state of remaking and reshaping his physique and performance.[53]

However, when Cena retires (or dies), new storylines will certainly introduce new champions and new faces but WWE will likely continue to find ways to capitalize on Cena's likeness and legacy. He will likely get to keep his name, but WWE will maintain all of the images and footage of him wrestling as well as his gestures and wrestling moves and catch phrases and myriad ephemera and, perhaps even more importantly, the rights to make more. The WWE brand, like other brands, will outlive those who work to support it and the products that bear its image.

Under this arrangement, wrestlers' likenesses can live on beyond the actual life of the wrestlers. WWE employs what it calls a "Legends Contract" as a way of capitalizing on the past careers of otherwise retired (and in some cases deceased) wrestlers. In 2005, Donna Goldsmith, then Senior Vice President of Consumer Products for WWE, was quoted in a press release announcing the program, that explained that

> WWE has a tremendous heritage on television, in the licensing industry, at retail and, most importantly, with our fans.... Through apparel, action figures, video games, DVDs, collectables, and other licensed products, WWE reminds our fans of our great heritage and those great members of the professional wrestling industry who remain their heroes.[54]

The press release promised "Legends action figures, apparel, books, and more DVDs."[55] A Trademark symbol followed the names of all current wrestlers and members of the Legends Initiative, none of whom are employees of the company, but contractually engaged to provide their images, gestures, and likenesses.

These residual traces of performers are not idle and fans actively engage with likenesses in a variety of ways, not limited to merchandise and video archives, but also to playable and social media. Tom Philips takes up the case of Chris Benoit, who was a beloved wrestler and fan favorite until he murdered his wife and child and committed suicide. Shortly following that horrendous event, WWE largely erased Benoit and his image and products from its website and company, including video games. Despite this erasure, wrestling fans still struggle with how to remember Benoit. In interviewing a number of wrestling fans, Phillips found that:

> In seeking to separate Benoit's celebrity and personal personas, some fans find the process easy. Respondent 710 notes: "I still remember him as one of the best workers of all time who had mental problems that led to his demise. I can easily separate the man and the wrestler." For others, the process is slightly more arduous. Respondent 14, for instance, notes that in working through his grief "I try to separate the man and the worker," with Respondent 25 adding that "I'm starting to separate the character of Chris Benoit from the man, but it is still difficult to watch him ... you know what he did and that is a hard pill to swallow." Yet regardless of whether the separation of Benoit's personas is easy or difficult for the individual, significantly it is a conscious and selective process.[56]

Benoit's character and in-ring work stand separate from his horrific acts, but the two are tightly melded. This is something that WWE regularly struggles with as its wrestlers are both part of its intellectual property and real people who sometimes say and do things that are not part of the intended image of the company.

WWE is finding new ways to use its aging "legends" in the ring with speculation that WWE may even institute a separate Legends league.[57] Like every other entertainment company, it also makes ample use of its intellectual property, even as the likenesses found on the action figures and in video games do not necessarily represent the current performing bodies of the wrestlers, but rather perform a nostalgic evocation of a now passed vitality and performance of masculinity. Indeed, the three options of gameplay in *WWE Legends of Wrestlemania* allow one to "Relive," "Rewrite," and "Redefine" wrestling history.[58]

Conclusion: Mick Foley's back

While under contract, the wrestlers are essentially laminated with their likeness, which is the intellectual property of the company. Despite the apparent difficulties of profit-making and circulating live, star performers, wrestling companies have found novel ways to peel the likenesses from the wrestlers that inhabit them and put them into circulation. Thinking of wrestlers as performing objects seems to be built into the profit-making mechanisms of professional wrestling and is something that Mick Foley learned early in his career. *Bleacherreport.com* notes that "While he had to risk his life and well-being to become successful, Foley is the personification of dedication."[59] Foley has benefitted from his painful performances in the ring, but what has been most personally profitable for him is his ability to parlay the perceived sideshow of wrestling and dangerous stunts into cultural production in other echelons of culture.

He has published "ten books; four memoirs, four children's books and two novels" and his first two memoirs, *Have a Nice Day: A Tale of Blood and Sweatsocks* and *Foley is Good: And the Real World is Faker Than Wrestling*, were *New York Times* bestsellers.[60] However, it is worth noting that Mick Foley is not alone in his suffering for professional wrestling. He may be an outlier less because of his many injuries and more because he has managed to survive the industry with so many injuries and, quite frankly, without dying. This may be attributed to Foley's masochistic attitude towards physical pain, which he says "always seemed to relieve emotional pain for me."[61]

Foley learned early on that fans will pay to see high-risk maneuvers. In addition, promoters seemed to appreciate it as well. Early in his career, after performing a painful fall that involved jumping from the edge of the wrestling ring to the floor and bleeding profusely, Foley was encouraged not only by the fans who cheered but also those backstage, including other wrestlers, while the promoter suggested Foley perform the maneuver on every stop of the tour.[62] Foley describes his experience:

> We started out in Nashville on a Saturday night. Boot to the head, off I flew with a sickening thud, fetal position, puddle of blood. Louisville on

Tuesday, ditto. By the time I got to Evansville on Wednesday, I was shot. My back was swollen and discolored to the point that there was actually a hump on my lower back. Truly hideous and, I'll be honest, it scared me because I really didn't know what to do about it. It certainly didn't look like a human back."[63]

And the problem was not just his back; rather, fans and promoter alike saw him as something other than human—a performing object:

That night, I ran into a problem that has become commonplace in my career. It seems that then, as now, people see me do so many things that look inhuman, that they start to believe that I'm not human. Well I may have a high tolerance for pain and I may have a body that has been conditioned to accept punishment, but my body is just like everybody else's—just a little less pleasing to look at.[64]

The format of professional wrestling almost guarantees this transformation from body to object. Likenesses are just one way of codifying and monetizing the process and circulating the labor of the wrestler beyond the ring. While perhaps unique to an industry that capitalizes on injurious labor, Foley's painful performances make him tangible and legible as a commodity and increase his value for promoters.

Nicholas Sammond describes "a short circuit of signification that moves from the hard plastic body of the toy, through the hard flesh of the performer, to the massive, processed image above them" on the stadium screen in which "the presence of the wrestler is consumed, fragmented, and multiplied in the flow of its commodity status."[65] The presence of the wrestler, the affective bodily self that is presented to the audience, is at the core of the exchange for professional wrestling. But that presence is carefully crafted and labored over in many different ways from body-building to toughening to beauty regimes to painful stunts and injuries. And given these constellations, wrestling may appear as "a celebration of oppression freely chosen—of the object mobilizing his, her, or its commodity status with a willful disregard for its effect on his, her, or its body or self."[66] Indeed, it may seem that regardless of the path, whether it be in the gym lifting weights or falling off tall structures, that the wrestler is ultimately in charge, crafting a likeness, an asset that can be sold on book covers and t-shirts and action figures and "printed paper labels, printed shipping labels; folders; general purpose plastic bags; paper tableware," etc.[67] It's an idea that perhaps does not seem so strange today—where one can be one's own brand, sold to the highest bidder as the accumulated labor in the body is extracted and repackaged.

But in the physical form of professional wrestling we see the real effects of the entrepreneurial and gig economy: disposable laborers, empowered by a personal sense of self-ownership to do whatever it takes to be productive, renting out everything, from legal names to muscles to movements both benign and dangerous. The living bodies of the wrestlers and their performances, like all performances, are ephemeral and transient, but create capital, accumulated labor, for the promoter. The wrestlers wear it as a likeness, a vendible commodity both separated from but intricately linked to the bodies of the wrestlers. In the performance of pain and shared embodied and affective labor, wrestlers perform the labor relations under contemporary capital wherein, regardless of the product, "living labour is but a means to increase accumulated labour."[68] Every action of the wrestler accumulates labor for the promoter, storing it to be deployed in a future performance or circulated long after the wrestler is gone.

Notes

1 David Bixenspan, "Mick Foley Believes That He Has Suffered Permanent Brain Damage From His Career in Pro Wrestling," TNA Impact, *Cageside Seats*, November 6, 2010, www.cagesideseats.com/2010/11/6/1798140/mick-foley-believes-that-he-has-suffered-permanent-brain-damage-from.
2 Mick Foley, *Have a Nice Day: A Tale of Blood and Sweatsocks* (New York: Regan Books, 1999), back cover.
3 Cory Barker and Drew Zolides, "WWE Network: The Disruption of Over-the-Top Distribution," in *From Networks to Netflix A Guide to Changing Channels*, ed. Derek Johnson (New York: Routledge, 2018), 385–394.
4 Christopher Olson, "Twitter, Facebook, and Professional Wrestling: Indie Wrestler Perspectives on the Importance of Social Media," *Popular Culture Studies Journal* 6, no. 1 (2018): 306–316.
5 Sam Ford, "WWE's Story World and the Potentials of Transmedia Storytelling," in *The Rise of Transtexts: Challenges and Opportunities*, ed. Benjamin W.L. Derhy Kurtz and Mélanie Bourdaa (London: Routledge, 2016), 169–186.
6 Disney, in particular, continues to push for the clear separation of the laboring performer and its intellectual property, the character, and recently warned performers to not reveal that they perform as costumed characters in Disney theme parks:

> Disney spokeswoman Jacquee Polak said the company has always expected the performers not to reveal the actors behind the characters. "We're proud of the role characters play in guest experience," Polak said. "This is in line with our longstanding expectation for cast members to uphold character integrity."
>
> (Associated Press, "Disney's Confidentiality Warning Riles Actor's Union, News, *CBSNews.com*, June 5, 2015, www.cbsnews.com/news/disneys-confidentiality-warning-riles-actors-union/.)

7 Mick Foley, "Bio," accessed August 1, 2013, www.realmickfoley.com/about/.
8 *Three Faces of Foley*, DVD (Stamford, CT: WWF Home Video, 2002).
9 Justin Labar, "15 Greatest Moments in Royal Rumble History," *Bleacher Report*, January 21, 2013, http://bleacherreport.com/articles/1494905–15-greatest-moments-in-royal-rumble-history.
10 NormanB, "Pay No Attention to the Man Behind the Curtain: AKA *The Death of Kayfabe*," *Lethal Wrestling* via *Internet Archive Wayback Machine*, accessed May 20, 2019, https://web.archive.org/web/20071201104107/www.lethalwrestling.com/opinions/news_content.php?fileName=298.

11 Richard E. Caves, *Creative Industries: Contracts Between Art and Commerce* (Cambridge, MA: Harvard University Press, 2000), 261.
12 Dan Rebellato, "Playwriting and Globalisation: Towards a Site-Unspecific Theatre," *Contemporary Theatre Review* 16, no. 1 (2006): 100.
13 David Savran, "Trafficking in Transnational Brands: The New 'Broadway-Style' Musical," *Theatre Survey* 55, no. 3 September 2014): 334.
14 Savran, "Trafficking in Transnational Brands," 335.
15 Caves, *Creative Industries*, 261. As some might imagine, there are some very popular and well-established wrestlers who are in a position to negotiate percentages of sales of merchandise and even ticket sales, but the wrestling promotions are not, by and large, set up on profit-sharing or co-op models.
16 David Shoemaker, *The Squared Circle: Life Death and Professional Wrestling* (New York: Gotham Books, 2013), 207.
17 Bruce Mitchell, "Hardcore Fans and the Wrestling Business," *The Wrestling Observer, 1990 Yearbook*, edited by Dave Meltzer (Campbell, CA: 1990), 64.
18 Sharon Mazer, *Professional Wrestling: Sport and Spectacle* (Jackson, MS: University of Mississippi Press, 1998), 48.
19 While both men and women wrestlers take up these regimens, such physical development and maintenance is not equally imposed—during the 2007 congressional inquiry into steroid use in the WWE, Stephanie McMahon stated that while she has not witnessed anyone asking a wrestler "be bigger or more muscular," she reported having conversations with women wrestlers about losing weight (Committee on Oversight and Government Reform, US House of Representatives, Transcript, "Interview of: Stephanie McMahon Levesque," 78, December 14, 2007, accessed May 15, 2019, http://muchnick.net/stephanietranscript.pdf.)
20 Broderick Chow, "Muscle Memory: Re-Enacting the *Fin-de-siècle* Strongman in Pro Wrestling," in *Performance and Professional Wrestling*, eds. Broderick Chow, Eero Laine, and Claire Warden (New York: Routledge, 2017), 150.
21 Geoff Winningham, *Friday Night in the Coliseum* (Houston: Allison Press, 1971), 45.
22 Drake Oz, "WWE's 15 Stupidest Name Changes Done For Legal Reasons," *Bleacher Report*, November 11, 2011, http://bleacherreport.com/articles/933313-wwes-15-stupidest-name-changes-done-for-legal-reasons.
23 Eric Lee, "Titan Sports, Inc. v. Hellwig: Wrestling with the Distinction between Character and Performer," 3 Tul. J. Tech. & Intell. Prop. 155 (2001). Charles B. Sears Law Library. 155–163, 156.
24 Lee, "Titan Sports," 162.
25 *Oxford English Dictionary*, oed.com, s.v. "Likeness."
26 Brian Massumi, *Semblance and Event: Activist Philosophy and the Occurent Arts* (Cambridge, MA: MIT Press, 2011), 44–45.
27 Jobs is taken up here as a particular kind of performing body. Jobs performed the role of the benevolent Silicon Valley guru-geek-chic CEO in his product launches and shareholder meetings. Especially as his health declined, Jobs' body stood in as a sort of marker of the health of Apple and Apple stock. For example: "Mr. Jobs didn't give a date for his return, and the 55-year-old CEO has looked increasingly frail with each public appearance. Few CEOs have been as closely linked to their company's success as Mr. Jobs has." (Roger Cheng and George Stahl, "Apple Shares Fall as Jobs Takes Medical Leave," Gadgets, *Wall Street Journal*, January 18, 2011, www.wsj.com/articles/SB10001424052748703954004576089633611009272.)
28 Rosa Golijan, "Apple Tries to Ban Realistic Steve Jobs Action Figure," Technology, *NBCNews.com*, January 5, 2012, www.nbcnews.com/technology/technolog/apple-tries-ban-realistic-steve-jobs-action-figure-118110). Another prominent example of someone copying an image of a likeness can be found in the Associated

Press' lawsuit against the artist Shepard Fairey for copyright infringement over his iconic red, white, and blue Obama "Hope" posters. The AP claimed the posters were nothing more than a "computerized paint by the numbers" replication of a photo to which the AP owned the copyright. The case was settled out of court in the AP's favor and seemingly amicably, with Fairey agreeing to work with the AP in the future and to share the rights to the iconic red and blue image. (David Kravets, "Associated Press Settles Copyright Lawsuit Against Obama 'Hope' Artist," *Wired Magazine*, January 12, 2012, www.wired.com/threatlevel/2011/01/hope-image-flap/). In this case, the AP was appealing to the law for redress over a painting of a copyrighted photo that had captured the likeness of Barack Obama. The AP was thus laying claim to the ownership of the photographic copy of the likeness. This is an important complementary example because what was at stake was a copy of a copy of a likeness, rather than the likeness itself.

29 Jamie Condliffe, "The Steve Jobs Action Figure is Cancelled," *Gizmodo*, January 17, 2012, http://gizmodo.com/5876722/the-steve-jobs-action-figure-is-dead.
30 David E Wellowitz and Tyler T. Ochea, *Celebrity Rights: Rights of Publicity and Related Rights in the United States and Abroad* (Durham, NC: Carolina Academic Press, 2010), 498.
31 Stacey L. Dogan, "An Exclusive Right to Evoke," *Boston College Law Review* 44, no. 2 (2003): 291.
32 Matt Novak, "Robot Vanna, Trashy Presidents and Steak as Health Food: Samsung Sells Tomorrow," *Smithsonian.com* February 20, 2013, www.smithsonianmag.com/history/robot-vanna-trashy-presidents-and-steak-as-health-food-samsung-sells-tomorrow-22348926/.
33 Lesley Goldberg, "Alex Trebek, Pat Sajak, Vanna White Renew Contracts Through 2022," *The Hollywood Reporter*, October 31, 2018, www.hollywoodreporter.com/live-feed/alex-trebek-pat-sajak-vanna-white-renew-contracts-2022-1156793.
34 Wellowitz and Ochea, *Celebrity Rights*, 498.
35 Dogan, "An Exclusive Right," 295.
36 Dogan, "An Exclusive Right," 292. Emphasis and brackets in original.
37 Wellowitz and Ochea, *Celebrity Rights*, 345.
38 Wellowitz and Ochea, *Celebrity Rights*, 345.
39 James J.S. Holmes and Kanika D. Corley, "Defining Liability for Likeness of Athlete Avatars in Video Games," *Los Angeles Lawyer* (May 2011): 17, www.lacba.org/docs/default-source/lal-back-issues/2011-issues/may-2011.pdf.
40 Holmes and Corley, "Defining Liability," 18.
41 Holmes and Corley, "Defining Liability," 19.
42 WWE, "Copyright," Community, wwe.com, accessed May 10, 2019, https://community.wwe.com/copyright.
43 WWE, "Live Events," *WWE Corporate*, accessed May 13, 2019, https://corporate.wwe.com/what-we-do/live-events.
44 Chris Smith, "Breaking Down How WWE Contracts Work," Sports Money, Forbes, March 28, 2015, www.forbes.com/sites/chrissmith/2015/03/28/breaking-down-how-wwe-contracts-work/#18e969426713.
45 Smith, "Breaking Down."
46 Smith, "Breaking Down."
47 "John Cena," United States Patent and Trademark Office, registration number 3169452, accessed May 11, 2019, uspto.gov.
48 "John Cena," United States Patent and Trademark Office, registration number 3088504, accessed May 11, 2019, uspto.gov.
49 "John Cena," United States Patent and Trademark Office, registration number 3074517, accessed May 11, 2019, uspto.gov.

50 WWE, "Licensing," What We Do, *WWE Corporate*, accessed May 12, 2019, https://corporate.wwe.com/what-we-do/consumer-products/licensing.
51 Nick Paglino, "John Cena's Brand Generates $100 Million Per Year For WWE, Brie Bella Reacts to Daniel Bryan Being Abducted by Wyatts," Wrestling News, *Wrestle Zone*, November 26, 2013, www.mandatory.com/wrestlezone/news/434619-john-cena-generates-100-million-per-year-for-wwe. In the same interview Cena revealed that he has some creative and financial control over his likeness:

> Essentially, the message of the clothing is to empower you through a positive message. I think that's why we were able to leverage our brand (WWE), my brand especially with Kmart, because it wasn't just a typical sponsor deal. A lot of athletes get a sponsorship—"here's your upfront money, we're going to use your likeness." I wanted to hold on to my asset, do it correctly, and create an inspirational line. So, it's not a "wrestling-driven" line. The line is called "Never Give Up," and truly my character on WWE plays one of aspiration, inspiration, and motivation. I try to defy all odds and do what I can to do the right thing…. Kmart picked up on this concept. And, from a branding standpoint, I just didn't outright leverage myself; I wanted a piece and equity in the brand. So, there was upfront money, plus equity in the brand.

(Paglino, "John Cena's Brand"). Note how Cena refers to his likeness as "an asset" to be held.

52 John Cena," United States Patent and Trademark Office, registration number 2957043, accessed May 11, 2019, uspto.gov.
53 The level of discipline and daily maintenance should not be understated. While likely an extreme example, former wrestler Dwayne "The Rock" Johnson's daily regimen begins at four in the morning and continues with multiple workouts, between which he consumes over 5,000 calories (or roughly ten pounds of food). This, of course, makes for a good story for the tabloids and such narratives are also part of his own brand. (Daily Mail Reporter, "Want to Look Like The Rock? Try Eating Like Him: Former WWE Champion Eats 10 POUNDS of Food a Day Over Seven Meals and Gets Up at 4am For His First Meal," News, *DailyMail.com*, May 9, 2015, www.dailymail.co.uk/news/article-3075270/Want-look-like-Rock-Try-eating-like-Former-WWE-champion-s-strict-5–165-calorie-daily-diet-contains-10-pounds-food-including-cod-eggs-steak-chicken.html.)
54 "WWE Legends Program Gives Former Professional Wrestlers Heroes New Life and WWE New Product," 2005 News, *WWE.com*, June 20, 2005, accessed via The Internet Archive, Wayback Machine, May 9, 2019, https://web.archive.org/web/20140313005648/http://corporate.wwe.com/news/2005/2005_06_20_2.jsp.
55 "WWE Legends Program"
56 Tom Phillips, "Wrestling With Grief: Fan Negotiation of Professional/Private Personas in Responses to the Chris Benoit Double Murder–Suicide," *Celebrity Studies* 6, no. 1 (2015): 78.
57 Christian Patterson, "Vince McMahon's Untapped Goldmine," *Underground Mall*, January 3, 2019, https://undergroundmall.xyz/2019/01/03/post-next-vince-mcmahons-untapped-goldmine/?fbclid=IwAR3bF4C_EanfxRdTSkiHEmDahw0MR00H6_03eunzMOY1E51IEK5tWgqUoZo.
58 *Legends of Professional Wrestling*, Video Game (Agoura, CA: THQ, 2009).
59 Bryan Flory, "Pro Wrestling: The Top 10 Richest Wrestlers," WWE, *Bleacher Report*, April 6, 2011, http://bleacherreport.com/articles/656507-pro-wrestling-the-top-10-richest-wrestlers.
60 Foley, "Bio."
61 Foley, *Have a Nice Day*, 52.

62 Foley, *Have a Nice Day*, 164.
63 Foley, *Have a Nice Day*, 165.
64 Foley, *Have a Nice Day*, 165.
65 Nicholas Sammond, "Introduction: A Brief and Unnecessary Defense of Professional Wrestling," in *Steel Chair to the Head: The Pleasure and Pain of Professional Wrestling*, ed. Nicholas Sammond (Durham, NC: Duke University Press, 2005), 7.
66 Sammond, "Introduction," 7.
67 "John Cena," registration number 3169452.
68 Karl Marx, "Chapter II. Proletarians and Communists," *The Communist Manifesto*, www.marxists.org/archive/marx/works/1848/communist-manifesto/ch02.htm.

Chapter 5

A stock theatre company
WWE and theatrical value

WWE may not be the only game in town when it comes to professional wrestling, but it is certainly the biggest and the most influential—there is no denying WWE's impact, reach, and appeal. Since the early 1980s, WWE has regularly found ways to integrate itself into larger social trends, news cycles, and controversies, and has with surprising consistency bought out or beat its competition. It has been publicly traded on the US stock market since 1999 and has a market capitalization of over one billion dollars—its stock price has traded in a range from $7.00 to nearly $100.00.[1] WWE is, in many ways, successful because of its easy creation and promotion of content and its ability to reach into many forms of media and entertainment. The company produces live events on a daily basis with a surprisingly traditional theatrical business model.

In the 1980s, the connection between WWE and theatre was vehemently, even violently, denied as when "Dr. D" David Schultz assaulted *20/20* reporter John Stossel during a taped interview after Stossel implied that wrestling was fake. Schultz recently confirmed that the direction to attack Stossel came from WWE owner Vince McMahon: "I did what I was told to do. Vince McMahon told me to blast him and tear his ass up and to stay in character and be Dr. D."[2] So, even as wrestling's theatricality was denied, the strength of the denial appears to have depended on a commitment to staying in character. Such issues seemed to fall by the wayside, however, after much of the deregulation of the late 1980s and 1990s and as the characters got more and more theatrical, especially in the early 1990s, and then less so by the end of the decade.

By the time WWE issued its first annual shareholder report in 2000, there was no question as to whether or not WWE was making theatre. Or at least theatre became an easy way to explain its business model to investors:

> Live events are the cornerstone of our business and provide the content for our television and pay-per-view programming. Each event is a highly theatrical production, which involves a significant degree of audience participation and employs various special effects, including lighting, pyrotechnics, powerful entrance music, and a variety of props.[3]

To me, this is still one of the clearest and most useful descriptions of just what exactly professional wrestling is and does. Even as elements of the live event are repackaged and resold through a variety of media, it is the live event with its audience interaction and special effects that anchors the whole endeavor. Today, WWE considers itself an "integrated media organization and recognized leader in global entertainment," but the live event remains a significant part of the WWE business model.[4] The shift in description may point towards WWE's ambitions to expand and overcome some of the limitations that live entertainment imposes on such goals. It may also just be a way of sounding more like a large and profitable corporation—in typical wrestling bravado, Stephanie McMahon indicated that WWE has their eyes set on surpassing Disney as an entertainment company.[5] While revenue from other ventures like media and merchandising described in the previous chapter may generate more money for WWE than ticket sales, those other wings of the business would not exist without the live event.

WWE is, arguably, the only publicly traded company that is primarily oriented towards a live, theatrical event. Looking at other publicly traded corporations that produce live entertainment, WWE's closest comparison might be Live Nation Entertainment, which generates revenue through concerts, ticketing, and sponsorship deals.[6] While Live Nation Entertainment is the self-described "global leader in live," it neither creates its own content nor is that content theatrical or narrative.[7] The model for selling and marketing merchandise and touring concert events is likely similar to WWE, but, again, Live Nation is not producing theatre.

I don't mean to take a hardline view of professional wrestling here as strictly theatre and somehow isolated from the rest of the economy and performing arts and entertainment. The business areas are all closely linked, of course. Live events can be broadcast across WWE's over-the-top streaming network, both of which drive interest in the product and push merchandise sales, online, in the stadium, and at retail locations. Even if the mechanisms for money making have expanded greatly and are now exploiting new legal contracts, the basic methods have not changed significantly since Sharon Mazer wrote about the sales-driven atmosphere of the wrestling event in her 1990 article in *TDR*, "The Doggie Dog World of Professional Wrestling."[8] Mazer describes the perhaps surprising numbers of spectators at live wrestling events, the impressive revenues, and merchandising schemes where "every move in the arena encourages the spectators to purchase products."[9] The basic business practices of professional wrestling (and WWE in particular) have largely remained the same, even if they have become more sophisticated and expanded significantly.

The chapters to this point have examined the productive labor of professional wrestling, attempted to disentangle the wrestling form from its troubling content, examined the sweaty and bloody labor of wrestling, and also unpacked the ways that wrestlers are sold and made saleable beyond the arena.

This chapter takes a slightly different tack, in that it looks closely at professional wrestling content—notably the most significant character in WWE and a recent storyline that betrays the confluence of finance and theatre at the heart of WWE. There are many, many studies that examine the various storylines of professional wrestling, in part because there are innumerable storylines to study.[10] Taking a more structural approach to the form itself and its overlapping interests with and practices of theatre, this book has to this point considered the form and its function as a productive performance. Considering two ideas central to theatre, character and plot, this chapter examines how they might function in WWE as a publicly traded theatre company.

WWE, in particular, presents a case study for the ways that capital overcomes the apparent limitations of live performance, borders, languages, and the costs of labor, turning the small, local institution of theatre and performance into a globalizing enterprise. It is noteworthy that the company also regularly stages these relations through highly theatrical segments. In the first example, Vince McMahon's in-ring character, Mr. McMahon, stages the relations of labor and its abuses in the ring, and does so unabashedly. Mr. McMahon is often reprehensible as a character, making evident the power dynamics between employee and employer. The idea is not uncommon in professional wrestling and the second example, Daniel Bryan's championship run, examines not only the ways that WWE stages workers fighting their bosses, but the ways that various audiences come to influence and impact such storylines. In considering WWE as a publicly traded theatre company, we see not only the ways that live theatre might relate to the stock market and investors, but also what a live theatre company, and especially one such as WWE, might reveal about US business itself. Before discussing these two examples, however, it is important to understand how WWE leverages the live event into media and how it has utilized its theatricality to avoid scrutiny.

WWE's mediated theatre

In February 2014, WWE launched a streaming, over-the-top, digital network where, for a monthly fee, viewers can access live events as well as thousands of hours of archival footage. Over the past decades, WWE has been buying the tape libraries of every wrestling promotion that is willing to sell and the footage is now digitized and made available on the streaming network. The WWE Network is thus both a live event streaming service and an enduring visual archive of a performance form that spans most of the previous century. By the standards of most video performance archives, the WWE Network is flatly impressive and important for theatre and performance scholars, if for no other reason than the sheer number of hours of live recorded performance that is made readily available.

Live broadcasts are not new for professional wrestling, even as many theatre companies such as the Metropolitan Opera and the National Theatre begin to follow in WWE's live pay-per-view footsteps. Throughout wrestling's history, television and pay-per-view have been deployed in a number of ways from advertising for the live event itself to a way of extending the audience and increasing revenues. The launch of the WWE Network allowed WWE to bring the telecast of its major events, still often referred to as "pay-per-views," in house. Rather than relying on and splitting revenues with cable and satellite companies selling one off events (for instance, WrestleMania or the Royal Rumble), WWE now has subscribers who pay a monthly fee and then have access to all of the special events of the year. These events are built up and promoted on cable network broadcasts and social media.

I am less interested in trying to distinguish where the live event begins and ends, or in wading into the ontological implications of live streaming theatrical events. Rather, what is useful, I think, is to see how WWE provides a model for the ways that live theatrical events are made profitable and circulated widely beyond the halls of performance. Here, I follow Sarah Bay-Cheng's ideas for a post-media criticality that is in part in response to Christopher Grobe's critique of the impulse to catalogue and describe every instance of media as it interacts with live performance.[11] Bay-Cheng points to "a kind of analysis that does not make great efforts to distinguish, document, and describe cultural objects in light of medial specificity."[12] Bay-Cheng thus considers a "postmedia approach that assumes all media are always already activated in every cultural object and begins a method of analysis from there."[13] Of course wrestling is mediated and of course the live event is resold across various forms of media and different technologies.

Even as WWE has become more adept at selling the live event more widely, it has significantly bolstered its roster of employees as a way of generating even more live content. Such moves allow WWE to perform in multiple cities night after night, both in the US and around the world. Describing its live entertainment activities in 2019, the WWE Corporate website states:

> Our multiple sports entertainment brands allow us to perform over 560 live events a year within the United States and abroad. WWE held 145 total events in the first quarter of 2019, with 141 held in North America and four held Internationally.[14]

Considered as a touring theatre company, WWE is quite busy. Averaging roughly a dozen events a week, there are only about two days a week wherein WWE stages just one event. Again, these are rough averages, but for a company that is fairly centrally organized it represents a significant logistical effort. Surely, if WWE could still maintain and expand the other parts of its business and hold wrestling shows at a single location, it would. Why continue to produce live events with all of their attendant complications and costs if live events were not absolutely necessary for the business model?

The idea of WWE as a stock theatre company plays on two registers. In one sense, it is a sort of stock theatre, a traveling troupe of players, who put on productions from its repertory of match styles, characters, and outcomes. Some may quibble with such a designation as a folksy way to describe a billion dollar corporation, but the mechanisms of traveling from city to city to perform familiar material with a set group of performers are really not much different than any other traveling theatre company. Thus, the other sense of the phrase "stock theatre company" might be more obvious, even as it is less common for theatre. Unlike most theatre companies, WWE has a publicly traded stock. Broadway producers may raise funds through private investment, selling shares for productions, but such arrangements are often restricted to those who are very wealthy and connected. Anyone, hypothetically, can purchase a share of WWE stock and WWE is also accountable to such shareholders, obligated to pursue profit and to protect shareholder value. Larger companies that produce live entertainment, such as Disney and DreamWorks, are publicly traded, but their theatrical wings are only a fraction of their total business. Thus as a stock theatre company, WWE offers theatre scholars a number of unique ways to consider the connections and networks of theatrical entertainment and finance.

WWE also trades on its theatricality in other ways, using the live event as a way of dismissing criticism, emphasizing its tackiness to dodge many more serious complaints. Dan O'Sullivan in *Jacobin* asserts that "The story of professional wrestling is the story of American capitalism."[15] O'Sullivan suggests that WWE is hiding in plain sight, masked by the crudely theatrical content it delivers:

> Pro wrestling's greater visibility as cheesy adolescent fantasy tends to mitigate the public backlash the industry *should* receive each time another wrestler dies young. This very quality of mainstream disrespect has largely served the interests of a blood-soaked business.[16]

While other studies have tracked the same path of the pro wrestling industry throughout the twentieth century as a sort of fixed racket and monopoly, O'Sullivan's essay stands out among other critiques for its attention to the intertwined threads of wrestling content and its institutionality.[17] According to O'Sullivan, as a lowbrow spectacle run by unsavory conmen, the wrestling industry ducks a number of criticisms that might be levied against most any other industry. Pro wrestling, as the argument goes, is so over the top as to be inscrutable or at least it is criticized for the wrong things (sensational storylines and offensive content) rather than what actually matters (wrestling's notoriously bad labor practices, including a fairly high rate of injury and early death among workers). Pro wrestling is the story of US capitalism in large part because it is a capitalist industry. However, what if we follow this line of thinking with a slight twist? What if the "mainstream disrespect" for professional wrestling is actually perturbation for flouting liberal fantasies of labor and market economies? That is, what if pro wrestling is breaking kayfabe on capitalism? For the establishment to criticize pro wrestling for its actual problems would be to criticize capitalism itself.

Indeed, the case of WWE prompts us to ask what pro wrestling reveals about the relation between live performance and global capital. While it is very likely true that "the notion that pro wrestling is a fixed, low-rent travesty, undeserving of serious mainstream scrutiny—is the single greatest angle ever sold by the wrestling industry," the focus of the critique should rather be on those institutions that allow pro wrestling to thrive among other corporations that only differ in content or the products produced.[18] In other words, the "blood-soaked business" of wrestling is not under-scrutinized because of its abuses, but rather for the ways that it lays bare and publicly performs the extractive and exploitative business of global, financial capital.[19]

Fighting the man

Vince McMahon, founder and CEO of WWE, may look like an exploitative, capitalist boss and he may act like an exploitative, capitalist boss, but don't be fooled—he really *is* an exploitative, capitalist boss! This is a bit of play on Groucho Marx's joke frequently taken up by Slavoj Žižek "where a lie assumes the form of factual truth."[20] ("He may look like an idiot and talk like an idiot, but don't let that fool you—he really *is* an idiot!") That is, the apparently false theatrical veneer contains the entirety of the performance. In acting like an exploitative, capitalist boss, Vince McMahon should not fool us into thinking he is not actually the same. Indeed, a tautology such as this, Žižek suggests, "renders the gap that separates knowledge from belief."[21] We know CEOs must be exploitive, capitalist bosses, but we may not always believe it or choose not to believe it—another bit of kayfabe as it plays out outside the wrestling ring.

Inside the ring, McMahon plays the part. In 1999, just months before WWE issued its initial public offering of stock, Vince McMahon appeared in a televised wrestling match that produced a tableau that is iconic among wrestling fans for the period. In a moment in the match, Mr. McMahon has wrestler "Stone Cold" Steve Austin trapped in the corner of the ring. Austin is seated looking up at McMahon who is grasping the middle ropes and screaming at Austin, spittle and froth flying from his mouth as he turns a shade of reddish-purple. The moment occurred during a performance of *Monday Night Raw*, where wrestler "Stone Cold" Steve Austin—middle finger-wagging, Budweiser-drinking, "blue-collar warrior for the common man"—was subjected to a gauntlet match against the members of "The Corporation," headed by Mr. McMahon.[22] Gauntlet matches, where one wrestler wrestles a series of other wrestlers without break and other seemingly grueling stipulations, are often used as part of storylines as a way for the bad guy (here,

Mr. McMahon) to punish the hero (here, "Stone Cold" Steve Austin). The dramaturgy of the gauntlet match allows for the hero to display superhuman-like strength and determination whether they are victorious in the end or not.

Within the ongoing narrative at the time, The Corporation was a team of wrestlers assembled to do the dirty work of Mr. McMahon and consisted of former mixed martial artist Ken Shamrock, the apparently demonic Kane, dominatrix-styled Chyna, and Big Boss Man, a fascistic police officer known for handcuffing his opponents to the ropes of the ring and beating them with his baton. Austin fought valiantly and with passion (of course), but in the end was overtaken by the members of The Corporation. After being pinned, Austin was held in the corner of the ring by the members of The Corporation to be berated and mocked by Mr. McMahon, who barked insults and foamed at the mouth and also took the time to pour what would have been Austin's celebratory beer onto him. It is a moment in wrestling that has stuck with many fans.[23] To see a boss abusively dressing down an employee after setting him up for a task that he was not likely to successfully complete is to see the regime of labor staged in a wrestling ring.

In many ways, this was just another moment in the countless hours of professional wrestling that are and have been recorded and broadcast, but it was also something different. In this moment of abject dominance and humiliation, and perhaps especially because of the overt theatricality afforded by the form of professional wrestling, the actual relations of labor crystalize in front of us. We see a CEO looming over, dominating, threatening, an employee too tired to continue their labor. The work of paid performance congeals in these actions, but rather than obscure the labor relations, it clearly stages them as a wealthy boss abusing a worker. As a stage picture it is expressionistic and has the subtlety of agit-prop. The boss abusing the worker, who tries to maintain his life and humanity in the face of near animalistic rage. Perhaps this reads too much into just another bit of pop culture, but perhaps hyperbolic readings are necessary for such hyperbolic material. To not take work like this on its face but to dismiss it is to fall into the trap described by O'Sullivan in *Jacobin*, where the content obscures the underlying labor structures. Given the nature of professional wrestling, its roots in carnival culture and tenuous grasp on truth, the inclusion of WWE among other publicly traded corporations reveals important slippages and elisions in the realms of business and finance.

Professional wrestling, and especially WWE, has often staged battles between classes, with the upper classes and business owners almost always portraying the heels or villains. In many narratives, characters team up to fight the evil CEO or boss. Indeed, many of the heels have been outsized versions of authority figures like Big Boss Man, The Mountie, Irwin R. Schyster (IRS) and the Million Dollar Man, Ted DiBiasi and, of course, Mr. McMahon. The content of pro wrestling stages these conflicts clearly with fans rooting for the underdog to beat the bullying bad guy who almost always has more institutional power or prestige. Theatrically, this is done by calling attention to its own capitalist business model—by staging a metatheatrical fight between owners and workers.

It is worth restating at this point that Mr. McMahon, the maniacal, power-hungry CEO character who fought and abused his employees in theatrical wrestling matches, was played by Vince McMahon, the CEO of the company producing these theatrical wrestling matches—the very same CEO who just months after the iconic match with Austin would try to convince investors on Wall Street to purchase shares in his company.[24] The image of McMahon constraining Austin in the corner of the ring is certainly emblematic, but by no means an isolated instance. Mr. McMahon and Austin took part in an ongoing feud that involved many other wrestlers over the course of months and years. Indeed, Austin is not the only wrestler to be theatrically abused by Mr. McMahon, and Austin is also not the only wrestler to, at times, beat (here, both literally and figuratively) Mr. McMahon.

Vince McMahon is thus fully integrated into and across professional wrestling content, its form, and its institutionality as a live, globalizing performance form. The *New York Times* notes that "It's hard to ignore an executive that uses profanity publicly."[25] Speaking to the *Times* readership, the article continues: "The temptation is to ignore McMahon, to leave him to his Wrestlemanias, bulky pecs, pompadour and quasi-pornographic shows. But you can't. He's a powerful marketer."[26] McMahon is too over the top—like contemporary professional wrestling itself, he's asking to be criticized, to be paid attention to. A self-made man of sorts, McMahon turned a regional wrestling company into a globally circulated brand. Vince McMahon's *Forbes* bio reads:

> A third generation wrestling promoter, McMahon grew up in a trailer park in North Carolina and joined his father's small wrestling company in 1972. Purchased the business 10 years later, then transformed the World Wrestling Federation from a regional operation into an international phenomenon. WWE went public in 1999 and today its programs are broadcast in nearly 150 countries and more than 30 languages.[27]

It is such a real-life reputation that set up the possibility of McMahon as a hated monster in the ring. He's the cocky face of the American Dream—from a trailer park to the global stage (with a little help from Dad). A billionaire who has battled Donald Trump in the ring and won a ratings war against Ted Turner, Vince McMahon might be the real face of US underdog gumption and bootstrappy determination, even (or maybe especially) as he physically attacks and degrades employees.

For many years, McMahon appeared at shows both suited and dressed to wrestle (sometimes in athletic pants and a tank top, sometimes shirtless). To take a corporate phrase, McMahon was leading by example. His willingness to get in the ring, to get thrown around, to bleed, led *Business Insider* to report that "Vince McMahon's dedication to his company is so great that he has at times put his body at risk inside the ring."[28] It certainly does mark a commitment to the business that few other CEOs have—imagine Bill Gates working on assembly lines or members of the Walton family working as late night greeters at Walmart. Or imagine Jeff Bezos punching in and out at an Amazon warehouse, working on holidays, urinating in trashcans because he is not allowed bathroom breaks, and being berated into working while injured.[29] Such examples may sound farfetched, but they follow the logic of McMahon's performances that assert his apparent dedication to the company and are intended to limit complaints from employees. If I can do it, McMahon seems to gloat, you should be able to as well.

At the same time, the performance of the evil Mr. McMahon character functions as a sort of theatrical deflection of possible criticism. McMahon can fall back on the idea that he is only playing a character, but he also avoids scandal and criticism because few would be surprised to find out he might have actually done something wrong. This, of course, inverts the usual CEO public image of a beneficent leader. If one is to believe his critics, there are more similarities than differences between Vince McMahon, the CEO of WWE, and Mr. McMahon, the maniacal and sadistic version of himself that he has played since the 1990s. By many accounts, Vince McMahon has built a performance and media empire through ruthless consolidation and monopolization on the backs of a contingent labor force while pandering to the lowest common denominator.[30] His larger-than-life wrestling gimmick, Mr. McMahon, has done nearly the same, even as he has also lost his share of matches and endured publicly embarrassing situations in the ring.

The cover of McMahon's DVD biography, which was produced by WWE, features a split image of his face. On one side he wears a smug smile of accomplishment, and on the other a malicious grimace. The effect is, of course, to show his two sides, successful businessman and in-ring terror. (But which one is which?) The performance of Mr. McMahon is in some ways supposed to discredit the possibility that this is actually how business might work—that hourly workers are not regularly abused and debased. Why would they show it if it was true? McMahon's entire performance seems to beg someone to call it out because, in the end, it's all just a show, right?

And his involvement in the ring is often interpreted by many media outlets not as a bit of character work or acting, but as the real thing. During Linda McMahon's failed US Senate campaign in Connecticut, her opponents and fellow detractors had only to string together clips from WWE live shows and broadcasts to create their attack ad. One video profiled by Fox News and created by the group Mothers Opposing McMahon, features Vince McMahon berating wrestler and WWE employee Trish Stratus to crawl around on her hands and knees and "bark like a dog" before McMahon

112 A stock theatre company

demands that she strip her clothes off.[31] That was just the first segment of many in the ad. As played by Vince McMahon, there is little to be redeemed about Mr. McMahon. Stratus did eventually get revenge as part of the narrative, but the segment stands on its own, perhaps for obvious reasons.[32] Of course, this negative political ad was made even more effective by the fact that the evil characters in WWE are played by the actual executives of the corporation, but it is a bit strange as well. Imagine, for instance, if during Arnold Schwarzenegger's California gubernatorial campaigns, his opponents compiled various offensive and violent clips from his films. And maybe they should have—I don't know—but for some reason it would have certainly been easier to defend against than the attacks on McMahon. We all know that films are made up, but why is wrestling different? Indeed, there is something about wrestling that seemingly eliminates the distance between theatre and not-theatre, making the form effective at staging that violence that might otherwise go unstaged (labor relations under capital), while both inviting and denying critique.

To see McMahon berating wrestlers, or to see McMahon strike his employees until they bleed in a cage match, or McMahon casually dropping the n-word during a pay-per-view event, or to witness any number of other indignities and offenses performed by McMahon, is to see the corporate world performed, staged as an obscene spectacle. Perhaps this is most evident in the storylines wherein McMahon regularly forced wrestlers to join his "Kiss My Ass Club," which involved his employees literally kissing his bare ass in the middle of the ring and in front of tens of thousands live spectators and millions of television viewers. While WWE may not use such footage in its current marketing materials or shareholder reports, the segments and other McMahon matches contributed significantly to WWE's popularity and profitability.

One might read McMahon's regular involvement in storylines alongside the sort of public performances regularly required of CEOs and other members of corporate boards. However, McMahon's overt theatricality, of playing the part of evil CEO who exploits and degrades his workers, is actually more honest than that of other CEOs who parade the ideology of teamwork and life changing products. To see McMahon require his employees to kiss his ass, literally place their lips on his exposed buttocks, is to see the labor relations of capital, well, laid bare. McMahon's performance is troubling and often hard to watch, but it is shockingly sincere in the context of a publicly traded company. This is the other side of McMahon's willingness to get in the ring and to do the work of his employees like almost no other CEO would do. To even approach a performance such as McMahon's Kiss My Ass Club, electronics company CEOs might hold their press conferences at the funerals of manufacturing employees who committed suicide on the assembly line or oil company executives place the next shareholder call from a ruined wilderness preserve, bank owners could star in a reality show that takes place in foreclosed houses, the boards of pharmaceutical companies could be cast as characters that sell opioids to kids and addicts in a gritty television drama.

This is not a celebration of McMahon's performance, but rather an argument that the overt theatricality of the wrestling event is perhaps more truthful than the apparent performance of other corporate meetings and good will initiatives. The character of Mr. McMahon and his real-life counterpart in this way open the world of capital for critique and function to expose the relations of wage labor. So, one more time with a twist: Mr. McMahon may look like an exploitative, capitalist boss and he may act like an exploitative, capitalist boss, but don't be fooled—like every other CEO, Vince McMahon really *is* an exploitative, capitalist boss.

McMahon's performance, despite its embarrassing earnestness, should point up and call to question the soft-spoken, TED Talk guru image of the CEO as just as much of a performance, but significantly less honest. The overtly and exaggeratedly offensive performance of pro wrestling reveals the hidden relations behind the corporate façade. Rather than viewing WWE as the peripheral exception to Wall Street corporations, it should instead be recognized as absolutely central to such operations as its theatricality is integrated into profit-making. Even as the performance of abuse and wage labor produces more capital—indeed, audiences were thrilled to watch Austin beat up McMahon—the value of the narrative becomes evident through the stock market. Whereas other entertainment companies might compare different products—a musical or film or album—in light of a larger portfolio of cultural products, WWE allows us to examine the correlation between plot and profit. If Vince McMahon stages and performs the real relations of wage labor, WWE also makes clear the ways that market forces come to bear on the wrestling product. WWE is enmeshed in the stock market and that relationship becomes evident in the following example.

Plotting profits

Daniel Bryan wasn't supposed to be the champion. In what has become the most studied character arc and wrestling storyline in recent memory, from the summer of 2013 to the late spring of 2014, the bearded, nice-guy underdog battled in and out of the ring for the chance to be the WWE World Heavyweight Champion.[33] Multiple times a week, in stadiums across the US and around the world, Bryan would make his way to the ring as a hard-rock version of Wagner's "Ride of the Valkyries" blared and thousands of spectators pointed their index fingers in the air and chanted "Yes! Yes! Yes!" And in each performance, Bryan would wrestle valiantly, overcome the odds and conquer the challenges laid before him with a fast-paced and acrobatic style. More often than not, however, Bryan's hard work was left unrecognized and debased by "The Authority," the wife and husband team of Stephanie McMahon (Vince McMahon's daughter) and her husband, Triple H, real-life

WWE executives who also play more sinister versions of themselves in WWE's sprawling wrestling narratives.

As the storyline went, Bryan was regularly denied opportunities to be champion by The Authority because they considered him only a "B+ player," unsuitable to be the "face of the company." The Authority regularly intervened in matches and set unusual stipulations that prevented Bryan from winning (or retaining) the championship belt. The Authority repeatedly stated that they were concerned that Bryan's unkempt looks would not sell tickets globally and that he didn't project a properly corporate image for the company.

The storyline clipped along for most of the summer and for many it seemed as if things were turning in Bryan's favor. However, at the end of the summer of 2013, according to sportswriter Jonathan Snowden, who interviewed many at WWE:

> Bryan ran into an even fiercer opponent—the stock market. The preliminary numbers for SummerSlam were in—and they weren't pretty. "They didn't buy the attraction," Vince McMahon told WWE investors during a conference call. "And these PPVs are attraction based … SummerSlam was not the right attraction. That was a swing and a miss." … Economics, combined with the early return of [leading wrestler John] Cena from a tricep tear, spelled the end of Bryan's run as the top good guy.[34]

In a confluence of reality and fiction that is both exceptional and commonplace in professional wrestling, investors seemed to take the side of The Authority against Daniel Bryan and his many fans. The storyline of the lovable but scruffy wrestler who is derided by management came full circle as Wall Street leaned hard on the underdog. However, many fans were extremely unhappy with what they saw as the decision to bury Bryan. The pro wrestling plot itself became a frontline between fans and executives, backed by financial considerations.

This situation is described as an example of a "worked shoot" by Wilson Koh, who also suggests that low pay-per-view buy rates

> could easily be read by followers of professional wrestling as the justification for the McMahon clan publicly humiliating Bryan on live WWE TV for months on end, and additionally keeping him out of the championship main event on a monthly basis.[35]

Koh's reading here is quite interesting as it pushes the ideas of stock performance and theatrical action even further than the idea that wrestling narratives are adjusted or rewritten in response to market dips and swings. Koh provocatively suggests that WWE executives were actually using the scripted weekly segments involving Bryan to punish him in front of his fans for his influence on the company's lagging performance. According to such a reading, McMahon and Triple H were not just playing abusive executives, they actually were abusive executives.

Typically, a worked shoot is where some aspect of the business is revealed intentionally or not (referred to as a *shoot* in wrestling argot) and then *worked* into the storylines—a backstage rumor is confirmed during a show or an actual wedding is held in the ring or the reasons are revealed for someone losing the belt (often because they are leaving the company), etc. However, the case of Daniel Bryan opens other possibilities as the theatrical aspects are weaponized by management to take out their frustrations on an employee. It may look like management is embarrassing and shaming an employee for lagging sales in front of a stadium of supporters, but don't let that fool you— they really are. However, this was not lost on fans as they responded at live events and on social media in defense of Bryan.

It is perhaps easy to interpret fans' reactions as some sort of overinvestment in an entertainment property, but considering the financial and corporate adversaries, the attempts to control the direction of the WWE plot by fans might rather be read as its own form of labor.[36] And if we take the considerable work of the fans into account, such protests and support of Daniel Bryan might even be read as a form of worker solidarity. Fans saw an employee being abused, both in the narrative of the wrestling storyline and in the humiliating ways he was treated in front of fans, and decided to do something about it all. Bryan's very vocal supporters organized themselves as what they called the Yes Movement, referring to the chant that Bryan led as he entered the ring. At various events throughout the winter, the Yes Movement cheered Bryan along, while booing and jeering not only The Authority, but even other wrestlers who were promoted over Bryan. This was especially evident at the annual Royal Rumble, where wrestler Batista surprisingly won after a hiatus from the company spent shooting movies. The crowd raucously disapproved, booing Batista and chanting for Bryan. This negative reaction to WWE's booking decisions was compounded by the fact that another fan favorite, wrestler CM Punk, walked out the following day.

Shortly thereafter, fans began "hijacking" live events by booing and chanting disruptively wherever the weekly *Monday Night Raw* performed. WWE could not silence an entire stadium of chanting spectators, and these outspoken and organized fans found themselves in a position to shape the wrestling narratives against the creative and authority figures at WWE and, notably, with little regard for shareholder value. The fan movement came to a head in CM Punk's hometown of Chicago, a city with a notoriously loud wrestling crowd. #HijackRaw trended on Twitter as the event approached. Fans who would be in attendance shared proposals for various protest actions to be performed in the stadium, from standing and turning their backs on The Authority to starting distracting and off topic chants to agreed upon responses when certain predictable things would take place during the show. Before the event, *Bleacher Report*'s Joe Johnson suggested, "Now, WWE is about to walk into a buzzsaw in the Windy City. Chicago is going to do its worst to destroy the flow of the program mere weeks before WrestleMania."[37] The financial implications of hijacking live events leading up to and possibly into WrestleMania were clear to fans and to WWE. The coordinated response at live shows was essentially a way for disaffected fans to destroy a live, theatrical corporate product—industrial sabotage for the social media age. Even more effective than simply not showing up, the fans were going to spoil WrestleMania, which is typically the biggest and most public event of the year for WWE, often attracting coverage in the news cycle and wider attention for its celebrity appearances and spectacular production elements.

However, WWE was prepared for the many possible disruptions. In what can only be considered a brilliant bit of dramaturgy, WWE turned the live audience's anger and protests into part of the story. WWE trolled the audience in return by playing CM Punk's music (CM Punk was not in attendance) and WWE also acknowledged #HijackRaw during the live show in one of Daniel Bryan's promos. The company managed to confront thousands of angry and coordinated fans and turn the audience's energy around to both support Bryan and to boo and jeer The Authority even more than they had before the show. A week later, WWE would incorporate that fan energy into a segment that is now known as #OccupyRaw, wherein Daniel Bryan and fans took over the wrestling ring and wouldn't give it up until Bryan was promised a match at Wrestlemania.[38] In the end, the fans felt victorious and WWE sold more tickets—after nearly a year of performances, of shareholder selling, and live audiences protesting, Daniel Bryan won the championship at the annual WrestleMania event in April.

This example highlights the ways that professional wrestling, where storylines are told over the course of weeks, months, and even years, is reliant on the live event, the actions of spectators, and the intricate connections between theatrical entertainment and finance. Just months after winning the championship belt in 2014, Daniel Bryan had to vacate the title due to a neck injury. Without an established storyline or conflict, it was unclear who would be the next champion and face of the company. This coincided with a slump in the stock price, leading Chris Smith of *Forbes* to suggest that John Cena's appeal to younger audience members is one of the main reasons he won the championship after WWE's stock price dipped in 2014.[39] In the same article, Smith charts WWE's quarterly revenue in relation to the championship runs of John Cena, Randy Orton, and CM Punk. In a for-profit, narrative form where storylines are told over the course of weeks, months, and even years, the popularity and profitability of each event and each appearance can be charted. The ongoing performance of professional wrestling sits neatly and in parallel to the ongoing performance of the market. This plotting, both in the theatrical sense and in setting points on a graph, is the plotting of finance and fiction. Professional wrestling is a market-driven performance and WWE's stock price is driven by theatrical performance.

Conclusion

WWE leverages its theatricality to create value for shareholders and itself as a corporation. This is perhaps not surprising considering that WWE is a publicly traded company, but WWE is an exemplary model for how theatre functions on a global scale and in conjunction with financial industries. There are, of course, many other theatre companies and corporations that produce live events for profit, but WWE is the only one where the live event is absolutely central to its operations. Of course, Disney has made arrangements to license its characters for *Disney on Ice* and *Disney Live* to Feld Entertainment for some time.[40] And since the debut of *Beauty and the Beast*, Disney and other media companies have also embraced theatrical live entertainment.[41] Such moves prompted the *New York Times* to rather naively pose the question: "has theater become just a derivative cog in brand machinery?"[42] Well, perhaps. But theatre has been productive for the capitalist classes for a long time and "brand machinery" is just a new mode for old labor relations. It has taken some time for the movie companies to come around to live performance, however, as studio executives still appear surprised at just how much revenue can be generated through live performances "charging 10 times more per ticket than movie theaters do."[43] It might be easier to consider Disney and DreamWorks as in the business of theatre than WWE because the live events produced by Disney and DreamWorks are performed in theatrical venues rather than stadiums. However, financially and organizationally there are few differences between them and WWE at least in the ways they actively pursue live, theatrical entertainment.

The impact of financial markets on the wrestling product (and vice versa) plays out in the ring itself. As the wrestling company that exerts the most influence on professional wrestling both in the US and around the world, WWE is both leading the field of pro wrestling and represents perhaps the most complete incarnation of a publicly traded, globalizing theatre company.

Notes

1 "World Wrestling Entertainment, Inc. (WWE)," *Yahoo! Finance*, accessed January 17, 2019, http://finance.yahoo.com/q?s=WWE.
2 Two Man Power Trip of Wrestling, "David Schultz Says He Slapped Reporter Because Of Vince McMahon, What Caused Rift With Hulk Hogan," *Wrestling INC*, February 24, 2018, www.wrestlinginc.com/news/2018/02/david-schultz-says-he-slapped-reporter-because-of-vince-637280/.
3 "Annual Report," Form 10-k, World Wrestling Federation Entertainment, Inc., *Edgar Online*, April 30, 2000, 3, http://yahoo.brand.edgar-online.com/display filinginfo.aspx?FilingID=1361985–1136–235098&type=sect&TabIndex=2& companyid=7520&ppu=%252fdefault.aspx%253fcik%253d1091907.

4 WWE, "Who We Are," *WWE Corporate*, accessed May 12, 2019, https://corporate.wwe.com/.
5 Jeremy Snodgrass, "Stephanie McMahon Thinks WWE Can Surpass Disney in Entertainment World," WWE, *ComicBook.com*, November 9, 2018, accessed May 13, 2019, https://comicbook.com/wwe/2018/11/08/stephanie-mcmahon-wwe-disney-can-surpass/.
6 Live Nation Entertainment, "Biz at Live Nation," accessed May 12, 2019, www.livenationentertainment.com/about/.
7 Live Nation Entertainment, "Biz at Live Nation."
8 Sharon Mazer, "The Doggie Dog World of Professional Wrestling," *TDR* 34, no. 4 (1990): 96–122.
9 Mazer, "The Doggie Dog World," 102.
10 To get a sense of just how expansive wrestling storylines might be, I recommend that you visit *The History of WWE*, a website researched and curated by Graham Cawthon (*The History of WWE*, www.thehistoryofwwe.com, accessed May 10, 2019). The site features details and results for wrestling matches stretching back decades and across promotions. Results from taped and televised matches, championship belt histories, matches at particular arenas—it is all meticulously recorded. For example, on April 26, 1981, WWF ran a program featuring Dominic DeNucci squaring off against Baron Mikel Scicluna in a high school gym in New Brighton, Pennsylvania, and at the Coliseum in New Haven, Connecticut, "Rick Martel & Tony Garea defeated Capt. Lou Albano (sub. for Moondog King) & WWF Tag Team Champion Moondog Rex via count-out" and "WWF IC Champion Pedro Morales defeated Sgt. Slaughter via disqualification," among other matches (*The History of WWE*, "1981," www.thehistoryofwwe.com/81.htm, accessed May 10, 2019.) One can presume that every one of those matches had a storyline or angle that may have been resolved during the match, but more likely continued. In just the month of April 1981, Pedro Morales defeated or was disqualified from nine matches with Sergeant Slaughter in as many cities. In looking closely at the accumulated records, it is hard not to see the wrestlers as a traveling troupe of actors going town to town to stage their matches.
11 Christopher Grobe, "Refined Mechanicals; Or, How I Learned to Stop Worrying and Share the Stage New Scholarship on Theatre and Media," *Theatre* 42.2 (2012), 139–146. Cited in Sarah Bay-Cheng, "Postmedia Performance," *Contemporary Theatre Review Interventions* 26, no. 2 (May 2016): www.contemporarytheatrereview.org/2016/postmedia-performance/.
12 Bay-Cheng, "Postmedia Performance."
13 Bay-Cheng, "Postmedia Performance."
14 WWE, "Live Events," What We Do, *WWE Corporate*, accessed May 12, 2019, https://corporate.wwe.com/what-we-do/live-events. Capitalization and formatting retained from original.
15 Dan O'Sullivan, "Money in the Bank: The Story of Pro Wrestling in the 20th Century is the Story of American Capitalism," *Jacobin*, August 11, 2014, www.jacobinmag.com/2014/08/money-in-the-bank/. Emphasis in original.
16 O'Sullivan, "Money in the Bank."
17 See for instance: Tim Hornbaker, *National Wrestling Alliance: The Untold Story of the Monopoly That Strangled Wrestling* (Toronto: ECW Press, 2007).
18 O'Sullivan, "Money in the Bank."
19 Also see Douglas Battema and Philip Sewell, "Trading in Masculinity: Muscles, Money, and Market Discourse in the WWF," in *Steel Chair to the Head: The Pleasure and Pain of Professional Wrestling*, ed. Nicholas Sammond (Durham, NC: Duke University Press, 2005), 260–294; Ted Butryn, "Global Smackdown: Vince McMahon, World Wrestling Entertainment, and Neoliberalism," in *Sport and*

Neoliberalism: Politics, Consumption, and Culture, eds. David L. Andrews and Michael L. Silk (Philadelphia: Temple University Press, 2012), 280–293.
20 Slavoj Žižek, *Absolute Recoil: Towards a New Foundation of Dialectical Materialism* (New York: Verso, 2014), 57.
21 Žižek, *Absolute Recoil*, 52.
22 "'Stone Cold' Steve Austin Bio," Superstars, *WWE.com*, accessed January 7, 2019, www.wwe.com/superstars/stonecoldsteveaustin.
23 "What Match is this Iconic Image of McMahon yelling at Stone Cold from?" R/SquaredCircle, Reddit.com, April 5, 2018, www.reddit.com/r/SquaredCircle/comments/89z8cm/what_match_is_this_iconic_image_of_mcmahon/
24 Douglas Battema and Philip Sewell offer a poignant critique of this slippage between selling shares in a company and selling the labor of workers. (Battema and Sewell, "Trading in Masculinity.")
25 Richard Sandomir, "Sports Business; W.W.F. Alters Script and Looks to Football," Sports Business, *New York Times*, February 4, 2000, www.nytimes.com/2000/02/04/sports/sports-business-wwf-alters-script-and-looks-to-football.html.
26 Sandomir, "Sports Business."
27 "Billionaires 2014: Notable Newcomers," *Forbes*, accessed May 10, 2019, www.forbes.com/pictures/fjlk45edee/vince-mcmahon/.
28 Aaron Taube, "9 Examples Of WWE CEO Vince McMahon's Insane Work Ethic," *Business Insider*, August 28, 2014, www.businessinsider.com/wwe-ceo-vince-mcmahons-work-ethic-2014-8.
29 Nina Godlewski, "Amazon Working Conditions: Urinating in Trash Cans, Shamed to Work Injured, List of Employee Complaints," U.S., *Newsweek*, September 12, 2018, www.newsweek.com/amazon-drivers-warehouse-conditions-workers-complains-jeff-bezos-bernie-1118849.
30 See for instance: Shaun Assael and Mike Mooneyham, *Sex, Lies, and Headlocks: The Real Story of Vince McMahon and World Wrestling Entertainment* (New York: Three Rivers Press, 2004; also the last chapter Scott M Beekman's *Ringside: A History of Professional Wrestling in America*. (Westport, CT: Praeger, 2006).
31 "Dems Mothers' Group Slams McMahon Over Former Role as WWE CEO," Senate, *FoxNews.com*, July 16, 2010, www.foxnews.com/politics/2010/07/15/mothers-group-slams-mcmahon-role-wwe-ceo/.
32 See Claire Warden, Broderick Chow, and Eero Laine, "Working Loose: A Response to 'Donald Trump Shoots the Match' by Sharon Mazer," *TDR: The Drama Review* 62, no. 2, T238 (Summer 2018): 201–215.
33 See also Brian Jansen, "'Yes! No! … Maybe?': Reading the Real in Professional Wrestling's Unreality," *Journal of Popular Culture* 51, no. 3 (June 2018): 1375–1392; Gino Canello, "Occupy Raw: Pro Wrestling Fans, Carnivalesque, and the Commercialization of Social Movements." *Journal of Popular Culture* 49, no. 6 (December 2016): 1375–1392; Eero Laine, "Stadium Sized Theatre: WWE and The World of Professional Wrestling," in *Performance and Professional Wrestling*, eds. Broderick Chow, Eero Laine, and Claire Warden (New York: Routledge, 2017), 39–47; Claire Warden, "'Might All Be a Work': Professional Wrestling at Butlins Holiday Camps,'" *The Journal of Popular Culture* 51, no. 4 (August 2018): 863–877; Wilson Koh, "'It's What's Best for Business'—'Worked Shoots' and the Commodified Authentic in Postmillennial Professional Wrestling," *Quarterly Review of Film and Video* 34, no. 5 (2017): 459–479.
34 Jonathan Snowden, "Inside WWE: An Exclusive Look at How a Pro Wrestling Story Comes to Life," Longform, *Bleacher Report*, January 21, 2015, http://bleacherreport.com/articles/2283701-inside-wwe-an-exclusive-look-at-how-a-pro-wrestling-story-comes-to-life.

35 Koh, "'It's What's Best for Business,'" 468.
36 Tyler Burnette and Birney Young, "Working Stiff(s): A Theory of Live Audience Labor Disputes," *Critical Studies in Media Communication* 36, no. 3 (2019): 221–234.
37 Joe Johnson, "WWE Will Face Most Hostile Audience Yet in Chicago on Monday Night RAW," WWE, *Bleacher Report*, February 27, 2014, http://bleacher report.com/articles/1976031-wwe-will-face-most-hostile-audience-yet-in-chicago-on-monday-night-raw.
38 Gino Canello offers a close analysis of the Occupy Raw movement and segment as an example, among others, of how "corporations, rather than combating social movements as the opposition, protect their capitalist interests by recognizing trends and creatively monetizing them." (Canello, "Occupy Raw," 1388.)
39 Chris Smith, "Is Making John Cena WWE Champ Really What's Best for Business?" SportsMoney, *Forbes*, July 1, 2014, www.forbes.com/sites/chrissmith/2014/07/01/is-making-john-cena-wwe-champion-whats-really-best-for-business/.
40 "History," Feld Entertainment, accessed May 21, 2019, www.feldentertainment.com/History/.
41 It is notable that Disney continues to license its intellectual property for the less prestigious popular entertainments that are staged in stadiums, while the Broadway productions are housed under Disney Theatricals, a direct subsidiary of Disney.
42 Patrick Healy, "Like the Movie, Only Different: Hollywood's Big Bet on Hollywood Adaptations," Movies, *New York Times* August 1, 2013, www.nytimes.com/2013/08/04/movies/hollywoods-big-bet-on-broadway-adaptations.html.
43 Healy, "Like the Movie."

Conclusion

It sometimes feels frivolous to study something like professional wrestling with such earnestness. It is as if to take something like professional wrestling seriously is to concede that it has won—you've been duped. The ruse might not have worked the way they wanted or intended it to, but it worked nonetheless. Today, professional wrestling perhaps seems too contemporary to be given the level of serious analysis of, say, popular entertainments from the nineteenth century, which are easily relegated to the past, tucked safely away from our contemporary sentiments, but interesting and worthy of study *historically*. However, in many ways, the fact that professional wrestling still exists is a rude reminder of what popular theatre actually looks like. Thus, I suspect the omissions of professional wrestling from the field of theatre or performance studies has less to do with an outright refusal to recognize the theatricality of pro wrestling performance and instead has more to do with the embarrassment of such recognition.

To study something is not to celebrate it. Professional wrestling, especially as it has manifested as an internationally commercial endeavor since at least the 1980s, is certainly complicit in a number of regressive and reactionary political projects. And it generally does so with a vigor that is at times painfully abrasive. As is often the case, reactionary aspects of art or performance forms that are more exclusionary, expensive, and highbrow are explained away as a misunderstanding or as an unfortunate and isolated incident rather than a key aspect of the form itself. On the other side, cultural products that are less esteemed, working class, and popular (e.g., pro wrestling) are more often viewed in such a way as to make the oppressive material endemic to the form itself.

There are, of course, myriad reasons to overlook wrestling as a form of theatre. With the exception of many of the design and technical elements (which also are shared with large concerts and touring musical productions) there is very little of pro wrestling that appears to directly overlap with legitimate theatrical forms, and most wrestlers and promoters have traditionally brushed off attempts to compare their business to theatre. Indeed, as discussed throughout this book, wrestling is frequently considered too overt, too crass, too objectionable, to merit comparisons to theatre. The situation is only heightened by a lack of a printable or purchasable scripts and the fact that professional wrestling history is most often held together by a community of fans and performers—most of whom would be more at home in sports arenas than in a proscenium theatre.

Professional wrestling matters for theatre studies because it is a form of theatrical, live performance with a history that spans the last century and encompasses numerous international traditions. Professional wrestling maps a global exchange of performers, styles, and verbal and physical vocabularies. It also offers a way of examining the intersections of theatre and capital through a contemporary case of a publicly traded theatre company that is finding ways to produce and circulate live performance on a global scale. However, it seems that what is at risk for theatre is the fact that the elements that make professional wrestling so offensive, exploitative, and backwards are also the very same elements that make it theatre. The assertion that WWE is a model for a publicly traded theatre company opens the possibility for many other incursions into commercial theatre. Indeed, the fact that professional wrestling encompasses a narrative form with characters and many other formal aspects of theatrical entertainment calls for a more comprehensive review of globalizing, commercial theatre companies.

It's funny, perhaps, but I do wonder if WWE included a little bit of Shakespeare in the opening of WrestleMania 35 just to see if someone might cite it in an article. In any case, I'll take the bait. Here is the text from the video package that opened the event:

> Shakespeare once said all the world's a stage and all the men and women merely players. Well tonight, we are the players, we are the storytellers, and this is our stage. This is our stage. A worldwide stage. Where opportunity awaits because here, tonight, in this showcase of immortals, we have the chance to live forever. All the world's a stage. We are the players. We are the storytellers. We are the storytellers. While tonight … I take it all. End of story.

The text was spoken by various WWE wrestlers and the last two sentences were spoken by Charlotte Flair, Becky Lynch, and Ronda Rousey, who would wrestle in the WrestleMania main event:

CHARLOTTE FLAIR: While tonight….
BECKY LYNCH: I take it all.
RONDA ROUSEY: End of story.

The text was part of a montage that featured video from previous matches, with images of wrestlers dancing or posing in a wrestling ring illuminated by lighted ring ropes, and was underscored by a version of the song "Never Die" written by Hopera, a hip hop opera group, featuring Adrian Dunn. The largest wrestling event of the year opened with a video sequence wherein an orchestra played behind rap vocals as wrestlers danced and referenced Shakespeare. It sounds spectacular, and it is, but it is also fairly normal for professional wrestling. Indeed, the high theatricality of WWE's glossy version of professional wrestling has always been present in professional wrestling. The differences between today's WWE and the lesser-known promotions are largely differences in production value. WWE has the money to recruit exactly who they want and to wrap everything up in a high-end media package. In leading with Shakespeare, WWE does seem to have reembraced the theatrical description of itself from its first report to shareholders ("Live events are the cornerstone of our business....")[1] Pro wrestlers are on stage, "a worldwide stage," as the largest wrestling company in the world asserts.

I can understand that some people don't like pro wrestling or that it doesn't sit well with their sensibilities or that they simply find it boring, but the largest wrestling company in the world launched its bid to financiers and investors with the idea that they are basically a theatre company and their opening to their largest event of the year involves a polished video about storytelling and theatre. If wrestling promoters used to deny the theatre of the event, they certainly don't any longer.

Because professional wrestling foregrounds issues that are central to theatre research—bodies, representation, character, plot, spectacle, labor, performance—it should not be too bold to claim that professional wrestling belongs in theatre studies. Without the stadiums, the live performances, the outsized characters, and other theatrical content and structures, professional wrestling would lack that which has made it a popular performance form for over a century. Indeed, it is perhaps strange that a form of theatre viewed and followed by millions of people around the world, should be so ignored by a profession devoted to uncovering even the most obscure forms of theatre and performance.

For theatre scholars, pro wrestling proves to be a very useful example in the classroom as well. If you want to help students understand theatricality or the difference between performance and theatre or characters or even, say, the political economy of live events, professional wrestling is an excellent place to start. Any student who is preparing to be a professional actor should understand how money is made off of their labor—why not show them performers who literally bleed for their work? That gig on the cruise ship might seem a bit more glamourous, but the economic mechanisms are the same. And students of technical theatre and design, in some cases, are already preparing for related fields of event design and stadium events that involve light shows, sound mixing, rigging, and set design and construction.

Of course, I have colleagues in professional wrestling studies who may disagree with such claims on the study of professional wrestling. I think that's ok. And I think they should also claim professional wrestling as central to their disciplines of media studies, celebrity studies, film studies, critical race theory, fan studies, sociology, anthropology, gender studies, business, transnational studies, dance, sports studies, and any other discipline that might take up pro wrestling. I can't make a claim to professional wrestling as essential for any other discipline than my own, but I also don't see this as simply a rhetorical strategy. I really do think theatre and performance studies needs to grapple with pro wrestling.

Professional wrestling should be central to many disciplines precisely because it is a popular form and because it taps into, comments upon, and interjects itself into many, many facets of culture and society. As what I think at this point we can call an emerging field, professional wrestling studies produces more useful and interesting results when we directly apply methodologies and disciplinary norms and histories and examples from our own fields. Many people have written dissertations and master's theses in particular academic programs with particular disciplinary methodologies and practices in part because there isn't a separate discipline of pro wrestling studies.[2] It is worth noting, perhaps especially in light of the nascent Professional Wrestling Studies Association, that professional wrestling studies still has quite a bit of room to develop its own theories and methodologies across disciplinary bounds.

As I hope is evident from most chapters in this book, pro wrestling also allows for an unobscured view of performance labor. A recent ESPN documentary on WWE and its developmental organization NXT offered this quote from WWE CEO Vince McMahon: "We're investing in human beings and the character they become. The healthier they are, the more longevity."[3] Here, WWE rather baldly engages the idea of a corporation considering people as an economic investment or human capital. WWE spends time and money on the development of its performers to make them more profitable, to extract larger and larger profits from their labor power. The decision to keep its wrestlers healthy (notably, not through comprehensive health insurance but through mandatory drug testing) is an economic one. The workers are protected by the corporation as assets first, as human beings only after that. This is perhaps not surprising at this point in the history of capital; however, the frankness with which professional wrestling, and WWE in particular, stages (with the full theatrical weight of the term) this encounter is notable.

The disjuncture between the fact of wrestlers' status as independent contractors on the one hand and the idea of the employer as an investor on the other, reveals theatrical performance as a business model that is thoroughly suited to today's labor markets. Professional wrestling thus asserts theatre and its profit-making potential rather bluntly in the face of the theatre arts. Professional wrestling is spectacular, frequently gruesome, and rarely polite. It foregrounds those aspects of performance that are often ignored, hidden backstage, or otherwise elided. In doing so, professional wrestling, in a way, pulls back the curtain on the economics of live performance as intertwined with the dangerous and frequently troubling aspects of live representational arts. Professional wrestling is theatre, and it models an economics of the stage that we might expect to see more of as performance companies seek wider and wider markets. These are just a few examples and there are many other possibilities that emerge from pro wrestling and cut across academic disciplines, even if each discipline might have something very particular to add to the conversation.

We might look to the actual act of wrestling for further methodologies and theories. This work is already underway. There have been numerous wrestlers who have written academically and in doing so have found ways to trouble the assumptions about the form from the vantage of one who has most directly engaged in it as a participant. Heather Levi trained in lucha libre in Mexico, Broderick Chow trained in London, Laurence DeGaris is a wrestler turned academic, Jamie Lewis Hadley has written academically about his work in wrestling, and the forthcoming *Professional Wrestling: Politics and Populism* features a number of wrestlers who are now studying professional wrestling academically. Claire Warden is running a wrestling company![4] These are precisely the methodologies that make professional wrestling both ripe for analysis and allow the form to speak across disciplines.

It is noteworthy that before the Professional Wrestling Studies Association, there was the Professional Wrestling Historical Society.[5] And fans have often driven the many archival and historical studies. Before academics were conducting anthropological and ethnographic field work in gyms, fan clubs and magazines and "dirt sheets" were publishing backstage gossip and news, not only about professional wrestling characters and performers and various plots and angles, but with a keen eye for the business itself. Pro wrestling fans are like those fans of opera, classical music, musical theatre, comic books, and other artistic forms with complex narratives and backstories. The academic field of fan studies likely has a lot to teach us, and wrestling fans themselves are really some of the most knowledgeable scholars of wrestling I know. And this is where my own background begins to show again: I would argue that wrestling fans are so knowledgeable and intensely focused on wrestler histories and championships because for most of wrestling history, the wrestling event, as any other theatrical event, was not otherwise recorded and the live event needed to be remembered and shared in print or in speech.

The 1980s changed some of that with video tapes, and wrestling fans acquired sometimes massive tape libraries. Wrestling documentation—"the tapes," as they're called—captures these deteriorating bodies and serves as a way of training others. R. Tyson Smith's ethnographic work with a small wrestling promotion outside of New York indicates that for many wrestlers "tape and video recordings are a primary vehicle for exchanging history, culture, and tricks of the trade."[6] Indeed, Smith suggests that

> These videos, dating back to the first popularity spike in the 1950s, are the subculture's recorded history. A knowledgeable, innovative pro wrestler scrutinizes these tapes as the veritable textbooks of the trade. Just as a conventional stage actor might have old copies of playbills or posters of Eugene O'Neil and Arthur Miller throughout the home, wrestlers have piles of taped matches from Hulk Hogan, Ric Flair, and Terry Funk. Viewing these classic bouts, wrestlers learn the history of the business, the moves, the gimmicks, the spectacle—and the legendary characters upon whose style they seek to build their own.[7]

Up until about a year ago, "tapes" were literally tapes and DVDs of matches and events that were packaged and sold by various wrestling promotions. Bought, traded, and sold by fans and wrestlers, they functioned as any other collectible might. Again, this changed radically with the introduction of the WWE Network, which features thousands of hours of old wrestling programming. The content and the history are now very much available, but the work of watching all of that old wrestling is really very time consuming. Still, the archive of recorded wrestling history exists and is very easily accessible. The field has not yet fully engaged, I think, with this massive trove of material.

This book is written from the perspective of my position as a theatre and performance studies scholar and I hope that it begins to indicate the significant work to be done on the many commercial forms of theatre and performance. Much of this work is happening under the guise of musical theatre studies and I have begun work on a project involving mascots as well as what I am calling "stadium theatre."

So much of live entertainment is fairly mundane. It is a sad middle-class endeavor to search for profound meaning where this is very likely none (a parlor, a kitchen table, and, yes, a wrestling ring), but at the same time such entertainments are meaningful precisely because they offer reflections and refractions of daily life today and throughout history. For professional wrestling studies, this book, I hope, opens some possibilities for future study. Also, in large part due to my disciplinary vantage, there is an attention to labor throughout the book. This is something that professional wrestling studies can also add to the wider discourse, especially as professional wrestling is writ through with the language of work.

This book did not deal much with any of the secret histories of professional wrestling, in large part because those histories are revealed and uncovered with quite a bit of success by the many fans sifting through old materials and tape libraries. At the professional wrestling halls of fame I visited, in Iowa and in Oklahoma, there were quite a few fan-made archival materials: binders full of citations and match descriptions, photocopied pictures from wrestling magazines, and the magazines themselves. These archives are massive, and rarely reported on—in part because, like all of popular culture, there is simply too much of it and it is scattered about. And really, this is another piece of work that needs to be done. There are halls of fame and libraries, but they need archivists, who need grants, and it all needs to be digitized. WWE is currently the best source for archival material and that is in large part because it has the funds to purchase video and has found an easy way to monetize that video. A huge swath of the history of professional wrestling exists in basements and attics and in a few halls of fame, sometimes coded and organized, sometimes not. The Smithsonian Museum lists just five images and a link to the website for the "Smithsonian Folklife Festival Features Hands-On Activities for Families and Children" from 2008, which evidently featured recreational activities from the country of Bhutan, including wrestling. Of the five images, really only two have to do with professional wrestling, and they show boots and a cape worn by Ric Flair. Both are housed in the National Museum of American History.[8] This is just the US—so think about Mexico, Japan, Australia, New Zealand, the UK, and nearly every country in South America and the EU. Since professional wrestling is a deeply commercial form, I will advertise here that if anyone is interested in working on such matters, I hope you will be in touch.

Popular culture is uncontainable, and as a form of performance, professional wrestling is especially unruly. Unlike many other aspects of pop culture, from comic books to advertising to music, pro wrestling doesn't have a collectible or a text. Or rather it has too many. There is no one thing that might be archived in its entirety. Once the shoulders hit the mat and the bell rings and the show is over, that's it. It's all ephemera. There are pictures, of course, and video and programs and written accounts and reports, and some may save bits of costuming or props, but none of that is wrestling itself. In many ways, this is the problem of theatre: an absence of the thing itself. Fans know this, promoters know this, wrestlers know this.

The National Wrestling Hall of Fame in Stillwater, Oklahoma has an impressive library of resources related to wrestling. There are a number of trade books and wrestler biographies and autobiographies, but there is even more material that has been collected and donated by fans, former wrestlers, and researchers, amateur and otherwise. What struck me when I visited this repository, however, were the fan-generated materials. There were scrapbooks with carefully pasted newspaper articles, organized by year and by wrestler or promotion. There were fan newsletters devoted to wrestlers with member rosters, and a carbon-copied and corner-stapled booklet on how to be a professional wrestler that included fitness tips and the mailing addresses of training schools. The National Wrestling Hall of Fame Dan Gable Museum in Waterloo, Iowa has scores of glossy magazines dating back to the mid-twentieth century, as well as some personal effects from wrestlers including journals and travel diaries. And the Professional Wrestling Hall of Fame and Museum, which I visited when it was located in Amsterdam, New York (it is currently in Wichita Falls, Texas) has an incredibly impressive collection of costuming and belts and photos, as well as a not-insignificant collection of DVDs and VHS tapes. (One of the people working at the museum kindly offered to put some tapes on as I was looking through the old magazines and other materials.) Professional wrestling is a visual form, it is a performance form. It is here tonight (one night only!) and then gone, maybe remembered or retold, but not reperformed.

I realize that calling for more work to be done is both a commonplace and yet deeply unsatisfying way to end a book-length study. There is, however, no real way around it. There is a lot of work to do in professional wrestling studies. Work that is more than telling and retelling biographies and recounting storylines and angles. Indeed, the work to be done is rooted in our own disciplines, even as we discuss and argue over professional wrestling together. Professional wrestling is an odd phenomenon and, I think, it is in this oddness that we find necessary examples and theories that help us better understand our social and cultural world.

There are wrestling storylines that last years, feuds that span careers, and really, if we want to, we might consider the entire history of wrestling as a single storyline stretching back through the WrestleManias to the territory days to the semi-legitimate fights in the early 1900s to carnivals. As a physical form, wrestlers have trained others into the discipline, setting up a genealogy of styles and move sets. Belts have changed hands and lasted for decades, only to be retired and replaced with new belts—championship lineages crossing borders and running through time. Wrestling opponents have worked together—learning, sharing, actually fighting sometimes—continuous, messy threads, weaving all the way back to the first wrestlers who worked something out together and thought they might make more money if they could guarantee the crowd an exciting fight, even it is wasn't a fair fight or a legitimate fight. It's easy to get nostalgic. That's built into wrestling.

I am always amazed to hear people's stories once they get past the idea that someone might study professional wrestling. Their uncle used to be a wrestler or their grandma used to make them watch it on TV, or they knew someone who knew someone whose child met John Cena through the Make a Wish Foundation, or maybe they dabbled in backyard wrestling when they were younger or they collect lucha masks. Or, like me, they're from Minnesota and have real opinions about Jesse Ventura. Or they went to a live show once or twice or every time a wrestling promotion came through town, like the circus, and found it fascinating or troubling or boring. Some people talk about seeing a wrestler in real life, sitting next to them on the train or plane, and others remember how huge they seemed in the stadium, how sweaty, how hairy, how toned or tanned. People used to tell me, remind me, that it's fake. In the past few years, however, I encounter more and more people who rather call it something else: entertainment, spectacle, or theatre even. Pro wrestling is theatre, but I think we can think about it from other perspectives as well. Even while I hope more theatre scholars might have a look at pro wrestling, I have always held out hope that scholars from other disciplines might look a little more closely at theatre. For that, I guess, we have wrestling.

Endings are hard for professional wrestling. There is always another match, another feud, another angle. What should be the neat closure of a story arc encounters a swerve. Someone runs in, someone is disqualified, their shoulders weren't down, it was a fast count, the bell never rang, and on and on and on and on. Or maybe you're already arguing about it with friends. Someone has the inside scoop. There is a report from backstage that a wrestler is retiring or their contract wasn't renewed or they failed a drug test and are not allowed to perform. Tomorrow, next week, on social media later tonight, you might find out what happened. Tune in next week. The show, as we say in theatre, must go on. And it goes on.

Notes

1 "Annual Report," Form 10-k, World Wrestling Federation Entertainment, Inc., *Edgar Online*, April 30, 2000, 3, http://yahoo.brand.edgar-online.com/display filinginfo.aspx?FilingID=1361985–1136–235098&type=sect&TabIndex=2&compa nyid=7520&ppu=%252fdefault.aspx%253fcik%253d1091907. Also see Eero Laine, "Stadium Sized Theatre: WWE and The World of Professional Wrestling," in *Performance and Professional Wrestling*, edited by Broderick Chow, Eero Laine, and Claire Warden (London and New York: Routledge, 2017), 39–47.
2 For further discussion of theses and dissertations, see Eero Laine, "Professional Wrestling Scholarship: Legitimacy and Kayfabe," *The Popular Culture Studies Journal* 6, no. 1 (2018): 82–99.
3 James Caldwell, "WWE TV RECAP: ESPN airs one-hour special on WWE – McMahon & Triple H interviewed, lives & careers of NXT stars focused on, more," *Pro Wrestling Torch*, 5 May 2015, http://pwtorch.com/artman2/publish/ wwsuperstarsreport/article_84815.shtml.
4 David Godsall, "Meet the Loughborough University Lecturer Who Combines Academia with Wrestling," Loughborough, *Leicester Live*, November 18, 2018, www.leicestermercury.co.uk/news/leicester-news/meet-loughborough-university-lecturer-who-2218941.
5 Professional Wrestling Historical Society, accessed May 20, 2019, www.pro wrestlinghistoricalsociety.com/.
6 R. Tyson Smith, *Fighting for Recognition: Identity Masculinity, and the Act of Violence in Professional Wrestling* (Durham, NC: Duke University Press, 2014), 53.
7 R. Tyson Smith, *Fighting for Recognition*, 45.
8 "Professional+Wrestling," Smithsonian, accessed May 20, 2019, www.si.edu/ sisearch/collection-images?edan_q=professional%2Bwrestling.

Bibliography

Amorosi, A.D. "There Will Be Blood ... And Weed Whackers." Naked City. *Philadelphia CityPaper*, February 13, 2008. http://archive.today/orGG#selection-359.463-363.147.

Aristotle. *Poetics*. Translated by S.H. Butcher. http://classics.mit.edu/Aristotle/poetics.1.1.html.

Arts Admin. "Jamie Lewis Hadley." Accessed May 22, 2019. www.artsadmin.co.uk/artists/supported/jamie-lewis-hadley.

Assael, Shaun and Mike Mooneyham. *Sex, Lies, and Headlocks: The Real Story of Vince McMahon and World Wrestling Entertainment*. New York: Three Rivers Press, 2004.

Associated Press. "Disney's Confidentiality Warning Riles Actor's Union, News." *CBSNews.com*, June 5, 2015. www.cbsnews.com/news/disneys-confidentiality-warning-riles-actors-union/.

Atkinson, Michael. "Fifty Million Viewers Can't Be Wrong: Professional Wrestling, Sports Entertainment, and Mimesis." *Sociology of Sport Journal* 19 (2002): 47–66.

Bahu. "FMW History." *Poruresu Central*, 2007, www.puroresucentral.com/FMW.html.

Ball, Michael. *Professional Wrestling as Ritual Drama in American Popular Culture*. Lewiston, NY: Edwin Mellen Press, 1990.

Balme, Christopher. "Selling the Bird: Richard Walton Tully's 'The Bird of Paradise' and the Dynamics of Theatrical Commodification." *Theatre Journal* 57, no. 1 (2005): 1–20.

Barker, Cory and Drew Zolides. "WWE Network: The Disruption of Over-the-Top Distribution." In *From Networks to Netflix A Guide to Changing Channels*, edited by Derek Johnson, 385–394. New York: Routledge, 2018.

Barthes, Roland. "The World of Wrestling." In *Steel Chair to the Head: The Pleasure and Pain of Professional Wrestling*, edited by Nicholas Sammond, 23–31. Durham, NC: Duke University Press, 2005.

Barthes, Roland. *Mythologies*. Translated by Annette Lavers. New York: Hill and Wang, 1972.

Battema, Douglas and Philip Sewell. "Trading in Masculinity: Muscles, Money, and Market Discourse in WWF." In *Steel Chair to the Head: The Pleasure and Pain of Professional Wrestling*, edited by Nicholas Sammond, 260–294. Durham: Duke University Press, 2005.

Baudrillard, Jean. *Simulation and Simulacra*. Ann Arbor: University of Michigan Press, 2008.

Bay-Cheng, Sarah. "Postmedia Performance." *Contemporary Theatre Review Interventions* 26, no. 2 (May 2016). www.contemporarytheatrereview.org/2016/postmedia-performance/.

Beekman, Scott M. *Ringside: A History of Professional Wrestling in America*. Westport, CT: Praeger, 2006.

Bennett, Susan. "Theatre/Tourism." *Theatre Journal* 57, no. 3 (October 2005): 407–428.

Billington, Michael. "Tanzi Libre—Review." Review of *Tanzi Libre*, by Claire Luckham. *Guardian*, May 22, 2013. www.theguardian.com/stage/2013/may/22/tanzi-libre-review.

Bixenspan, David. "Mick Foley Believes That He Has Suffered Permanent Brain Damage from His Career in Pro Wrestling." TNA Impact. *Cageside Seats*. November 6, 2010. www.cagesideseats.com/2010/11/6/1798140/mick-foley-believes-that-he-has-suffered-permanent-brain-damage-from.

Blair, B. Brian. "About." Accessed February 20, 2019. www.brianblair.com/about.html.

Blair, B. Brian. *Smarten Up!: Say it Right*. St. Petersburg, FL: Kayfabe Publishing Company, 2001.

Boehm, Eric, "In Pennsylvania, Pro-Wrestling is Taxation Without Regulation." Features. *Pennsylvania Independent*. July 22, 2013. http://paindependent.com/2013/07/in-pennsyvania-wrestling-is-taxation-without-regulation/.

Boyle, Michael Shane. "Performance and Value: The Work of Theatre in Karl Marx's Critique of Political Economy." *Theatre Survey* 58, no. 1 (January 2017): 3–23.

Brecht, Bertolt. "Emphasis on Sport." *Brecht on Theatre: The Development of an Aesthetic*, translated by John Willet, 6–9. New York: Hill and Wang, [1926] 1964.

Broadway League, The. "Broadway Season Statistics." Research & Statistics. Accessed April 19, 2019. www.broadwayleague.com/research/statistics-broadway-nyc/.

Brooker, Nathan. "Tanzi Libre." Review of *Tanzi Libre*, by Claire Luckham. *Exeunt Magazine*. May 22, 2013. http://exeuntmagazine.com/reviews/tanzi-libre/.

Bureau of Economic Analysis. "Arts and Cultural Production Satellite Account, U.S. and States 2016." Arts and Culture. bea.gov. March 19, 2019. Accessed April 19, 2019. www.bea.gov/data/special-topics/arts-and-culture.

Burnette, Tyler and Birney Young. "Working Stiff(s): A Theory of Live Audience Labor Disputes." *Critical Studies in Media Communication* 36, no. 3 (2019): 221–234.

Butryn, Ted. "Global Smackdown: Vince McMahon, World Wrestling Entertainment, and Neoliberalism." In *Sport and Neoliberalism: Politics, Consumption, and Culture*, edited by David L. Andrews and Michael L. Silk, 280–293. Philadelphia: Temple University Press, 2012.

Caldwell, James. "WWE TV Recap: ESPN Airs One-Hour Special on WWE—McMahon & Triple H Interviewed, Lives & Careers of NXT Stars Focused On, More." *Pro Wrestling Torch*, May 5, 2015. http://pwtorch.com/artman2/publish/wwsuperstarsreport/article_84815.shtml.

Canello, Gino. "Occupy Raw: Pro Wrestling Fans, Carnivalesque, and the Commercialization of Social Movements." *Journal of Popular Culture* 49, no. 6 (December 2016): 1375–1392.

Carlson, Marla. *Performing Bodies in Pain: Medieval and Post-Modern Martyrs, Mystics, and Artists*. New York: Palgrave Macmillan, 2010.

Cavendish, Dominic. "Tanzi Libre, Southwark Playhouse, Review." Review of *Tanzi Libre*, by Claire Luckham. *Telegraph*, May 22, 2013. www.telegraph.co.uk/culture/theatre/10073756/Tanzi-Libre-Southwark-Playhouse-review.html.

Caves, Richard E. *Creative Industries: Contracts Between Art and Commerce*. Cambridge, MA: Harvard University Press, 2000.

Cawthon, Graham. *The History of WWE*. Accessed May 10, 2019. www.thehistoryofwwe.com.

Cawthon, Graham. "1981." *The History of WWE*. Accessed May 10, 2019. www.thehistoryofwwe.com/81.htm.

Chamberlin, Wilt. "The Wrestler – Mickey Rourke – Stunt Double." YouTube.com. February 15, 2008. www.youtube.com/watch?v=5n9UeLiCUrk.

Cheng, Roger and George Stahl. "Apple Shares Fall as Jobs Takes Medical Leave." Gadgets. *Wall Street Journal*. January 18, 2011. www.wsj.com/articles/SB10001424052748703954004576089633611009272.

Chow, Broderick. "Work and Shoot: Professional Wrestling and Embodied Politics." *TDR: The Drama Review* 58, no. 2, T222 (Summer 2014): 72–86.

Chow, Broderick. "Muscle Memory: Re-Enacting the *Fin-de-siècle* Strongman in Pro Wrestling." In *Performance and Professional Wrestling*, edited by Broderick Chow, Eero Laine, and Claire Warden, 143–153. New York: Routledge, 2017.

Chow, Broderick and Eero Laine. "Audience Affirmation and the Labour of Professional Wrestling." *Performance Research* 19, no. 2 (June 2014): 44–53.

Chow, Broderick, Eero Laine, and Claire Warden, editors. *Performance and Professional Wrestling*. London: Routledge, 2017.

Cillizza, Chris. "Why Pro Wrestling is the Perfect Metaphor for Donald Trump's Presidency." The Point with Chris Cillizza. *CNN*. July 2, 2017. www.cnn.com/2017/07/02/politics/trump-wrestling-tweet/index.html.

Cohen, Eric. "Secrets of the Wrestler." Professional Wrestling, *About.com* via *Internet Archive Wayback Machine*. Accessed January 22, 2019. https://web.archive.org/web/20090211151910/http://prowrestling.about.com/od/beginnersguide/tp/secretsofthewrestler.htm.

Committee on Oversight and Government Reform, US House of Representatives, Transcript. "Interview of: Stephanie McMahon Levesque," December 14, 2007. http://muchnick.net/stephanietranscript.pdf.

Condliffe, Jamie. "The Steve Jobs Action Figure is Cancelled." *Gizmodo*, January 17, 2012. http://gizmodo.com/5876722/the-steve-jobs-action-figure-is-dead.

Cornette, Jim. "The Slippery Slope of Hardcore Wrestling." *jimcornette.com*. Accessed January 15, 2019. https://jimcornette.com/cornettes-commentary/slippery-slope-hardcore-wrestling.

Craven, Gerald and Richard Moseley. "Actors on the Canvas Stage: The Dramatic Conventions of Professional Wrestling." *Journal of Popular Culture* 6, no. 2 (Fall 1972): 326–336.

CZW, "[FREE MATCH] CZW Tournament of Death 8: Jon Moxley Vs Brain Damage." YouTube.com, December 31, 2018. www.youtube.com/watch?v=Z_ZJZ-r9t8E.

Daily Mail Reporter. "Want to Look Like The Rock? Try Eating Like Him: Former WWE Champion Eats 10 POUNDS of Food a Day Over Seven Meals and Gets Up at 4am For His First Meal." News. *Daily Mail*, May 9, 2015. www.dailymail.co.uk/news/article-3075270/Want-look-like-Rock-Try-eating-like-Former-

Bibliography 133

WWE-champion-s-strict-5-165-calorie-daily-diet-contains-10-pounds-food-including-cod-eggs-steak-chicken.html.

Dalzell, Tom, ed. *The Routledge Dictionary of Modern American Slang and Unconventional English*. New York, Routledge: 2008.

DeGaris, Laurence. "The 'Logic' of Professional Wrestling." In *Steel Chair to the Head: The Pleasure and Pain of Professional Wrestling*, edited by Nicholas Sammond, 192–212. Durham: Duke University Press, 2005.

DeGaris, Laurence. "The Money and the Miles." In *Professional Wrestling: Politics and Populism*, edited by Nell Haynes, Eero Laine, Heather Levi, Sharon Mazer. Enactments. Richard Schechner, series editor. Calcutta: Seagull Books, forthcoming.

Dell, Chad. *The Revenge of Hatpin Mary: Women, Professional Wrestling, and Fan Culture in the 1950s*. New York: Peter Lang Publishing, 2006.

Diaz, Kristoffer. *The Elaborate Entrance of Chad Deity*. New York: Samuel French, 2011.

Di Benedetto, Stephen. "Playful Engagements: Wrestling with the Attendant Masses." In *Performance and Professional Wrestling*, edited by Broderick Chow, Eero Laine, and Claire Warden, 26–36. London: Routledge, 2017.

Dogan, Stacey L. "An Exclusive Right to Evoke." *Boston College Law Review* 44, no. 2 (2003): 291–321.

Dunn, Carrie. "'Most Women Train with Men, so Why Not Wrestle Them?': The Performance and Experience of Intergender Wrestling in Britain." In *Performance and Professional Wrestling*, edited by Broderick Chow, Eero Laine, and Claire Warden, 95–104. London: Routledge, 2017.

Elsy, Hannah. "Review: Tanzi Libre." Review of *Tanzi Libre*, by Claire Luckham. *A Younger Theatre*, May 27, 2013. www.ayoungertheatre.com/review-tanzi-libre-southwark-playhouse/.

Enders, Jodi. *Murder by Accident: Medieval Theater, Modern Media, Critical Intentions*. Chicago: University of Chicago Press, 2009.

Everard, David Eugene. "Wrestling Dell'arte: Professional Wrestling as Theatre." MA Thesis, University of Victoria, 2002.

Feld Entertainment. "History." Accessed May 21, 2019. www.feldentertainment.com/History/.

Fink, Joel G. "*Trafford Tanzi* by Claire Luckham. Half Moon Theatre, London. August 9, 1982." Review of *Trafford Tanzi*, by Claire Luckham. *Theatre Journal* 35, no. 1 (March 1983): 117–118.

Flory, Bryan. "Pro Wrestling: The Top 10 Richest Wrestlers." WWE, *Bleacher Report*, April 6, 2011. http://bleacherreport.com/articles/656507-pro-wrestling-the-top-10-richest-wrestlers.

FMWWrestling.us. Accessed May 19, 2019. http://fmwwrestling.us/FMWHistory.html.

Foley, Mick. *Have a Nice Day: A Tale of Blood and Sweatsocks*. New York: Regan Books, 1999.

Foley, Mick. "The Wrestler is Good." Life and Art. *Slate*. December 18, 2008. www.slate.com/articles/news_and_politics/life_and_art/2008/12/the_wrestler_is_good.2.html.

Foley, Mick. "Bio." Accessed August 1, 2013. www.realmickfoley.com/about/.

Forbes. "Billionaires 2014: Notable Newcomers." Accessed May 10, 2019. www.forbes.com/pictures/fjlk45edee/vince-mcmahon/.

Ford, Sam. "WWE's Story World and the Potentials of Transmedia Storytelling." In *The Rise of Transtexts: Challenges and Opportunities*, edited by Benjamin W.L. Derhy Kurtz and Mélanie Bourdaa, 169–186. London: Routledge, 2016.

Fox News. "Dems Mothers' Group Slams McMahon Over Former Role as WWE CEO." Senate. *FoxNews.com*. July 16, 2010. www.foxnews.com/politics/2010/07/15/mothers-group-slams-mcmahon-role-wwe-ceo/.

Foy, Matt. "The Ballad of the Real American: A Call for Cultural Critique of Pro-Wrestling Storylines." *The Popular Culture Studies Journal* 6, no. 1 (2018): 173–188.

Gobetz, Wally. "NYC – Queens – Astoria: Museum of the Moving Image – forehead wound from The Wrestler." April 2, 2011. www.flickr.com/photos/wallyg/6456719717/.

Godlewski, Nina. "Amazon Working Conditions: Urinating in Trash Cans, Shamed to Work Injured, List of Employee Complaints." *Newsweek*, September 12, 2018. www.newsweek.com/amazon-drivers-warehouse-conditions-workers-complains-jeff-bezos-bernie-1118849.

Godsall, David. "Meet the Loughborough University Lecturer Who Combines Academia with Wrestling." *Leicester Live*, November 18, 2018. www.leicester mercury.co.uk/news/leicester-news/meet-loughborough-university-lecturer-who-2218941.

GoFundMe. "'Necro Butcher' Dylan Summers' Medical Expenses." September 11, 2013. www.giveforward.com/fundraiser/sfw2/dylan-summers-medical-expenses.

Goldberg, Lesley. "Alex Trebek, Pat Sajak, Vanna White Renew Contracts Through 2022." *The Hollywood Reporter*, October 31, 2018. www.hollywoodreporter.com/live-feed/alex-trebek-pat-sajak-vanna-white-renew-contracts-2022-1156793.

Golijan, Rosa. "Apple Tries to Ban Realistic Steve Jobs Action Figure." *NBCNews.com*, January 5, 2012. www.nbcnews.com/technology/technolog/apple-tries-ban-realistic-steve-jobs-action-figure-118110.

Gordon, Jeremy. "Is Everything Wrestling?" *New York Times*, May 27, 2016. www.nytimes.com/2016/05/27/magazine/is-everything-wrestling.html.

Griffin, Marcus. *Fall Guys: The Barnums of Bounce: The Inside Story of the Wrestling Business, America's Most Profitable and Best Organized Sport*. Chicago: Reilly Lee Company, 1937.

Grobe, Christopher. "Refined Mechanicals; Or, How I Learned to Stop Worrying and Share the Stage: New Scholarship on Theatre and Media." *Theatre*, 42 no. 2 (2012): 139–146.

Hackett, Thomas. *Slaphappy: Pride, Prejudice & Professional Wrestling*. New York: Ecco, 2006.

Hadley, Jamie Lewis. "The Hard Sell: The Performance of Pain in Professional Wrestling." In *Performance and Professional Wrestling*, edited by Broderick Chow, Eero Laine, and Claire Warden, 154–162. New York: Routledge, 2017.

Hadley, Jamie Lewis. *We Will Outlive the Blood You Bleed*. Spill Festival of Performance, October 29, 2014. http://spillfestival.com/show/we-will-outlive-the-blood-you-bleed/.

Hagan, Darrin. "Why I Hate Wrestling (the Sport, Not the Foreplay!)." *Torquere: Journal of the Canadian Lesbian and Gay Studies Association/Revue de la Societe Canadienne des Etudes Lesbiennes et Gaies* 1 (1999): 114–119.

Hall, Kira, Donna M. Goldstein, and Matthew Bruce Ingram. "The Hands of Donald Trump: Entertainment, Gesture, Spectacle." *HAU: Journal of Ethnographic Theory* 6, no. 2 (Autumn 2016): 71–100.

Hall, Stuart. "Notes on Deconstructing the Popular." In *People's History and Socialist Theory*, edited by Raphael Samuel, 227–240. London: Routledge, 1981.

Harkulich, Christiana Molldrem. "Sasha Banks, the Boss of NXT: Media, Gender, and the Evolution of Women's Wrestling in WWE." In *Identity and Professional Wrestling: Essays on Nationality, Race and Gender*, 148–161. Jefferson, NC: McFarland, 2018.

Haynes, Nell. "Global Cholas: Reworking Tradition and Modernity in Bolivian Lucha Libre." *The Journal of Latin American and Caribbean Anthropology* 18, no. 3 (2013): 432–446.

Haynes, Nell. "UnBoliviable Bouts: Gender and Essentialisation of Bolivia's Cholitas Luchadoras." In *Global Perspectives on Women in Combat Sports: Women Warriors around the World*, edited by Alex Channon and Christopher R. Matthews, 267–283. London: Palgrave Macmillan, 2015.

Haynes, Nell. "Kiss with a Fist." *Journal of Language and Sexuality* 5, no. 2 (2016): 250–275.

Haynes, Nell, Eero Laine, Heather Levi, and Sharon Mazer, eds. *Professional Wrestling: Politics and Populism*. Enactments. Richard Schechner, series editor. Calcutta: Seagull Books, forthcoming.

Healy, Patrick. "Here, a Careful Body Slam Is as Vital as Deft Dialogue." *New York Times*, May 16, 2010. www.nytimes.com/2010/05/17/theater/17wrestle.html.

Healy, Patrick. "Like the Movie, Only Different: Hollywood's Big Bet on Hollywood Adaptations." *New York Times*, August 1, 2013. www.nytimes.com/2013/08/04/movies/hollywoods-big-bet-on-broadway-adaptations.html.

Hedges, Chris. *Empire of Illusion: The End of Literacy and the Triumph of Spectacle*. New York: Nation Books, 2009.

Henry, Justin. "Real by Nature: Combat Zone Wrestling Celebrate 15 Years of Signature Anarchy." *CCB*, January 29, 2014. http://camelclutchblog.com/combat-zone-wrestling-15-years/.

Hewitt, Mark S. *Catch Wrestling: A Wild and Wooly Look at the Early Days of Pro Wrestling in America*. Boulder, CO: Paladin Press, 2005.

Hoberman, J. "Mickey Rourke and Darren Aronofsky Both Make Visceral Comebacks in *The Wrestler*." *The Village Voice*, December 17, 2008. www.villagevoice.com/2008-12-17/film/mickey-rourke-and-darren-aronofsky-both-make-visceral-comebacks-in-the-wrestler/.

Holmes, James J.S. and Kanika D. Corley. "Defining Liability for Likeness of Athlete Avatars in Video Games." *Los Angeles Lawyer* (May 2011): 17–43. www.lacba.org/docs/default-source/lal-back-issues/2011-issues/may-2011.pdf.

Hornbaker, Tim. *National Wrestling Alliance: The Untold Story of the Monopoly That Strangled Wrestling*. Toronto: ECW Press, 2007.

Horton, Aaron D., ed. *Identity in Professional Wrestling: Essays on Nationality, Race and Gender*. Jefferson, NC: McFarland and Company, 2018.

Jackson, Sharyn. "Interview: Five Questions for *The Wrestler*'s Necro Butcher." *The Village Voice*, March 20, 2009. http://blogs.villagevoice.com/music/2009/03/interview_five.php.

Jansen, Brian. "'Yes! No! … Maybe?': Reading the Real in Professional Wrestling's Unreality." *Journal of Popular Culture* 51, no. 3 (June 2018): 1375–1392.

Jeffries, Dru, ed., *#WWE: Professional Wrestling in the Digital Age*. Indiana University Press, forthcoming.

Jenkins III, Henry. "'Never Trust a Snake': WWF Wrestling as Masculine Melodrama." In *Steel Chair to the Head: The Pleasure and Pain of Professional Wrestling*, Edited by Nicholas Sammond, 33–66. Durham, NC: Duke University Press, 2005.

Johnson, Joe. "WWE Will Face Most Hostile Audience Yet in Chicago on Monday Night RAW." *Bleacher Report*, February 27, 2014. http://bleacherreport.com/articles/1976031-wwe-will-face-most-hostile-audience-yet-in-chicago-on-monday-night-raw.

Kerr, Peter. "Now It Can Be Told: Those Pro Wrestlers Are Just Having Fun." *New York Times*. February 10, 1989. www.nytimes.com/1989/02/10/nyregion/now-it-can-be-told-those-pro-wrestlers-are-just-having-fun.html.

Kluber, Warren. "Character-World Dialectics on the Contemporary American Stage: Gaming, Role-Playing, and Wrestling with Idioculture." *Theatre Journal* 70, no. 2 (June 2018): 209–227.

Koh, Wilson. "'It's What's Best for Business'—'Worked Shoots' and the Commodified Authentic in Postmillennial Professional Wrestling," *Quarterly Review of Film and Video* 34, no. 5 (2017): 459–479.

Kravets, David. "Associated Press Settles Copyright Lawsuit Against Obama 'Hope' Artist." *Wired Magazine*, January 12, 2012. www.wired.com/threatlevel/2011/01/hope-image-flap/.

Labar, Justin. "15 Greatest Moments in Royal Rumble History." *Bleacher Report*, January 21, 2013. http://bleacherreport.com/articles/1494905-15-greatest-moments-in-royal-rumble-history.

Laine, Eero. "Professional Wrestling: Creating America's Fight Culture." In *Sports at the Center of Popular Culture: The Television Age*. Vol. 2 of *American History Through American Sports: From Colonial Lacrosse to Extreme Sports*, edited by Daniel Coombs and Bob Batchelor, 219–236. Santa Barbara: Praeger, 2013.

Laine, Eero. "Stadium Sized Theatre: WWE and The World of Professional Wrestling." In *Performance and Professional Wrestling*, edited by Broderick Chow, Eero Laine, and Claire Warden, 39–47. London: Routledge, 2017.

Laine, Eero. "Professional Wrestling Scholarship: Legitimacy and Kayfabe." *The Popular Culture Studies Journal* 6, no. 1 (2018): 97–99.

Laine, Eero. "World Building in the WWE Universe." In *#WWE: Professional Wrestling in the Digital Age*, edited by Dru Jeffries. Bloomington, IN: Indiana University Press, forthcoming.

Laine, Eero. "Kayfabe: Optimism, Cynicism, and Critique." In *Professional Wrestling: Politics and Populism*, edited by Nell Haynes, Eero Laine, Heather Levi, Sharon Mazer. Enactments. Richard Schechner, series editor. Calcutta: Seagull Books, forthcoming.

Lazar, Louie. "Bronx Wrestlers Punch, Body-Slam for Glory." *Wall Street Journal*, March 19, 2014. http://blogs.wsj.com/metropolis/2014/03/19/bronx-wrestlers-punch-body-slam-for-glory/.

Lee, Eric. "Titan Sports, Inc. v. Hellwig: Wrestling with the Distinction between Character and Performer," 3 Tul. J. Tech. & Intell. Prop. 155 (2001). Charles B. Sears Law Library. 155–163.

Leonard, H.F. and K. Higashi. "American Wrestling vs. Jujitsu." *The Cosmopolitan*, May 1905.

Levi, Heather. "Sport and Melodrama: The Case of Mexican Professional Wrestling." *Social Text*, no. 50 (Spring 1997): 57–68.

Levi, Heather. "The Mask of the Luchador: Wrestling, Politics, and Identity." In *Steel Chair to the Head: The Pleasure and Pain of Professional Wrestling*, edited by. Nicholas Sammond, 96–131. Durham, NC: Duke University Press, 2005.

Levi, Heather. *The World of Lucha Libre: Secrets, Revelations, and Mexican National Identity.* Durham, NC: Duke University Press, 2008.

Levi, Heather. "Why It Mattered: Wrestling Dramaturgy in the 2016 Presidential Election." In *Professional Wrestling: Politics and Populism*, edited by Nell Haynes, Eero Laine, Heather Levi, Sharon Mazer. Enactments. Richard Schechner, series editor. Calcutta: Seagull Books, forthcoming.

Levine, Lawrence W. *Highbrow/Lowbrow: The Emergence of Cultural Hierarchy in America.* Cambridge, MA: Harvard University Press, 1988.

Legends of Professional Wrestling, Video Game (Agoura, CA: THQ, 2009).

Lister, John. "Professional Wrestling's Clandestine Jargon." *Verbatim* 31, no. 2 (Summer 2006): 6+. NOVELny.

Litherland, Benjamin. *Wrestling in Britain: Sporting Entertainments, Celebrity and Audiences.* London: Routledge, 2018.

Litherland, Benjamin. "Breaking Kayfabe is Easy, Cheap and Never Entertaining: Twitter Rivalries in Professional Wrestling." *Celebrity Studies* 5, no. 4 (2014): 531–533.

Live Nation Entertainment. "Biz at Live Nation." Accessed May 12, 2019. www.livenationentertainment.com/about/.

Liverpool Eric's. "Eric's – April 1978." May 30, 2016. http://liverpoolerics.blogspot.com/2016/03/erics-april-1978.html.

Liverpool John Moores University. "Tuebrook Tanzi, The Venus Fly Trap." Digital Collections. Accessed May 5, 2019. http://digitool.jmu.ac.uk:8881/R/GSV45LA6 11RKNXRK8J2S1PLLMT9STHPXETA8N4SFG5TGH7YUA9- 00292?func=dbin-jump-full&object_id=16464&local_base=GEN01&pds_ handle=GUEST and the record itself: digitool.jmu.ac.uk:1801/webclient/Delivery Manager?pid=16464&custom_att_2=direct.

Loverro, Thom. *The Rise and Fall of ECW: Extreme Championship Wrestling.* New York: Gallery Books, 2007.

Luckham, Claire. *Plays.* London: Oberon, 1999.

Luckham, Claire. *Trafford Tanzi: Her Hopes, Her Fears, Her Early Years.* London: Quartet Books, 1983.

Lukowski, Andrzej. "Tanzi Libre." Review of *Tanzi Libre*, by Claire Luckham. *Time Out: London*, May 29, 2013. www.timeout.com/london/theatre/tanzi-libre-southwark-playhouse-29-may-2013.

MadManAmbrose. "Jon Moxley (Dean Ambrose) talks about his first Tournament of Death." YouTube.com, June 9, 2015. www.youtube.com/watch?v=eQhj Uz5LLMc.

Magee, Bob. "As I See It 12/27: Arena History, Part 2.... The Post-ECW Era." *Gerweck.net*, December 27, 2013. www.gerweck.net/2013/12/27/as-i-see-it-1227-arena-history-part-2-the-post-ecw-era/.

Magee, Bob. "As I See It 6/8." *Pro-Wrestling Between the Sheets.* Accessed 22 June 2014. www.pwbts.com/columns/2009/b060809.html.

Marx, Karl. "Chapter II. Proletarians and Communists." *The Communist Manifesto.* www.marxists.org/archive/marx/works/1848/communist-manifesto/ch02.htm.

Marx, Karl. "Chapter IV: Theories of Productive and Unproductive Labour." *Theories of Surplus Value*. www.marxists.org/archive/marx/works/1863/theories-surplus-value/ch04.htm.
Marx, Karl. *Grundrisse: Foundations of the Critique of Political* Economy. Translated by Martin Nicolaus. New York: Penguin Classics, 1993.
Marx, Karl. "Wages of Labor." *The Economic Manuscripts of 1844*. www.marxists.org/archive/marx/works/1844/manuscripts/wages.htm.
Massumi, Brian. *Semblance and Event: Activist Philosophy and the Occurrent Arts*. Cambridge, MA: MIT Press, 2011.
Mazer, Sharon. "The Doggie Dog World of Professional Wrestling." *TDR: The Drama Review* 34, no. 4 (1990): 96–122.
Mazer, Sharon. *Professional Wrestling: Sport and Spectacle*. Jackson, MS: University of Mississippi Press, 1998.
Mazer, Sharon. "'Real Wrestling'/'Real' Life." In *Steel Chair to the Head: The Pleasure and Pain of Professional Wrestling*, edited Nicholas Sammond, 67–87. Durham, NC: Duke University Press, 2005.
Mazer, Sharon. "Donald Trump Shoots the Match." *TDR: The Drama Review* 62, no. 2, T238 (Summer 2018): 175–200.
Mazer, Sharon. "Sharon Mazer Responds to Warden, Chow, and Laine." *TDR: The Drama Review* 62, no. 2, T238 (Summer 2018): 216–219.
Mazer, Sharon. "A Mega Power Implodes: Donald Trump, Presidential Performativity, and Professional Wrestling." In *Professional Wrestling: Politics and Populism*, edited by Nell Haynes, Eero Laine, Heather Levi, Sharon Mazer. Enactments. Richard Schechner, Series Editor. Calcutta: Seagull Books, forthcoming.
McBride, Lawrence B. "Professional Wrestling, Embodied Morality, and Altered States of Consciousness." MA Thesis, University of South Florida, 2005.
McQuarrie, Fiona A. E. "Breaking Kayfabe: 'The History of a History' of World Wrestling Entertainment." *Management & Organizational History* 1, no. 3 (2006): 227–250.
Merrifield, Nicola. "*Tanzi Libre* Cancelled After Lead Actor Suffers Injury." *The Stage*, May 28, 2013. www.thestage.co.uk/news/2013/tanzi-libre-cancelled-after-lead-actor-suffers-injury/.
Mitchell, Bruce. "Hardcore Fans and the Wrestling Business." *The Wrestling Observer, 1990 Yearbook*, edited by Dave Meltzer. Campbell, CA: 1990.
Monsiváis, Carlos. "The Hour of the Mask as Protagonist: El Santo versus the Skeptics on the Subject of Myth." In *Steel Chair to the Head: The Pleasure and Pain of Professional Wrestling*, edited by Nicholas Sammond, 88–95. Durham: Duke University Press, 2005.
Montez, Noe. "The Heavy Lifting: Resisting the Obama Presidency's Neoliberalist Conceptions of the American Dream in Kristoffer Diaz's *The Elaborate Entrance of Chad Deity*." *Theatre History Studies* 37 (2018): 305–312.
Morgenstern, Joe. "Takedown!: Rourke Reigns as Failed 'Wrestler'" Review of *The Wrestler*, directed by Darren Aronofsky. *Wall Street Journal*, December 19, 2008. http://online.wsj.com/news/articles/SB122963414294619431.
Morton, Gerald W. and George M. O'Brien. *Wrestling to Rasslin: Ancient Sport to American Spectacle*. Bowling Green, OH: Bowling Green State University Popular Press, 1985.

Murphy, Tim. "Hate Wrestling? Blame Rick Santorum." *Mother Jones*, March 16, 2012. www.motherjones.com/politics/2012/03/rick-santorum-wwf-pro-wresting.

Mysterio, Rey with Jeremy Roberts. *Behind the Mask*. New York: Pocket Books, 2009.

Nark, Jason. "Nick Gage, Jailed Icon of Violent Wrestling, Speaks of Drugs & Bank Heist." *Philly.com*, January 8, 2011. http://articles.philly.com/2011-01-08/news/27017192_1_addictions-facebook-fans-heist.

Novak, Matt. "Robot Vanna, Trashy Presidents and Steak as Health Food: Samsung Sells Tomorrow." *Smithsonian.com*, February 20, 2013. www.smithsonianmag.com/history/robot-vanna-trashy-presidents-and-steak-as-health-food-samsung-sells-tomorrow-22348926/.

Nevitt, Lucy. "Popular Entertainments and the Spectacle of Bleeding." *Popular Entertainment Studies* 1, no. 2 (2010): 78–92.

Nevitt, Lucy. "'The Spirit of America Lives Here': US Pro-Wrestling and the Post-9/11 'War on Terror.'" *Journal of War and Culture Studies* 3, no. 3 (2010): 319–334.

New York Times. "Wrestling Placed Under New Status." April 9, 1930. www.nytimes.com/1930/04/09/archives/wrestling-placed-under-new-status-commission-rules-clubs-must-list.html?searchResultPosition=1.

New York Times. "Muldoon Denounces Bouts in Civic Centre." May 15, 1931. www.nytimes.com/1931/05/15/archives/muldoon-denounces-bouts-in-civic-centre-sees-desecration-in-staging.html?searchResultPosition=1.

NormanB. "Pay No Attention to the Man Behind the Curtain: AKA *The Death of Kayfabe*." *Lethal Wrestling* via *Internet Archive Wayback Machine*. Accessed May 20, 2019. https://web.archive.org/web/20071201104107/www.lethalwrestling.com/opinions/news_content.php?fileName=298.

Olson, Christopher. "Twitter, Facebook, and Professional Wrestling: Indie Wrestler Perspectives on the Importance of Social Media." *Popular Culture Studies Journal* 6, no. 1 (2018): 306–316.

Oppliger, Patrice A. *Wrestling and Hypermasculinity*. Jefferson, NC: McFarland and Company, 2004.

O'Sullivan, Dan. "Money in the Bank: The Story of Pro Wrestling in the 20th Century is the Story of American Capitalism." *Jacobin*, August 11, 2014. www.jacobinmag.com/2014/08/money-in-the-bank/.

Oxford English Dictionary, oed.com, s.v. "Likeness."

Oz, Drake. "WWE's 15 Stupidest Name Changes Done For Legal Reasons." *Bleacher Report*, November 11, 2011. http://bleacherreport.com/articles/933313-wwes-15-stupidest-name-changes-done-for-legal-reasons.

Paglino, Nick. "John Cena's Brand Generates $100 Million Per Year For WWE, Brie Bella Reacts to Daniel Bryan Being Abducted by Wyatts." *Wrestle Zone*, November 26, 2013. www.mandatory.com/wrestlezone/news/434619-john-cena-generates-100-million-per-year-for-wwe.

Patterson, Christian. "Vince McMahon's Untapped Goldmine." *Underground Mall*, January 3, 2019. https://undergroundmall.xyz/2019/01/03/post-next-vince-mcmahons-untapped-goldmine/.

Phillips, Tom. "Wrestling with Grief: Fan Negotiation of Professional/Private Personas in Responses to the Chris Benoit Double Murder–Suicide." *Celebrity Studies* 6, no. 1 (2015): 69–84.

Playbill. "Teaneck Tanzi: The Venus Flytrap." *Playbil.com.* Accessed May 5, 2019. www.playbill.com/production/teaneck-tanzi-the-venus-flytrap-nederlander-theatre-vault-0000013345.

Professional Wrestling Historical Society. Accessed May 20, 2019. www.prowrestlinghistoricalsociety.com/.

Professional Wrestling Studies Association. Accessed May 20, 2019. https://prowrestlingstudies.org/.

"Professional+Wrestling," Smithsonian. Accessed May 20, 2019. www.si.edu/sisearch/collection-images?edan_q=professional%2Bwrestling.

Pro Wrestling Doctor. "Blood's Arm and Leg are Severely Gashed by Light Tubes." *Pro Wrestling Doctor*, June 2, 2011. www.pro-wrestling-doctor.robtencer.com/wrestling-injuries/bloods-arm-and-leg-are-severely-gashed-by-light-tubes

Prowrestling.net. "Fundraiser Launched for Injured Wrestler Necro Butcher." August 15, 2013. www.prowrestling.net/artman/publish/miscnews/article10032888.shtml.

Quint, "Wanna see Mickey Rourke and Darren Aronofsky in the Ring? Footage From the Shooting of *The Wrestler* is Here!" *Ain't It Cool News*, February 12, 2008. www.aintitcool.com/node/35591.

Rahilly, Lucia. "Is *RAW* War? Professional Wrestling as Popular S/M Narrative." In *Steel Chair to the Head: The Pleasure and Pain of Professional Wrestling*, edited by Nicholas Sammond, 213–231. Durham: Duke University Press, 2005.

Ramirez, Kimberly. "Let's Get Ready to Rumba: Wrestling with Stereotypes in Kristoffer Diaz's *The Elaborate Entrance of Chad Deity*." *Label Me Latina/o* 3 (Fall 2013): 1–12.

Rebellato, Dan. "Playwriting and Globalisation: Towards a Site-Unspecific Theatre." *Contemporary Theatre Review* 16, no. 1 (2006): 97–113.

Reddit. "What Match is this Iconic Image of McMahon yelling at Stone Cold from?" R/SquaredCircle. Reddit.com, April 5, 2018. www.reddit.com/r/SquaredCircle/comments/89z8cm/what_match_is_this_iconic_image_of_mcmahon/.

Reinhard, CarrieLynn D. and Christopher J. Olson, eds. *Convergent Wrestling: Participatory Culture, Transmedia Storytelling, and Intertextuality in the Squared Circle*. London: Routledge, 2019.

Reinhard, CarrieLynn D. "Kayfabe as Convergence: Content Interactivity and Prosumption in the Squared Circle." In *Convergent Wrestling: Participatory Culture, Transmedia Storytelling and Intertextuality in the Squared Circle*, edited by CarrieLynn D. Reinhard and Christopher J. Olson, 31–44. London: Routledge, 2019.

Reinelt, Janelle. "Beyond Brecht: Britain's New Feminist Drama." *Theatre Journal* 38, no. 2 (May 1986): 154–163.

Ridout, Nicholas. "Animal Labour in the Theatrical Economy." *Theatre Research International* 29, no. 1 (2004): 57–65.

Roach, Joseph. *The Player's Passion: Studies in the Science of Acting*. Newark, DE: University of Delaware Press, 1985.

Rodman, Gil. "Notes on Reconstructing the 'Popular'." *Critical Studies in Media Communication* 33, no. 5 (2016): 388–398.

Russell, Carol L. and Thomas E. Murray. "The Life and Death of Carnie." *American Speech* 79, no. 4 (Winter 2004): 400–416.

Salmon, Catherine and Susan Clerc. "'Ladies Love Wrestling, Too': Female Wrestling Fans Online." In *Steel Chair to the Head: The Pleasure and Pain of Professional*

Wrestling, edited by Nicholas Sammond, 167–191. Durham: Duke University Press, 2005.

Saltz, David. "Editorial Comment: Popular Culture and Theatre History." *Theatre Journal* 60, no. 4 (December 2008): front matter.

Sammond, Nicholas. "Squaring the Family Circle: WWF Smackdown Assaults the Social Body." In *Steel Chair to the Head: The Pleasure and Pain of Professional Wrestling*, edited by Nicholas Sammond, 132–166. Durham: Duke University Press, 2005.

Sammond, Nicholas. "Introduction: A Brief and Unnecessary Defense of Professional Wrestling." In *Steel Chair to the Head: The Pleasure and Pain of Professional Wrestling*, edited by Nicholas Sammond, 1–22. Durham, NC: Duke University Press, 2005.

Sandomir, Richard. "Sports Business; W.W.F. Alters Script and Looks to Football." *New York Times*, February 4, 2000. www.nytimes.com/2000/02/04/sports/sports-business-wwf-alters-script-and-looks-to-football.html.

Saunders, Terry McNeil. "Play, Performance and Professional Wrestling: An Examination of a Modern Day Spectacle Of Absurdity." PhD Diss., University of California, Los Angeles, 1998.

Savran, David. "Toward a Historiography of the Popular." *Theatre Survey* 45, no. 2 (November 2004): 211–217.

Savran, David. *Highbrow/Lowdown: Theatre, Jazz, and the Making of the New Middle Class*. Ann Arbor: University of Michigan Press, 2010.

Savran, David. "Trafficking in Transnational Brands: The New 'Broadway-Style' Musical." *Theatre Survey* 55, no. 3 (September 2014): 318–342.

Scarry, Elaine. *The Body in Pain: The Making and Unmaking of the World*. New York: Oxford University Press USA, 1987.

Schulze, Daniel. "Blood, Guts, and Suffering: The Body as Communicative Agent in Professional Wrestling and Performance Art." *Contemporary Drama in English* 1, no. 1 (2013): 113–25.

Scott, A.O. "Hard Knocks, Both Given and Gotten." Review of *The Wrestler*, directed by Darren Aronofsky. *New York Times*, December 16, 2008. www.nytimes.com/2008/12/17/movies/17wres.html.

Shoemaker, David. *The Squared Circle: Life Death and Professional Wrestling*. New York: Gotham Books, 2013.

Sehmby, Dalbir Singh. "Professional Wrestling, Whooo!: A Cultural Con, an Athletic Dramatic Narrative, and a Haven for Rebel Heroes." MA Thesis, University of Alberta, 2000.

Serrato, Phillip. "Not Quite Heroes: Race, Masculinity, and Latino Professional Wrestlers." In *Steel Chair to the Head: The Pleasure and Pain of Professional Wrestling*, edited by Nicholas Sammond, 232–259. Durham: Duke University Press, 2005.

Slagle, Steve. "Carlos Colon." *The Professional Wrestling Hall of Fame Presented by The Ring Chronicle*. Accessed May 25, 2019. www.wrestlingmuseum.com/pages/wrestlers/carloscolon2.html.

Smith, Adam. *Wealth of Nations*, edited by Jim Manis. Old Main, PA: Electronic Classics Series Publication, 2005. https://web.archive.org/web/20150218062802/www2.hn.psu.edu/faculty/jmanis/adam-smith/Wealth-Nations.pdf.

Smith, Chris. "Is Making John Cena WWE Champ Really What's Best for Business?" *Forbes*, July 1, 2014. www.forbes.com/sites/chrissmith/2014/07/01/is-making-john-cena-wwe-champion-whats-really-best-for-business/.

Smith, Chris. "Breaking Down How WWE Contracts Work." *Forbes*, March 28, 2015. www.forbes.com/sites/chrissmith/2015/03/28/breaking-down-how-wwe-contracts-work/#18e969426713.

Smith, R. Tyson. "Passion Work: The Joint Production of Emotional Labor in Professional Wrestling." *Social Psychology Quarterly* 71, no. 2 (2008): 157–176.

Smith, R. Tyson. *Fighting for Recognition: Identity and the Performance of Violence in Professional Wrestling*. Durham, NC: Duke University Press, 2014.

Snodgrass, Jeremy. "Stephanie McMahon Thinks WWE Can Surpass Disney in Entertainment World." *ComicBook.com*, November 9, 2018. https://comicbook.com/wwe/2018/11/08/stephanie-mcmahon-wwe-disney-can-surpass/.

Snowden, Jonathan. *Shooters: The Toughest Men in Professional Wrestling*. Toronto: ECW Press, 2012.

Snowden, Jonathan. "Inside WWE: An Exclusive Look at How a Pro Wrestling Story Comes to Life." *Bleacher Report*, January 21, 2015. http://bleacherreport.com/articles/2283701-inside-wwe-an-exclusive-look-at-how-a-pro-wrestling-story-comes-to-life.

Soulliere, Danielle M. "Wrestling with Masculinity: Messages about Manhood in the WWE." *Sex Roles* 55 (2006): 1–11.

Stages of Half Moon. "Trafford Tanzi (1980)." Accessed May 4, 2019. www.stagesofhalfmoon.org.uk/productions/trafford-tanzi/.

Taube, Aaron. "9 Examples Of WWE CEO Vince McMahon's Insane Work Ethic." *Business Insider*, August 28, 2014. www.businessinsider.com/wwe-ceo-vince-mcmahons-work-ethic-2014-8.

Theatricalia. "Trafford Tanzi by Claire Luckham." Accessed May 5, 2019. https://theatricalia.com/play/980/trafford-tanzi-by-claire-luckham.

Thompson, Lee Austin. "Professional Wrestling in Japan—Media and Message." *International Review for the Sociology of Sport* 21, no. 1 (1986): 65–81.

Three Faces of Foley, DVD. Stamford, CT: WWF Home Video, 2002.

Turan, Kenneth. "As Fake as Wrestling." Review of *The Wrestler*, directed by Darren Aronofsky. *Los Angeles Times*, December 17, 2008. http://articles.latimes.com/2008/dec/17/entertainment/et-wrestler17.

Turowetz, Allen. "An Ethnography of Professional Wrestling: Elements of a Staged Contest." MA Thesis, McGill University, 1974.

Two Man Power Trip of Wrestling. "David Schultz Says He Slapped Reporter Because Of Vince McMahon, What Caused Rift With Hulk Hogan." *Wrestling INC*, February 24, 2018. www.wrestlinginc.com/news/2018/02/david-schultz-says-he-slapped-reporter-because-of-vince-637280/.

United States Patent and Trademark Office. "John Cena." Registration number 2957043. Accessed May 11, 2019. www.uspto.gov/.

United States Patent and Trademark Office. "John Cena." Registration number 3074517. Accessed May 11, 2019. www.uspto.gov/.

United States Patent and Trademark Office. "John Cena." Registration number 3088504. Accessed May 11, 2019. www.uspto.gov/.

United States Patent and Trademark Office. "John Cena." Registration number 3169452. Accessed May 11, 2019. www.uspto.gov/.

Wall Street Journal. "World Wrestling Entertainment Inc. Cl A." Accessed April 19, 2019. https://quotes.wsj.com/WWE/financials/annual/income-statement.

Wandor, Michelene. *Carry On, Understudies: Theatre & Sexual Politics*. London: Routledge & Keegan Paul, 1981.
Warden, Claire, Broderick Chow, and Eero Laine. "Working Loose: A Response to 'Donald Trump Shoots the Match' by Sharon Mazer." *TDR: The Drama Review* 62, no. 2, T238 (Summer 2018): 201–215.
Warden, Claire. "'Might All Be a Work': Professional Wrestling at Butlins Holiday Camps.'" *The Journal of Popular Culture* 51, no. 4 (August 2018): 863–877.
Weinstein, Eric. "Kayfabe." *Edge*, 2011. http://edge.org/q2011/q11_16.html#weinstein.
Wellowitz, David E and Tyler T. Ochea. *Celebrity Rights: Rights of Publicity and Related Rights in the United States and Abroad*. Durham, NC: Carolina Academic Press, 2010.
Wikipedia. "Kayfabe." Accessed April 6, 2019. http://en.wikipedia.org/wiki/Kayfabe.
Williams, Joe. "The Hippo Hippodrome." *Judge*, reprinted in *The Literary Digest*, February 6, 1932.
Williams, Scott E., *Hardcore History: The Extremely Unauthorized Story of ECW*. New York: Sports Publishing, 2011.
Winningham, Geoff. *Friday Night in the Coliseum*. Houston: Allison Press, 1971.
Wolf, Stacy. "Musical Theatre Studies." *Journal of American Drama and Theatre* 28, no. 1 (Winter 2016). https://jadtjournal.org/2016/03/23/musical-theatre-studies/.
Wood, Rachel and Benjamin Litherland. "Critical Feminist Hope: The Encounter of Neoliberalism and Popular Feminism in *WWE 24: Women's Evolution*." *Feminist Media Studies* 18, no. 5 (2018): 905–922.
Workman, Mark Elliot. "The Differential Perception of a Dramatic Event: Interpretations of the Meaning of Professional Wrestling Matches." PhD Diss., University of Pennsylvania, 1977.
World Wrestling Federation Entertainment, Inc. "Annual Report." Form 10-k. *Edgar Online*, April 30, 2000. http://yahoo.brand.edgar-online.com/displayfilinginfo.aspx?FilingID=1361985-1136-235098&type=sect&TabIndex=2&companyid=7520&ppu=%252fdefault.aspx%253fcik%253d1091907.
Wrenn, Marion. "Managing Doubt: Professional Wrestling Jargon & the Carnival Roots of Consumer Culture." In *Practicing Culture*, edited by Craig Calhoun and Richard Sennett, 149–170. London: Routledge, 2007.
Wrestlenomics. Accessed May 15, 2019. https://sites.google.com/view/wrestlenomics/home.
WWE. "Copyright." Accessed May 10, 2019. https://community.wwe.com/copyright.
WWE. "Live Events." Accessed May 13, 2019. https://corporate.wwe.com/what-we-do/live-events.
WWE. "Licensing." Accessed May 12, 2019. https://corporate.wwe.com/what-we-do/consumer-products/licensing.
WWE. "Who We Are." Accessed May 12, 2019. https://corporate.wwe.com/.
WWE. "'Stone Cold' Steve Austin Bio." Accessed January 7, 2019. www.wwe.com/superstars/stonecoldsteveaustin
WWE. "WWE Legends Program Gives Former Professional Wrestlers Heroes New Life and WWE New Product." June 20, 2005. *WWE.com* via *Internet Archive Wayback Machine*, Accessed May 9, 2019. https://web.archive.org/web/20140313005648/http://corporate.wwe.com/news/2005/2005_06_20_2.jsp.

Yahoo! Finance. "World Wrestling Entertainment, Inc. (WWE)." Accessed January 17, 2019. http://finance.yahoo.com/q?s=WWE.

Zazzali, Peter. *Acting in the Academy: The History of Professional Actor Training in US Higher Education*. New York: Routledge, 2016.

Žižek, Slavoj. *Absolute Recoil: Towards a New Foundation of Dialectical Materialism*. New York: Verso, 2014.

Zolides, Andrew. "The Work of Wrestling: Struggles for Creative and Industrial Power in WWE Labor." In *#WWE Professional Wrestling in the Digital Age*, edited by Dru Jeffries. Bloomington, IN: Indiana University Press, forthcoming.

Index

AAA 65–6
Abdullah the Butcher 67
Abramović, Marina 73
actors 1, 22, 27, 30, 45–6, 49, 53, 60, 68, 123
Andre the Giant 68
Apple, Inc 82, 88–9, 92
Aristotle 2
Aronofsky, Darren 63, 70, 72
art galleries *versus* sporting arenas 62
artwork-as-commodity, notion of 6
Attitude Era of the late 1990s 40
auditions 84
Austin, Steve 108–10, 113
authenticity of bleeding, in pro-wrestling 61
axis of evil 41

barbed-wire matches 67
Barthes, Roland 1–2, 9–10, 41, 50, 64
Beauty and the Beast 91, 117
Bezos, Jeff 111
Big Boss Man 109
Big Japan Pro-Wrestling (BJW) 62, 69
Bleacher Report 87, 96, 116
bloodletting, displays of 62
bloody brawling matches 67
body building 69, 97
brain damage, due to wrestling 80
branded wrestling body 80–2; legal likeness 87–91; living gimmicks 82–7
Brecht, Bertolt 41, 50, 53
Broadway musical 6, 83, 91
Bryan, Daniel 101, 105, 113–16
business model, of professional wrestling 18, 20, 32, 82, 94, 103–4, 106, 110, 124
Butcher, Necro 67, 70–2; injuries 75–6

cable network broadcasts 106
capitalism 6, 43, 107–8
capitalist commodity 22
Capitol Sports 67
celebrity rights 89
Cena, John 75, 85, 92, 94, 114, 116, 128
chain matches 67
Chyna 87, 109
circuses 27, 128
CM Punk 60, 115–16
code of conduct, wrestlers 34
Colon, Carlos 67
Combat Zone Wrestling (CZW) 70; promotional material 63; *Tournament of Death* 62–4, 74; type of wrestling 65
contact sports 65
Cornette, Jim 69
costumes 1, 42, 81–4, 98n6
copyright 13, 82, 87, 89–91

death match 66–7; Exploding Barbed Wire Death Match 67; in Puerto Rico 67
Diaz, Kristoffer 11, 43–7
Disney Theatricals 7, 81, 83, 91, 104, 107, 117
doubleness, idea of 88
DreamWorks 81, 107, 117

Edinburgh Festival 49
Elaborate Entrance of Chad Deity, The 11, 43, 44–7, 49, 54
Electronic Arts 90–1
emotional labor 23, 25
Everyman Theatre Company 49
Exeunt Magazine 53
exploding barbed wire death match 67
extreme authenticity, notion of 12, 62

146 Index

Extreme Championship Wrestling (ECW) 62, 66

Fabian, Kay 30
Fall Guys: The Barnums of Bounce (1937) 18
feminism 48, 51, 53
feud 2, 128–9
Flair, Charlotte 85, 122
Flair, Ric 126–7
Foley, Mick 63, 80, 82, 86, 96–8; battle with The Undertaker 83; "Hell in a Cell" match 83; "King of the Deathmatch" tournament 82; match against Vader 82; popularity of 83; Three Faces of Foley 83; wrestling career 82–3; as WWE Champion 83
forearm smash 64
for-profit theatre 4, 6–7, 21, 116
Frontier Martial-Arts Wrestling, in Japan 66–7
Funk, Terry 67, 126

garbage wrestling 59, 76n1
Gates, Bill 111
gimmick, wrestling 80, 82–5, 87, 111
GLOW (Netflix show) 48
Gotch, Frank 33
Greco-Roman wrestling 66
Griffin, Marcus 18, 20

Hadley, Jamie Lewis 25, 64, 73–4, 125
hardcore wrestling: accusations of fakeness 60; agony and the suffering of participants 60; authenticity of bleeding in 61; bleeding wounds 59; bloody performances in 62; conventions of 59; death match 67; deregulation and great spectacles of suffering 64–70; development of 63; extreme authenticity 62; as form of professional wrestling 59; idea of kayfabe in 62; markers of pain 60; Mass Transit Incident 77n23; pain in 59–60; performance of 61; physical pain in 71; popularity of 62; and power tool theatrics 72–5; reward for performers 60; staple gun art 72–5; style of 59; *Tournament of Death* 62–3, 74; YouTube video 71
Hassan, Mohammad 45
Have a Nice Day: A Tale of Blood and Sweatsocks 80

Hellwig, James 87
highbrow suffering of bodies 73
high-flying moves 24
#HijackRaw 115–16
Hogan, Hulk 68, 126
hookers 27, 29

intellectual property 13, 89, 91–2, 95–6
intercollegiate wrestling 66

Jacobin 107, 109
Japanese professional wrestling: history of 33; and *Kōdōkan* Judo 33; Rikidōzan 33; training facility 33
Japan Professional Wrestling Association 33–4
jiujitsu 66
Jobs, Steve 82, 88–9, 99n27

Kane 109
Kasai, Jun 69
Kaufman, Andy 49
kayfabe 83; code of conduct for workers 34; concept of 11, 19, 26; etymology and practice 26–32; fabrication of 31–2; in hardcore wrestling 62; physical implications of 31; production of 31
Kayfabe Publishing Company 29
Kōdōkan Judo 33
Kogyo, Yoshimoto 34

labor: of actor 22; emotional labor 23, 25; manual labor 23, 74; productive labor 24; wage labor 45; of wrestling 23
labored performance, of professional wrestling 26
Legends Contract 94–5
likeness, legal notion of 87–91
Lion King 12, 91
Live Nation Entertainment 104
live performance, economics of 125
living gimmicks 82–7
Los Angeles Times, The 72
Louis, Joe 33
lucha libre (Mexico) 1; matches 67; training of 65–6
Luckham, Claire 11, 43, 47–8, 50–1
Lunatic Wrestling Federation (LWF) 60
Lynch, Becky 122

masks 83, 85

McMahon, Vince 67–8, 85, 103, 108–12; DVD biography 111; performance of 111, 113
McMahon, Linda 68, 111
Mamet, David 54
manual labor 23, 73
Marx, Groucho 108
Marx, Karl 11, 21–2, 68
masculine performance, theory of 9
Mass Transit Incident 77n23
melodrama 9, 41–2
Mermaid Theatre 49
Metropolitan Opera 20, 54, 105
Monday Night Raw 108, 115
Moxley, Jon: CZW's Tournament of Death 74; match with Brain Damage 74–5
musical theatre studies 5, 126
Mysterio, Rey 66

National Football League Players Association (NFLPA) 90–1
national television contracts 85
National Wrestling Alliance (US) 33
Nederlander Theatre 49, 105–6

#OccupyRaw 116
Olympics 33; Olympic Wrestling Association 49
Onita, Atsushi 67
Onyehara, Olivia 53

passion work: concept of 23; emotional response to 23; ideal performances of 23
pay-per-view 80, 103, 106, 114
performance art 12, 64, 72–3
poruresu (Japan) 1
powerbomb 46
power tool theatrics 72–5
productive and unproductive labor, concept of 22
productive labor 22–3, 25, 80, 104; idea of 11
productive labourer: definition of 22; for promoters 23
productive theatre: labor of the actor 22; and professional wrestling 21–6, 81; quantity of labour 22
Professional Wrestling Historical Society 125
Professional Wrestling Studies Association 5, 124, 125

profit 18, 20, 26, 32, 46, 51, 68, 92, 94, 107
profit motive 7
profit making, act of 20, 80, 96, 113, 124
publicity, right of 18, 20, 49, 89–90

repertory theatres, state-sponsored 4
representational arts 39, 125
Rikidōzan 33–4
rippers 28–9
Rourke, Micky 70–1
Rousey, Ronda 122

sameness, idea of 88
Santorum, Rick 68
Schwarzenegger, Arnold 112
secrets of professional wrestling 28
self-preservation, sense of 65
Shamrock, Ken 109
shooters 27–9
skilsaws 75
Smith, Adam 11, 21–2
Smithsonian Museum 127
social media 41, 80, 95, 106, 115–16, 129
social safety net 70
Spill Festival of Performance (2014), London 73
sporting event, legitimacy of 33, 41–2, 62, 69
sports entertainment 7, 67, 92, 106
staple gun art 72–5
stock market, the 13, 103, 105, 113–14
stock theatre company 103; idea of WWE as 107
Stossel, John 103

Tanzi Libre 48, 53
Theatre of the Half Moon 49
Theories of Surplus Value 22
THE Wrestling 44
touring carnivals 27
touring theatre 21, 106
Tournament of Death 62–4, 74
toxic masculinity 40
trademark 12, 81, 82, 87, 90–2, 94–5
Trafford Tanzi 11, 43, 47–54, 55
Trump, Donald 7–8, 110
Tuebrook Tanzi 48
Turner, Ted 110

Ultimate Warrior 87
"unproductive" laborers 22

Index

Valentine, Johnny 86
Venus Fly Trap, The 48
vulgarization, of professional wrestling 65

wage labor 12, 22, 45, 69, 76, 113
Wheel of Fortune 89
White v. *Samsung* case 89–90
working class 6, 41–2, 48–51, 121
World Championship Wrestling (WCW) 66
World Heavyweight Champion 113
World Tag Team Championship 33
World Wrestling Entertainment, Inc. (WWE) 4, 11, 21, 68, 80, 82, 87, 104, 110, 123; Attitude Era of the late 1990s 40; intellectual property of 92; Legends Contract 94–5; live performance of touring show 40; mediated theatre 105–8; as stock theatre company 107; World Heavyweight Champion 113; *WWE Legends of Wrestlemania* 96
World Wrestling Federation *see* World Wrestling Entertainment, Inc. (WWE)
WrestleMania 96, 106, 110, 116, 122, 128
wrestlers, productive labor of 22
Wrestler, The (film) 63, 70, 79n56
wrestling likenesses 91–6
Wrestling Observer, The 85
wrestling's iconography, limits of 64
wrestling violence, implications of 40

Printed in the United States
By Bookmasters